RITUAL MAGIC

An Occult Primer

The proportions of man
and their Occult numbers, *Agrippa, c.* 1533

RITUAL MAGIC

An Occult Primer

DAVID CONWAY

A Dutton  *Paperback*

E. P. DUTTON
NEW YORK

4|10

Pronaque cum spectent animalia cetera terram
Os homini sublime dedit, coelumque tueri
Jussit, et erectos ad sidere tollere voltus.

Ovid, *Metamorphoses* I

All other creatures look down towards the earth,
but man was given a face so that he might turn
his eyes towards the stars and his gaze upon the sky.

CONTENTS

FIGURES

FOREWORD

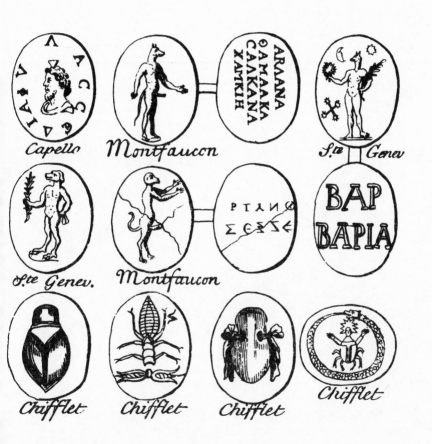

Capello   Montfaucon   S.te Genev

S.te Genev.   Montfaucon

Chifflet   Chifflet   Chifflet   Chifflet

This strikes me as one of the best books on magic that has been written in the twentieth century, and one of the best introductions to magic (an altogether rarer phenomenon), written in any century. I have only one minor criticism. The author is a genuine magician; consequently, he fails to grasp the extent to which the rest of us find the whole idea of magic frankly absurd. Let me see if I can make the proposition sound any less illogical.

In August 1888, a young man named Charles Johnston was sitting in the room of Helena Petrovna Blavatsky, the founder of Theosophy. Madame Blavatsky was playing patience; her friend Colonel Olcott, on a visit to her, was writing a letter at a side table; Johnston was sitting nearby, carrying on a desultory conversation with both. Madame Blavatsky became impatient as the cards refused to 'come out'; she frowned and drummed her fingers on the table top. Then, quite unconsciously, she raised her hand well above the table, continuing to drum with her fingers. The tapping sounds on the table continued. Realising that Johnston was watching her with interest, she turned towards him and began to tap on the back of his hand—without rising from her seat. He was five or six feet away from her. Now amused by her game, she transferred the taps to the top of his head. Johnston writes: 'I could both feel and hear them. It was something like taking sparks from the prime conductor of an electric machine; or, better still perhaps, it was like spurting quicksilver . . .'

Johnston goes on to say that this was 'a quite undoubted

miracle.' It was, of course, nothing of the sort. It was a perfectly ordinary phenomenon which has been observed hundreds—probably thousands—of times by psychic researchers. It is known as a 'poltergeist effect.' Madame Blavatsky was particularly good at it; when she first met her disciple Sinnett, he told her that he had tried spiritualism, but could not even get the spirits to rap on a table. 'Raps are the easiest to get' said Madame Blavatsky, and made raps sound from all over the room. A vagabond named William Drury had made the same discovery two hundred years earlier; he was arrested at the small town of Ludgershall, in Wiltshire, in 1661; his drum was confiscated and he was sent to jail. Immediately afterwards, the house of the magistrate who had sentenced him was disturbed by loud drumming noises, which went on every night, together with other strange phenomena. The case—known as 'the phantom drummer of Tedworth'—is attested by dozens of witnesses. Drury admitted to a visitor that it was he who was somehow causing the disturbances, and when he was transported out of the country, they ceased.

Perhaps the most amazing and convincing case is one that has been published since Mr Conway first wrote this book. In the early 1970s, the Toronto Society for Psychical Research, under the direction of Dr George Owen and his wife Iris, decided to try to create a ghost. A group of researchers invented the life story of a seventeenth century cavalier called Philip who had a tragic love affair with a gypsy girl and committed suicide. They then sat around and tried to persuade the imaginary ghost to rap on a table. For months, nothing happened, although they tried hard. Then, one day when they had *stopped* trying, loud raps began to sound from the table. The 'spirit' identified itself as Philip and told his life story in detail; it also made the table waltz around the room. Philip eventually became such a professional performer that he even made the table levitate in front of a television audience.

In short, there can be no reasonable room for doubt that 'poltergeist effects' originate in the human subconscious mind—more often than not in the minds of disturbed adolescents. Yet we do not have the slightest idea of *how* the mind can cause an object to fly through the air or make rapping noises all over the room. What energies are involved? How do they work? At the moment, no one has even managed to offer a convincing explanation.

Now I would submit that this is what is usually meant by 'magic.' It is true that the legendary 'great magicians'— from Merlin to Gandalf—could do far more spectacular things; Merlin is supposed to have transported the great trilithons of Stonehenge from Ireland by magic. (He didn't —they were there two thousand years before King Arthur's time.) But if you read any book about the history of men who were supposed to be able to perform magic, from Apollonius of Tyana to Aleister Crowley, you will discover that their feats were far less spectacular. Crowley once demonstrated his powers to an acquaintance in New York; he fell into step behind a respectable looking gentleman, imitating his walk exactly. Suddenly, Crowley allowed himself to crumple at the knees; the man in front of him also fell on to the pavement; he got up looking puzzled and frightened, wondering what had happened.

And now, I think, my own basic theory of magic should be emerging. 'Magical powers' originate in the unconscious mind. And the reason that we are very naturally sceptical about their existence is that what you call 'you' and I call 'me' is our *conscious* egos. Disturbed adolescents can cause 'poltergeist effects' because their unconscious minds are far more highly charged than the average person's by tensions due to physical changes. (For the same odd reason, menstruating women can sometimes produce the same effects— a fact that is recognised by most primitive tribes.) In most of us, the unconscious has adjusted itself to the routine of everyday life, and sees no good reason to make unusual efforts. So it yawns and relaxes. A man like Crowley deliberately kept his 'unconscious' supercharged by practising strange magical rituals and by behaving in a way that would strike most of us as deplorable. (For example, he filed his teeth so as to be able to draw blood from his girlfriends, who were usually masochists.)

Now all this sounds incredible enough. But in the past two or three years, there has emerged at least one piece of scientific evidence whose value seems to me incalculable. I am speaking of the discoveries made by R W Sperry and others in the field called 'split brain research.' What they have discovered, basically, is that there are *two* people living inside our heads. The right and left sides of our brains have quite different functions—this has been known for more than a century. The left deals with language, with ideas, with analysis; the right with recognition, with intuition. In other words, to put it crudely, the left is a scientist and the right is an artist. But the two halves are joined by a knot of nerve fibre which keeps them in close contact, like the hot line between two neighbouring states. If this fibre is separated (as it sometimes is to cure epilepsy), the results can be rather odd. If the left eye is shown an apple, and the right eye is shown an orange, and the person is *asked* what he has just seen, he replies: 'An orange.' But if he is asked to *write* what he has seen with his left hand, he writes 'apple.' If asked what he has just written, he will reply: 'orange.' (It should me mentioned that, for some reason, the right hemisphere of the brain governs the left side of the body, and vice versa.) Moreover, if the right side of the brain is shown an obscene picture, the patient will blush; asked why he is blushing, he replies: 'I don't know.' And he doesn't. In other words, the person who calls himself 'I' is actually only the left side of the brain; sitting only a few centimeters away, there is another 'you', who exists as a completely independent person. The right hemisphere is silent; yet it is just as much an individual as the left.

This explains, at least, how it is possible for a person to cause poltergeist effects and yet be totally unaware that he is the cause. (This is so almost invariably—Dr Owen warns psychical researchers against telling young people who are the focus of such disturbances that they are to blame; it can cause severe shock.) The left is genuinely ignorant of what the right is up to.

The inference would seem to be that the left side of our brain is what Freud called the 'ego'; the right is, presum-

ably, what he called the 'id', or the unconscious. Or, at least,
is the gateway to the unconscious. For there are other mysterious 'lower regions' of the brain—the cerebellum, the
limbic system, the 'reptile brain', a relic of our remote past
in primeval seas. The psychologist Stan Gooch is convinced
that it is the cerebellum—the so-called 'old brain'—that is
responsible for 'paranormal experience.' We know almost
nothing about the brain. Meanwhile, the experts—like
Sperry, Robert Ornstein, Sir John Eccles—are not too happy
when amateurs like me begin to evolve curious theories,
pointing out that some new discovery tomorrow may change
everything. I take their point but—forgive me—decline to
stop speculating.

And in the present case, it is easy to see why. These discoveries could be the great breakthrough in the field of
paranormal research. Moreover, they suggest all kinds of
revolutionary experiments. For example, in the last century,
when hypnosis had only recently been discovered, there
were many experiments to try to determine whether it could
endow people with paranormal powers. There is an immense amount of evidence that it could—certain hypnotised
subjects were able to display 'travelling clairvoyance', and
describe places that they had never visited. (All this can be
found in the four volumes of E J Dingwall's classic *Abnormal Hypnotic Phenomena*.) But this new knowledge of the
functions of left and right hemispheres suggests that when
a person is hypnotised, it is only the left side of the brain
that is put to sleep; the right remains as active as ever.
(This, at any rate, is my own conviction.) And if, as we
suspect, the right brain lies at the root of paranormal phenomena, then it might be possible to train it to make more
deliberate use of its powers through hypnosis. Another
obvious possibility is to attempt to train people who have
had the 'split brain' operation, which might be even more
rewarding. . . .

Any good book on psychical research will tell you that
'poltergeist effects' are not the only 'strange powers' at the
command of certain human beings. There are, for example,

many well-authenticated examples of genuine glimpses of the future. This taxes our credulity far more than poltergeist phenomena, because it seems to contradict the common sense recognition that the future has not yet happened. Then there is a vast amount of evidence for the phenomenon known as 'out of the body experience'—people at certain moments find themselves apparently hovering outside their own bodies. The majority of these are not remotely interested in 'occultism'; they are perfectly ordinary people who have had just one single abnormal experience. (It happened to the biologist Lyall Watson, for example, when his Landrover overturned in Africa; in his 'out of the body' state he saw the position of one of the passengers, halfway through the roof. He recovered consciousness moments later and verified that his observation had been correct.) The evidence for telepathy and 'second sight' is also impressive.

Now all this is, I would argue, a form of what our ancestors called 'magic.' We do not think of such things as magic because the word conjures up Merlin and Dr Faust and Gandalf. This is a mistake, and it explains the understandable and universal scepticism about magic. If, in fact, we can accept that 'paranormal phenomena' are somehow produced by that 'other self' inside the brain, then we have acknowledged that every one of us contains a magician.

At which point, I have to acknowledge that this is not all there is to it. Anyone who has been more than half convinced by my arguments so far may find the second part harder to swallow. I do myself, and I have to admit that I am by no means totally convinced about it.

Let me begin by speaking of a subject that most of us know at least a little about: astrology. Few people can resist surreptitiously reading their horoscope in the daily newspaper, even if they insist—quite truthfully—that they regard the whole thing as a joke.

I agree with the sceptics. Of course astrology is a joke. Of course it is preposterous to suppose that the position of the stars and planets could exert the slightest influence on the life of human beings. . . . Having said which, I have to shamefacedly admit that, in many cases, it really seems to work. I am willing to agree that it could all be coincidence; yet it *does* seem true that many people born under Cancer are home-lovers with an over-developed protective streak; that Geminis tend to be clever and changeable; that Capricorns are plodders; that Leos are show-offs; that Virgos are precise and tidy; that Pisces are romantics; that Aquarians are detached but kindly; that Scorpios have powerful and often violent emotions. . . . Moreover, people also display characteristics of their rising sign—the sign that was coming up over the horizon at the moment of their birth. This was investigated by two French statisticians, the Gauquelins, who convinced themselves that this was more than coincidence. They turned over their result to a thoroughly tough-minded psychologist named H J Eysenck, who was convinced that the whole thing was nonsense, and that it would only take him a few hours to prove it. Eysenck has ended up by publicly acknowledging that, for some totally unknown reason, people *are* influenced by their rising sign.

In short, it is one of the basic principles of traditional magic that, in some unknown way, there is a link between man and the heavens. 'As above, so below' said Thrice Great Hermes. It may be some purely mechanical link, as mechanical as the genes that determine the colour of our eyes. One student of astrology, the late Rodney Collin, suggested that when a person is born, something inside him responds like a light meter to the precise configuration of the planets (and, of course, to their gravitational forces.) So each of us is stamped at the moment of our birth like a branded cow. My own theory, for what it is worth, is that the major influence on human beings is the earth itself, which exerts all kinds of strange forces on our minds and emotions. But the delicately balanced magnetic forces of the earth change from moment to moment, as the tides are influenced by the moon. If I am correct, then we are more closely connected to the earth than we realise.

Which brings me to the oddest part. It is only in recent centuries that we have learned about the relation of the heavens to the earth, of the way in which the moon influences the tides and sunspots influence the growth of plants and trees. Yet our ancestors of three thousand years ago had already worked out an elaborate science of man's relation to the universe. If Professors Alexander Thom and Gerald Hawkins are correct, the earliest part of Stonehenge, constructed five thousand years ago, is an elaborate computer for working out eclipses of the sun and moon. We not only have no idea how our neolithic ancestors acquired such knowledge, but *why* they acquired it. My guess—and in an introduction like this I lack the space to justify it—is that they had a thorough but *instinctive* (i.e., right brain) knowledge of such matters; they knew about the relation between heaven and earth 'in their bones.'

Now it is important to realise that ancient 'magic' is not merely a collection of absurd superstitions—although it inevitably contains plenty of these—but an elaborate knowledge system, as precise and complex as our tables of atomic weights. Like most people, I had always assumed that it was something of a joke, until I was asked to write a book on 'the occult.' What surprised me as I read about Babylonian and Assyrian and Egyptian and Greek and Roman and Celtic magic was that they were so incredibly similar. If magic was merely crude pre-scientific thinking, you would expect the magic of the Eskimoes to differ as much from that of the Central Africans as their climate; and you would certainly expect to find no resemblance whatever between the magic of the Norsemen and the ancient Chinese. This is not so; not only are there dozens of similarities, there is an obvious basic *identity*. They were talking about the same thing. Jungians might explain this by saying that the human race possesses a collective unconscious—which could be stretched to mean that both Chinese and African alcoholics will see pink elephants, and that this proves nothing. Yet it seems to me more accurate to say that all primitive 'shamans' (or witch doctors) were trying to describe something they saw in the *outside* world—an underlying 'order of nature.' This, at any rate, is my own impression.

This notion that there is some kind of connection between the universe and man—the macrocosm and the microcosm—is the basic principle of all magic; it is called a 'correspondence.' And, according to the ancients, there was not only a system of correspondences between man and the planets (the stars do not really count in astrology, being merely the equivalent of the figures around the edge of a clock), but between the planets and various animals, colours, scents, gods and so on. And, perhaps most important, between the planets and the various sephira (or emanations—wishes made manifest) of the Kabbala. The system of Jewish mysticism known as the Kabbala is the basis of western magic, its atomic table of the elements, so to speak. It is such an incredible and fascinating study that I am tempted to devote a few paragraphs to it here; but Mr Conway has explained it all so well in the book that it would be pointless. Anyone who is curious about my own views can find them in my book *The Occult*.

I have to admit that when I first opened David Conway's book on magic—it was sent to me for review by its English publisher—I was inclined to feel dismissive. A history of magic would have been respectable enough, but a book that professes to teach students how to perform simple magic seemed altogether too much of a gimmick. But as soon as I began to read, I was impressed by a certain quality of the author's mind—a sense of genuineness. When I had finished the book, I realised that it *is* a good general introduction to the subject of magic, the kind of thing that would serve a student of anthropology who was writing a paper on the subject. And since the author believes that magic really works, it is only common sense that he should try to offer some basic rules and procedures.

Who is David Conway? The name is, in fact, a pseudonym. Soon after I reviewed the book, we had some correspondence, and he explained that his reason for using the alias was that he was working for the government, and his colleagues in the department might look at him a little oddly if they knew he was a magician. Since then he has left government service and gone to live in Germany. And now, knowing a little more of him, I realise that it was not entirely because of his government job that he preferred to

keep his identity a secret. For there is nothing of the phoney
or exhibitionist about David Conway. He is not merely a
magician, but a genuine mystic, an intensely private person
who is absorbed in what Blake called 'the inner worlds' and
their mystery.

This became clear to me when I asked him for some personal details. He is, to begin with, a Welshman—that is, a
Celt. For some odd reason, the Celts are the most 'mystical'
race on earth. They include, of course, the Irish, the Welsh
and the Scots, and certain tribes of Spain. 'Second sight' is
common among them. David Conway's experiences of the
occult began as a baby, when two strange old ladies used
to come to his bedside and talk to him. They also tickled
him, and his parents would rush in, wondering why he was
shouting. When he told them about the old ladies they took
it for granted that he was dreaming, although they were
struck with the exactness of his descriptions of the women—
he even knew their pet names (they told him to call them
Auntie). Then one day, the local doctor called, and the
five year old boy described the old ladies. After that, his
parents moved him to another bedroom, and he saw no
more of them. It was only years later that his parents told
him that the old ladies *had* once lived in the house—forty
years earlier. One had died in the bedroom; the other had
committed suicide there some months later.

David Conway's explanation of this curious episode is
that the old ladies had somehow left 'memory traces' of
their presence imprinted on the room, and the small boy's
unconscious mind had picked up these traces when he was
relaxed, on the point of sleep, and had 'translated' them
into real people. The 'memory trace' theory of 'ghosts' is
fairly well-known in psychic circles—it was first suggested
by Sir Oliver Lodge around the turn of the century—and is
to my mind highly plausible. But in this case, I do not feel
that it fits. I get the feeling that Mr Conway is leaning over
backwards to try to sound logical when it might be better to
acknowledge that this is one of those matters that, at the
moment, we cannot even begin to explain.

In order to understand David Conway, it is necessary to

accept that there are certain human beings who, from their earliest days, have a strong sense that the solid physical world is only half the story, and that hidden behind it there is a world of 'invisible' reality. William Blake was such a person; so was Emanuel Swedenborg; so was Rudolph Steiner; so was George Russell, better known as the poet AE. All had what would be termed 'supernatural' experiences in childhood; yet all were far more interested in what they felt to be this perfectly natural world concealed behind the visible world of solid objects. It is also worth noting that Blake, Swedenborg, Steiner and Russell were all basically realists, hard-headed men with a definite scientific or practical bent. The same is true of David Conway, as the first chapter of this book shows.

Conway was brought up in a remote country district of Wales. Anyone who knows such areas—I live in a similar one myself—will also know that there are many aspects of the 'supernatural' that are taken for granted there; for example, there are 'wart charmers' who really *can* make warts disappear in a day or so by muttering a charm. There are dowsers who can not only locate underground water, but who can discover the sex of an unborn child by swinging a pendulum over the mother's stomach. When David Conway was four, he was taken to see a local farmer, a Mr James of Plynlimon, who made up various herbal remedies that he dispensed throughout the district. The odd thing about these remedies is that they worked. Conway was so fascinated by it all that he learned all that Mr James could teach him about herbal law (and has since written a book about it). At the age of seven, he found an adult reader's ticket to the local library, which had a fairly good 'occult' section —no doubt consisting largely of works like Harry Price's *Most Haunted House in England;* young Conway hurled himself on it, and soon had a wide and comprehensive working knowledge of 'the occult.' But Mr James remained his chief mentor, introducing him to astrology as well as herbalism, and to the simple basic principles of ordinary 'white magic.' Someone should persuade him to write a book about his apprenticeship with the Welsh farmer; from hints he has dropped, I suspect it would be as fascinating as Carlos Castaneda's accounts of Don Juan, as well as being rather more truthful.

Meeting Mr James was the best piece of luck of Conway's early years, for he was able to absorb all the basic principles of 'mysticism' (for that is what it amounts to), at an early age, before the 'shades of the prison house' began to close on the growing youth. For he admits that at University, he did his best to seem like all the other graduates, and forgot magic. His few attempts to explore Spiritualism, theosophy and contemporary witchcraft soon ended in disillusionment —or boredom. He does not explain why, but I presume it was for the same reason that I felt repelled by my own contacts with Spiritualism as a child and teenager—my grandparents were Spiritualists; it seemed somehow too vague, too imprecise, too human—*all* too human. But his early magical training provided him with a solid foundation, and in his early thirties, David Conway decided that he would try to do what no one seemed to have attempted —to write about magic from the point of view of an objective observer *and* a believer. The result was the present volume, which seems to me to be wholly successful in achieving its aims.

And do I actually believe in magic? The question embarrasses me, because I dislike the word. It is a pity we cannot have done with it, and invent some other word, or phrase, that links the subject with psychical research and paranormal phenomena. Then I would not have the least hesitation in answering in the affirmative.

I believe that man has *two* 'wills'—one associated with left-brain consciousness, the other with the right. The left will can bring great precision to bear, but it lacks force. The right will, like an elephant, has great force, but it lacks precision. Magical disciplines must be seen as an attempt to somehow teach the 'right will' (which some occultists prefer to call 'the true will'), how to discipline its own forces. Like a snake in a basket, this consciousness responds to music (or symbols) rather than to ideas. I would draw the reader's attention particularly to Chapter 4 of Part One, where Mr Conway describes the art of 'visualisation.' It underlines the important point that the only certain way of calling upon the forces of the right hemisphere is through the use of controlled imagination.

If anyone wishes to take this as an admission that the whole subject is moonshine, neither I nor Mr Conway will be in the least bothered. This book is plainly not for them. Those of a more enquiring turn of mind may care to ponder why the word 'moonshine' is so often used as a synonym for imagination. The answer will provide them with a good introductory insight into the world of the paranormal.

—Colin Wilson

Cornwall, England
June, 1978

INTRODUCTION

Capello

Capello

Chifflet

Chifflet

Chifflet

Capello

Capello

Ste. Genev.

Ste. Genev.

In recent years there has been something of an occult revival. Scarcely a month goes by without the appearance of a new book on the subject and the number of its adherents keeps growing apace. Many observers are baffled by this interest in such subjects as astrology, magic and witchcraft, an interest that seems at first glance quite alien to our scientific age. And yet it is itself a product of our age, being a natural reaction against the crass materialism propounded by science. Each of us, it seems, hopes there is more to him and to life than the bundle of molecules the experts allow. The more our betters set out to dismiss such hopes, the more we seek grounds for holding them.

Some have attributed this resurgence of interest to a yearning for the supernatural which all men inherit. That yearning is, after all, the basis of every religion. But whereas religion confines the supernatural within a formal theology which the faithful have to accept, occultism invites its followers to experience the supernatural for themselves. To this pragmatic approach it owes its survival, for unlike religion, occultism is not the custodian of elderly dogmas which science has shown to be untenable. Instead, it encourages the inquirer to work everything out for himself.

Interest in the occult – that is, in things concealed from the senses – is, of course, as old as mankind. However, only since the development of experimental science has it had to contend with a widespread belief that nothing exists outside our empirical experience. On one level this, the dominant belief of our age, seems inescapable, given the materialistic conclusions of science. And yet in subscribing to it we are in effect seeking to limit reality to the evidence of our senses; it is as if we were to say that America did not exist until

Columbus first saw it. People interested in occult matters are un-willing to limit themselves in this way. They take the view that there may be a reality beyond the physical world with which we are familiar. For them occultism is a search for that other reality.

This search can take many forms. At the turn of the century interest in the occult was dominated by spiritualism, a movement that began in America and spread rapidly to Europe. Eastern ideas, too, gained a following, thanks largely to the Theosophical Society which was founded by the Russian émigrée Helena Blavatsky. Other groups – for example the various Rosicrucian fraternities and Rudolf Steiner's Anthroposophical movement – also sprang up, most of them still active today. However, much of their early appeal has been lost since each has gradually confected its private theology which, as in the case of orthodox religion, is rarely consistent with science. For that reason most contemporary occultists prefer to search independently for their own meaning to life.

This is just as it should be, for one of the blessings of occultism, as we have noted, is that it offers each of us his own personal experience of the supernatural. By supernatural, let me repeat, I mean that dimension which is inaccessible to the senses, but is no less real for all that. Meditation techniques, about which we have lately heard a great deal, are among the means of approaching this transcendental reality. So too, in a less disciplined way, are the drugs and acoustic or visual experiments which are a part of the current pop scene. At the same time, others are turning to telepathy, astrology and allied subjects with such enthusiasm that we seem well and truly to live in an Age of Aquarius, full, as the song says, of dreams and visions and mystic revelations.

In this book we shall examine the theory and practice of ritual magic. Such a book is, in my view, important because magic offers us the most effective way of contacting the supernatural reality we have been discussing. This I know from personal experience, which has further taught me that magic holds the key to many mysteries. That key is now within your grasp, for magic has one unique advantage over other forms of mystical tuition: it is the only one which guarantees that anyone who follows its procedures can appre-hend and, equally important, comprehend the things that lie outside sensory experience. For those who long for immortality and those who, through meditation, drugs or E.S.P., have intimations of it, this book reveals the shortest and the surest path towards fulfilment.

That, at least, is what I hope to have shown by the time you reach the final page. Before then, however, I hope also to have demonstrated that ritual magic, though long dismissed as empty superstition, is compatible with common sense and reason. It is compatible, too, with the most recent scientific thinking, which is why, in our approach to the subject, we shall dispense with the weird and the wonderful in order to concentrate on what science has to teach us about the world and ourselves. Unless the theories of magic fit in with this teaching, they are clearly suspect from the start. If, on the other hand, they are found to be consistent with the postulates of science – however materialistic these are – then magic will have shown itself worthy of serious attention.

An exercise of this sort has not to my knowledge been attempted before. The truth is that in the past magic has fared rather badly at the hands of those who have written about it. What scholarly interest the subject has attracted comes from sociologists or anthropologists who are more concerned with the behaviour of magicians than the art they practise. In the same way, studies of old magical texts tend to dwell on the virtues of their literary style and not on the magic they taught. As for the few practising magicians who have put pen to paper, almost without exception they have preached only to the converted. Because of that their grandiloquent musings seem very remote from the world of today and seem to confirm the impression that magic has no contemporary significance whatever.

This book, therefore, is a belated defence of magic. It is also much more than that since it will give instructions for a number of magical operations which can be performed to one's advantage in everyday life. Magic, you see, does not demand to be taken on trust: the rites and spells described later really do work, as you will certainly discover if you turn your hand to them. Thanks to these, everyone, converted or not, has the chance of seeing for himself why magic, brought up to date, is supremely relevant to the occult-minded times in which we now live.

D. C.

PART ONE

MAGICAL THEORY

1

T HE WORD 'magic' is commonly applied to any effect that has no observable cause. To small children the appearance of a rabbit in the conjurer's hat is a great feat of magic, although wiser folk know that the beast was put there before the performance began. One of the distinctions between the magic our book is about and party tricks of this sort is that in the former the causes responsible for certain effects escape even the wisest among us. These causes exist, of course, but they owe nothing to the physical laws of our everyday world. Hence their magical aspect and our consequent difficulty in believing them possible.

The aim of this book is quite straightforward. It is to show that such magic actually works. To that end precise instructions will be given later and any reader so inclined can try a little magic for himself. First of all, however, for the benefit of those who consider magic an illusion, we shall set about examining the theory behind it. We shall see whether the supernatural retains its credibility in an age when science claims that only those things exist which can be objectively experienced under given conditions. For unless we can establish the validity of magic within this scientific context it deserves to remain the historical curiosity the sceptics believe it to be.

Throughout this chapter we shall try to maintain the empirical approach demanded by science. We will adopt the view that there is no such thing as the supernatural: whatever exists must be natural, and will therefore not contradict what we already know about the workings of nature. Even so, we shall ultimately have to deduce certain conclusions from the evidence presented to us. There is nothing too unscientific about this. Far from being a body of absolute knowledge, modern science is itself largely speculative and offers its own tentative generalizations from the facts it has experimentally obtained.

In his monumental work *The Golden Bough*, Sir James G. Frazer describes magic as a spurious system of natural law. He means presumably that it is based on imaginary laws which have nothing in common with the natural laws known to science. To some extent the criticism is deserved, for successive magicians have been content to elaborate their system without pausing to consider the value of the premises on which it is based. Unfortunately, we are handicapped in our desire to take natural law as our starting-point because in spite of recent developments in radio-astronomy and physics even scientists remain very much in the dark as to the real nature and manner of working of the cosmos. We cannot even say whether our universe had a beginning, since all that a study of galaxies suggests is that it is expanding all the time. This expansion has led some cosmologists to argue that matter is being continuously created throughout space and so is constantly pushing outwards. Others suggest, however, that thousands of millions of years ago the universe, which was then a dense mass, exploded, hurling matter in all directions. According to them the present expansion is simply the prolonged after-effect of that primordial bang. The latter theory is the more widely accepted but, interesting though it is, it tells us nothing about the genesis of the original dense mass nor the ultimate destiny of its fragments.

What we do know for certain is that in the vast cosmos there exists one particularly bright igneous star which embraces nine major planets within its gravitational field. That bright star is the Sun, which together with the planets and several assorted asteroids makes up what we call the solar system. Of these planets our Earth is perhaps the most fortunate, since its surface and atmosphere are, we are told, conducive to the production of stable molecular structures formed from atoms of carbon and charged with electrons. These molecules have the knack of extending themselves into chains, linking with their neighbours to form an organized sequence and finally producing bigger structures called polymers. Among the polymers are those extremely complicated substances known as proteins which by a subtle variation of their constituent amino-acids are able to generate a wide range of complex forms. The most important of these molecular structures are the nucleoproteins. These are the self-replicating raw materials which, as chromosomes, make up the bricks of life that are known as living cells. Biological evolution begins when these single living cells, their nuclei swimming in cytoplasmic jelly, develop into higher life forms. From the earliest times the immediate ambition of each cell would have been to ensure its own survival and this must have led to competition for the raw materials required for that purpose. In this way a pattern was established which characterizes all subsequent organic evolution, for it is the fight for survival that has determined the twin processes of genetic mutation and natural selection.

Summed up very briefly, the doctrine of organic evolution contends that a unified and common ancestor is responsible for the diversity of complex organisms that exists in the world today. This was dimly perceived by the philosophers of ancient Greece and revived by the scientist-philosophers of the eighteenth century. It was Charles Darwin, however, who first stated the doctrine as we now know it and backed up that statement with a wealth of data from all fields of biology. Since then palaeontology has increased our knowledge of early forms so that we can now regard it as adequately proven that 'life' on earth has always consisted of an orderly progression from relatively simple structures to the wonder that is man himself. Despite the wonder, however, the appearance of man was no mere accident, and *Homo sapiens* like all else in nature has his appropriate place on the evolutionary tree. Sharing the same branch on that tree are his closest cousins, the apes.

The physical resemblances between apes and man are too obvious to be stated. It is reported that when the first orang-outang was exhibited in Paris in the eighteenth century, the archbishop of that city waited outside its cage to baptize the creature as soon as it emitted a sound resembling human speech. Since then zoologists and anatomists have confirmed the fundamental similarity between man and ape, archbishop and orang-outang. Psychologists have even drawn on their observations of ape behaviour in order to explain human conduct. Small wonder then that for purposes of classification man and ape have been lumped together in the order known as Primates, and that evidence of our common ancestor is sought among the fossilized remains of monkeys. So far the search for the first *Homo sapiens* or even the so-called 'missing link' between him and his simian forebears has been unrewarding and we cannot say for certain where or when man emerged from some advanced type of anthropoid. In terms of geological time the transformation may well have been an abrupt one. Certainly by the end of the Pleistocene era, varieties of *Homo sapiens* had achieved quite a wide geographical distribution.

What we do know is that somewhere about this period the evolutionary process had reached a point at which the potential hominid embodied all the characteristics required to accomplish the transition from animal to man. Among these characteristics were an upright posture, vocal cords which already allowed him to communicate in a rudimentary way with his fellows and hands with which he could manipulate objects. But above all man's brain provided the impetus for what would finally set him apart from other animals. It has been attributed variously to divine inspiration, spontaneous intuition and a cervical irrigation of nucleic acid, but whatever the reason man suddenly became aware of his own individuality and of his independence from the world around him. This stupendous realization turned what had formerly been a brute consciousness based on instinct to the self-consciousness that is born of an idea. Man had stepped outside himself into the realm of conceptual as opposed to merely perceptive experience. Language enabled him to give verbal expression to that experience and gradually he started to fashion and use ideas in the same way that his supple fingers already fashioned tools. He was still an animal, but an animal that reasoned. He was still a creature of the Earth, but now he inhabited what Teilhard de Chardin has termed its noosphere (from the Greek *vôus*, mind). From then on man was endowed with the unique gift of being able to control his own development.

This rapid and all-too-superficial review of evolution makes it abundantly clear that the human mind is indissolubly linked with the physiological process of evolution. We must at once discount the idea that at a certain point in prehistory God breathed into man a soul which gave him his humanity and a special place in the natural (and 'supernatural') scheme of things. Evolution is dramatic enough without having recourse to a *deus ex machina*. By insisting on the link between physical and mental development we are from the outset avoiding also any suggestion of dualism, according to which man may be viewed in terms of a mind and a body, the ghost inside the machine. Such a view is quite untenable if only because of what we know of the causal links between body and mind. From our own experience most of us are well aware of how excessive alcohol in the bloodstream can affect our thinking processes. Similarly the use of certain hallucinogenic drugs may bring about alarming and beautiful mental reactions.

Now if, as we have said, mind is organic inasmuch as it is completely identifiable with and attributable to bodily processes, it follows that it must coexist in some form or other with all living forms of physical life. Not only must it coexist with them, but it must also develop with them throughout their evolutionary course. Although man began to think conceptually only when his brain, the necessary physiological apparatus, had developed to a point of refinement capable of it, there is no reason to suppose that his immediate ancestors were completely incapable of thought. Who would deny, for example, that a chimpanzee possesses a mind of its own? Indeed, assuming, as we must, that mind and matter are inextricably linked, then the mere fact that the chimpanzee has a body is sufficient proof that it also has a mind.

Philosophical proofs are unnecessary, however, since Nature herself shows us quite plainly that all living things can think. We have already mentioned the instinctive consciousness that man has always shared with the lower animals. Even now much of his thinking differs only in degree and not in kind from their own. But this type of thought must not be confused with the conceptual variety which, thanks to the peculiar complexities of his cervical cortex, is man's special privilege. We are now discussing those thoughts which arise from the stimulation of one or more of our senses, and which represent our reactions to the outside world. This is the type of thinking that is said to stem from an organism's awareness of its environment and of the effect that environment will have on its well-being. For example, if I see a large obstacle in my path when I am walking down the road I shall try to avoid it if it is going to impede my progress. A dog will do the same thing in a similar situation. So too will a worm. Can we infer from this that the worm has a mind? I think we must; if we grant that the higher vertebrates have minds, there is no reason why, in view of evolution, some degree of mentation should not take place within lesser creatures. Indeed, scientists have shown that flat worms are capable of memory and that even single-celled protozoa will react to things around them in the manner they deem best for themselves. If it comes to that, even plants, consciously or unconsciously, will turn towards the sun so as to benefit from its light. The inescapable conclusion from all this is that nature must be psychologically directed towards the satisfaction of its needs;

the bee[1] stores honey in a hexagonal cell, a form which mathematicians have shown to be the most economical for this purpose; the ant establishes for itself a well-ordered society; the homing pigeon crosses hundreds of miles of unknown sky to regain its loft. Clearly, proof that nature has a mind is as much the result of observation as it is of logical deduction from the very existence of matter.

That there is something which may be called 'mental' coexistent with life is a fundamental belief of magic, and is a belief shared by a great many scientists.* However, while the scientists are prepared to accept this as a working hypothesis which experience seems to confirm, the magician ventures to speculate on the nature of this universal mind. In doing so he is bound to incur the displeasure of those who insist that only a rigorously scientific approach confined to empirical observation can possess any real validity. It is true that once he abandons such restraints the magician is bound to be led to conclusions that are as yet scientifically unproven. However, these conclusions, provided they satisfy the essential conditions of observation and experience, do not deserve to be rejected out of hand. Reason and induction are perfectly respectable aids to knowledge. These led Democritus in the fifth century B.C. to describe the atom, although only in the second half of the last century could technology produce the instruments needed to show he was right. It is an all-too-common presupposition of allegedly non-presupposing scientists that nothing can exist until it has been detected by them or the apparatus they have invented.

We have said that the magician speculates on the nature of the *universal* mind. For to him this mind is universal, although it is experimentally observable only in the behaviour of living organisms. But the distinction between living matter and dead matter is at best a vague one. After all, the origin of life itself is now accredited to an adventitious combination of 'dead' chemicals subjected to various gases. In any case all matter, by its very existence in the universe, has 'life'; so to say that a stone 'lives' is not as ridiculous as it may at first appear. This is especially true if one recalls that in the stone's molecular structure there are tiny electrons all whizzing around in a manner that seems far from dead. We have

* Other scientists hold a different view. They contend that evolution may on occasion produce novel features such as the emergence of the living from the non-living. In the same way the 'mental' is said by them to be a novel feature that has emerged from the 'non-mental'.

in any case already noted that if the evolutionary theory were carried to its logical conclusion, then mind or life would have to be regarded as implicit in all things, an essential aspect of that same reality of which matter is merely the external appearance.

The assumption that life is natural to matter means that nature is both self-generating and self-perpetuating. In addition, because some form of mentation is present in matter, it must follow that these are to some extent conscious processes. Every plant and animal must share spiritually in the life process of the world's 'soul' just as it participates materially in the organization of the world's 'body'. This interpretation is by no means new; it is that of the early Greek philosophers, in particular of the Stoics, and reappeared during the Renaissance. It may also be latent in Descartes, whose dualist assertion 'I think, therefore I am' can lead quite happily to the Hobbesian paraphrase 'I think, therefore matter can think' and, later, to Bergson's theory of the *élan vital*. Nor has any of this been contradicted by modern science. On the contrary, the recent discovery of ribonucleic acid (RNA) and subsequent views on the molecular origin of thought serve only to confirm it.

When we observe the life force that permeates the universe we see that it manifests itself in process and movement. Because this movement is reducible to rational laws of motion we may safely conclude that the universe, or rather its all-pervading vitalism, is itself both orderly and rational. And yet the world has its share of disorder and destruction – at times it may even seem that chaos rather than unity or harmony characterizes the universe. However, even if we admit that the actual creation of the universe, if it ever was created, is nothing more than a vast cosmic accident, the fact remains that it is subject to certain laws which arise from the very nature of matter. The disorder and destruction, the freaks and curiosities, can all be explained by material causes, that is, by natural law working out its irrevocable process when physical conditions happen to be uncommon. Far from proving the absence of law in the universe, the apparent exceptions serve only to emphasize its efficacy. Nature never contradicts herself. Were she to do so, there would be no causality.*

* Recently, it is true, physicists have encountered molecular behaviour that is both irrational and non-causal, but it may be that such apparent exceptions are due more to gaps in our understanding than to a perverse quirk in an otherwise rational system. This will be considered further in Chapter 3.

So far we have posited that a certain life force is present every-where. It follows then that the world we know may be only a small part of the external manifestation of that force. There is a strong likelihood of its having manifested itself elsewhere in the cosmos, although it is too soon to be certain. It is also possible that though at present identifiable only when bound up with matter, life may in certain circumstances exist independently of it or, to remain true to materialism, in material forms not directly recognizable by our senses. There is no need to stress again the inadequacy of our sense organs: viewed through the microscope a drop of water is seen to contain myriad living forms all invisible to the naked eye; there may be myriad other forms invisible to the microscope.

After its ubiquity the most important thing about the life force is the rational motivation which can be discerned behind the work-ings of natural law. It is on account of this that pan-vitalism has often been expressed in metaphysical terms like universal law, Providence or simply God. To do this, however, is to bring in the *deus ex machina* we have been at such pains to keep out. The atheist will be all too ready to tell us that to deify a natural, albeit un-fathomable, process is to explain one mystery by substituting another. It is like the old story-teller who claimed that the world rested on the back of a tortoise, and when asked what the tortoise was standing on replied that it rested on the back of an elephant.

Having said that, I am afraid that at this point we are nevertheless going to try to smuggle in the tortoise. We may even need the ele-phant as well. The fact is that provided we know exactly what we mean, there is no real harm in calling the life force 'God'. Those confirmed atheists who are still with us need not drop out, how-ever, for we shall attribute to 'God' nothing more than what can reasonably be attributed to the life force. God is merely another name for it. A better name, too, for those words 'life force' have a curiously old-fashioned ring to them reminiscent of the 'twenties and 'thirties when New Thought, eurhythmics and George Bernard Shaw were all the vogue. Admittedly the word 'God' is of even older vintage, but at least it is more economical. In using it, however, we are not indulging in that parochial type of pantheism which sees the solar universe as a living being with God as its soul and the sun as its heart. On the contrary – and, alas, here comes the elephant – there are grounds for arguing that if the universe is but a visible manifestation of God, then God the unmanifest may also exist. If the Creator is within everything, He must also transcend everything, for the Creator cannot be confined within the created. If this is true, then God becomes the formless one behind the world of form, transcendent as well as immanent. Again, the atheists need not despair, for by accepting the possibility of a transcendent deity we are simply accepting, possibly without much philosophical justification,* a Great Unmanifest, which some agnostic philosophers have likened to x, the unknown quantity in algebra. Fortunately the whole question is irrelevant to the practice of magic, which involves no more than the application of certain natural laws. It is quite immaterial whether or not these laws presuppose a divine law-giver.

Because he knows that mind characterizes the entire universe, the magician is able to enjoy what we may call a unitary view of nature. For him the universe is exactly what the word implies – a unity. This in turn leads him to postulate that a law manifestly in operation in one part of the universal system is equally operative throughout the whole. The consequence of this last premise is that, since the universe is in itself a complete whole, some characteristic of the major components must be shared by the lesser components, animal, vegetable or mineral. We have, for example, seen how varying combinations of identical molecules lie behind the evolution of all matter; the visible results may differ but the essential properties of matter remain the same. All things therefore have the same components and obey the same natural law, and behind their outward form there is but one mind. In magic it is this universal 'oneness' that has long been an object of study and research. It represents for the magician, as it must also for the scientist, the secret of nature. It is the unifying principle behind the intricacy of natural phenomena, reconciling the unity of substance with the heterogeneity of form.

In magic the underlying similarity between different things is

* Roman Catholicism is now the only important religion still to claim that the existence of God is deducible by reason alone. Three arguments are commonly used in support of this natural theology: (1) The ontological argument, according to which the concept of an infinite God, since it is greater than the mind conceiving it, must mean that God has an independent existence. (2) The cosmological argument, which is really the old Aristotelian argument from first causes and which makes God the first cause and the material universe its effect. (3) The teleological argument, which posits that the complex organization of the universe testifies to the existence of a Supreme Intelligence. Many modern philosophers have exercised themselves in refuting these arguments, Kant and Hume being among the most successful.

systematized by identifying certain correspondences between them. From time immemorial magicians have sought to establish the natural affinity that exists between certain planets, metals, jewels, birds, beasts, herbs, colours, flowers and scents. A great deal of patience and ingenuity have been expended on this formidable task, but observation and experiment have also played their part. Magic is, after all, much more than an academic exercise. Nowadays many of the correspondences that have been elaborated may appear crude and naive, but the fault often lies not in the correspondences themselves but in the archaic way in which they are expressed or the quaint reasons once thought up to justify them. We must allow for the fact that much extant magical writing dates from the Middle Ages or earlier and reflects the mental and cultural climate of its time. Some of these writings may be downright silly and many others will be inconsistent with what we now know to be true. However, while it is only right to discard everything that strikes us as foolish, it would clearly be imprudent to reject the rest out of hand.

The most important of the universal correspondences are those that exist between ourselves and God. Although we know well enough that man is no more than the product of a natural evolutionary scheme, we must nevertheless accord him a special place within that scheme. He is its fulfilment. If the material world is but a reflection of God, it is in man that God is truly reflected. Like the universe itself, only on a far smaller scale, man is a psycho-biological unit; by studying that unit, the microcosm, we are able to gain a more profound understanding of the universe, the macrocosm, for we can confidently expect God, the sum of all things, to be everything that we ourselves are, only much magnified. We may even go as far as to liken Him and the universe in which He expresses Himself to the human organism expressed on a vast scale. Man, the miniature organism, is able by introspection to expand his consciousness so that his inner self reaches out and embraces the universe. Clearly, the closer the miniature resembles its subject, the greater the expansion that is possible. Thus it is above all the complete man who, once he has experienced every human impulse and integrated them in one balanced personality, is able to reach the heart of the universe wherein lies union with God. This is the supreme achievement of magic, and it is summed up by Aleister Crowley as 'the raising of the whole man in perfect balance to the power of Infinity'. In short, it is the apotheosis of the self.

If the universe is man on a gigantic scale, the mysterious forces that move it may be equated with those that move man. Through them is woven the fabric of all visible things and it is the magician's task to discover their true nature. To this end he need only cultivate the forces already latent in himself, for they are, of course, the same as those that regulate our world and propel the furthermost star. 'Know thyself' was the good advice given at Delphi. In order to make them easier to comprehend, however, the major cosmic forces have been named in magic after various planets and the gods and goddesses of the ancient world. However, this personification is merely a device to help us to appreciate their real significance: the friendly figure of Mr Therm was always more evocative than the vague concept of High Speed Gas. Even more personalized are the lesser forces, which are dubbed angelic or demonic according to their function. In the Western hemisphere these often have Jewish names which are ceremonially invoked in magical operations based on a system known as the kabbalah. Elsewhere in the world their names are different, as we shall see in Chapter 7 when we describe an Egyptian ritual, but that need not disturb us; the forces they represent are still the same.

Apart from the results they achieve and the names they have been given, little is known about these forces. They presumably represent different aspects of the universal mind, its thoughts and intentions which, unseen and inexorable, move through the universe in pursuit of some divine ambition. There are forces that sponsor growth and conservation; others cause decay and destruction; still others promote love and peace; while others, no less potent, are harbingers of hatred and war. Because of these differences it is possible to describe some forces as positive and others as negative. No moral judgment is implied by this classification, and both types of force are equally necessary. Indeed, the theory of opposites is very ancient, and many ethical systems advise us to achieve a balance between the opposites in our own character. The philosopher Hegel is well known for his emphasis on the need for a negative as well as a positive element in life. Because the first of these discards the old and the second ushers in the new, progress is possible only when they act together. This synthesis between the two is the goal of the dedicated magician who, having experienced and mastered all things, becomes the complete man, the true likeness of God.

The power that is used in magic is derived from the forces we have been describing and so comes from both within and outside ourselves. It is formed by linking one aspect of the magician's personality with a corresponding aspect of the cosmic mind. This at once sets up a current of power which the magician can draw upon for his own purposes. It is not unlike flicking a switch to turn on the electric light. However, just as electricity requires an efficient wiring system, so magical power always needs a suitable conductor through which to flow. This conductor is established by the performance of an appropriate ritual, every detail of which contributes to the final influx of power. It is because each detail is so important that the rituals given in this book must be scrupulously followed. This is not only because the success of the whole operation will depend on it, but because, as in the case of electricity, magic can be dangerous when tampered with.

In the beginning of this chapter we compared man to a glorified monkey and we have finished by likening him to God. You will recall that the reason for his elevation was his unique ability to think in conceptual terms. This meant that he could form thoughts that were not directly prompted by sense-perception, though possibly based on perceptive experience, and then go on to examine their content objectively. All along, however, we have been careful to insist that even conceptual thinking is based only on molecular processes inside the brain cells and is susceptible to physiological changes; our judgment as well as our sense-perceptions may be impaired by alcohol or narcotics. But perhaps we have not sufficiently stressed that the influence of the mind on bodily functions is equally strong. Only as we learn more about the psychosomatic origin of many diseases are we slowly beginning to realize how powerful our thoughts can be. We must now consider the nature of thought itself. For our difficulty, as we come to the end of this chapter, is that so far we have not been able to identify in man anything which might suggest that he can transcend the all-too-mortal flesh of which he is made. Unless we do find something, however, we shall never succeed in getting him or magic off the ground.

The first thing to be said about thought is that it cannot be destroyed. It appears that every thought leaves an indelible imprint on the neuron that sponsored it; a suspension of consciousness, as for example under hypnosis, is all that is needed to revive it. That is why most psychoanalytic therapy is concerned with teaching a patient how to cope with the subconscious memories stored in his brain. Thus once they are born, thoughts may exist quite independently of the original thinking process. The most obvious examples outside the store-rooms of the subconscious are the things men create – from buildings to ball-bearings, from poetry to pin-tables – all of which are the material expression of what were once only ideas.

Most thoughts, however, remain in the mind of the thinker. Yet there are grounds for stating that even these enjoy a form of existence. This is because thought is the energy generated by the molecular reaction involved in thinking and, like all energy, it cannot be destroyed. What happens to it, then? The occultist will answer that if the thought is powerful enough it may imprint itself on the etheric or astral atmosphere. Etheric and astral are fancy, but unavoidable, words intended to convey the notion of a non-material or, possibly, a semi-material dimension that is not normally recognizable by our senses. The latter are, of course, able to respond only to the material world of which our body is part. This imprinting of thought on the etheric planes is the explanation often given for the characteristic atmosphere surrounding certain places. It is known that people who are in some way more sensitive than the rest of us react at once to the atmosphere of a former battlefield, or a room where, for example, a murder has taken place. It is as if the feelings of those participating in the tragedy were raised to such a pitch of intensity that they still linger in the air. A great many hauntings can probably be explained in this way. So much for intense thoughts, but that still leaves us with the less forceful ones that come into being almost constantly. The occult explanation is that if these are too weak to enjoy any lasting permanence they simply dissolve with whatever aspect of the cosmic mind corresponds most closely with them.

Perhaps the best illustration of the occultist view of thought is by means of the over-worked comparison with a radio wave. The brain then becomes the broadcasting studio from which the thought radiates. We become aware of radio waves only if they are picked up and densified by a suitable receiver, but they exist, nevertheless. All the receiver has done is to make them accessible to our senses, just as printed verses express a poet's vision in a form others can appreciate. The theory that thoughts, like radio waves, are imprinted on the ether is not without scientific foundation. We know, for example, that the thinking process is accompanied by tiny rhythmic variations in the electric charges that go on in the brain. It is possible that these charges may somehow mould the ether into what we might call a thought form. Nor is such a theory confined to a few starry-eyed occultists; it has also been put forward by Professor H. H. Price, who imagines the universe populated by mental images, each with a semi-physical existence in the 'psychic ether'.[2] According to him these ideas are independent entities which, given certain conditions, may integrate to form vast patterns that transcend the individual consciousness. This, of course, is remarkably similar to the occult view that powerful thoughts impose their own peculiar imprint on the astral, while weaker ones blend with related aspects of the cosmic mind. The psychic patterns described by Professor Price may also provide the images that make up the group mind which is so important a feature of Jungian psychology. Interesting though these theories are, however, they remain only theories. Fortunately for us, therefore, the independent existence of thought is also confirmed by the phenomenon of telepathy.

Researchers all over the world are now beginning to admit that the evidence adduced in favour of telepathy is so impressive as to merit serious consideration. Indeed, a few years ago Sir Alister Hardy, Emeritus Professor of Zoology at Oxford University, told the British Association for the Advancement of Science that the existence of telepathy had been[3] scientifically demonstrated. A similar view has been expressed by Professor C. D. Broad.[4] Much of this evidence is the result of patient research conducted by Dr J. B. Rhine at Duke University, North Carolina, and is complemented by equally meticulous work carried out by Dr S. G. Soal and the Society for Psychical Research. Even in Soviet Russia, where all forms of parapsychology were once dismissed as bourgeois superstition, the eminent scientist Professor Vasiliev, of the University of Leningrad, has admitted the possibility of telepathic communication. For our purpose we may state that however rarely telepathy occurs under scientifically acceptable conditions, the few times it has done so are enough to show that whereas brain and mind may be two aspects of the same entity, the thoughts they jointly produce achieve an identity that is independent of both.

Of the thoughts we have, the vast majority concern ourselves. These consist not only of the thoughts that spring from our day-to-day experience, like going to work or filling in our income-tax returns, but also of that deeper self-awareness which only conceptual thinking permits, an unremitting consciousness of our own identity.[5]

As a result of such preoccupation, an exact replica of ourselves is built up in thought form on the astral planes or, if you prefer, the psychic ether. In occultism the name given to this etheric extension of our physical selves is the astral body, or the body of light. It is believed to be composed of a finer and subtler material than our physical bodies, but even so can on occasion become visible. The well-attested phenomenon of bilocation, as in the case of the late Padre Pio, may probably be explained as the appearance of the astral self in one place while the physical self is elsewhere. The fact that the physical self is usually asleep when bilocation occurs suggests that consciousness may sometimes be transferred from the physical body to its astral counterpart. With practice the transference can be made voluntarily, and then it becomes known as astral projection. In Chapter 8 we shall explain how this is done. To step out into the astral body and observe one's physical self sleeping beside one is an exhilarating experience. In one second it refutes materialism more effectively than hours of argument or a successful canter through the Zener cards.

The fact that the astral body enjoys an existence of its own has one further consequence which will not have escaped the astute reader; being independent of the physical body it can survive physical death. Here lies our only hope of immortality, for we must agree with the materialists that when our brain ceases to function our existence should logically come to an end. Such is probably the fate of most living creatures. In the case of man, however, his consciousness can on death pass to the astral body he has spent a lifetime creating. His personality, having survived intact, can then withdraw to the astral planes where it will begin the next phase of its existence. Even so, our astral bodies, like the incarnate personalities from which they are derived, are really no more than an outward expression of ourselves. With time they too must be shed, so that only the individual self, a spark of consciousness which is the quintessence of many personalities, is left. If it then still has lessons to learn from the world, or, in occult language, if it still has a karmic debt to satisfy, it must return there. This is not done by direct incarnation, which would be contrary to the scientific view of man as the psycho-biological product of evolution, but by associating, in some way at present unknown to us, with the nascent astral personality which a new-born baby creates as it slowly becomes aware of itself. If, on the other hand, the individual has no further cause to return to the world, he is free to proceed on the path of spiritual evolution which leads eventually to the sublime vision of God's true self. A secret benefit of magic is that by understanding and practising the art we can move along that path now. In the following pages we shall step a little closer towards the glory of the light.

2

FTER OUR bird's-eye view of magical theory we must examine a little more closely certain aspects of it before going on to tackle the practical consequences. Magic works regardless of whether the magician knows the reasons for it, but this should not deter us from trying to understand why. To go through the ritual motions with no clear idea of what they are all about is mere superstition, not magic. In any case, the magician should expect more from his magic than mere signs and wonders. If these are all he is after, he would be better advised to take up conjuring, which is far less trouble. The real rewards of magical study are not temporal benefits but a spiritual maturity which affords a more profound understanding of the universe in which we live. Let us examine that universe in occultist terms, beginning, appropriately enough, at the beginning.*

God and the universe which is His self-expression have always existed: visible and invisible, both make up the divine being. Because the universe is God's awareness of Himself, at once the product and expression of His divine mind, creation is conceived by most occultists as a series of thoughts emanating simultaneously from the divine source and often described as a series of ineffable lights. The analogy with light is a useful one, for just as white light is composed of different colours, so the creative thought has been said to contain the potentialities of all the various types of force that are manifest throughout the universe. In all, God brought into being ten of these lights, each containing less and less of the divine essence until the final one formed the world of dense matter. This

* I am afraid that the theologizing which follows will not appeal to everyone, but as it is intended only to provide us with a working hypothesis it need not be taken too seriously by those who prefer to work things out for themselves.

initial emanation of divine energy may also be viewed as the unfolding of a divine language, for occultists have long assumed that these creative thoughts must have been expressed verbally, like our own more humble thoughts. For this reason they often speak of creation in terms of words and the holy letters of which they are composed, thus making the secret world of God a world of language in which powerful names unfold in accordance with the divine will.

This particular theory of creation is principally derived from an occult tradition known as the kabbalah, the *hokmahnistarah* or secret wisdom of the Jewish people. The word 'kabbalah' means tradition, and it was evidently bequeathed by one generation to the next long before it came to be written down.* What exactly is the knowledge it contains? In its essence it is a mystical vision of the ultimate reality behind the world of form. Like all mysticism it is a confrontation between the individual and his creator, a deeply personal experience which no one else can share. Fortunately for us, however, most mystics have endeavoured to describe or formulate their experience as best they can, although the words at their disposal can never adequately depict the full wonder of what they have seen. To a large extent a mystic is always forced to use the language and ready-made symbolism of his community, because these alone are comprehensible to his fellows and, possibly, to himself as well. In this way he ends up by fitting what was a moment of sudden illumination within a conventional framework, a *corpus symbolicum* representative of his time and cultural background. Thus although mystics everywhere, whether Hindu, Christian or Buddhist, perceive the same reality, they inevitably clothe it in whatever religious trappings are most familiar to them. That is why Hindu visionaries never see the Virgin Mary and Christians are not brought face to face with Vishnu.

* The chief books of the kabbalists are the *Sefer Yetsirah*, or Book of Creation, which is thought to date from the 6th century, and the *Sefer Hazzohar* (known as the *Zohar*), or Book of Brightness, which appeared in the 13th century. There is some controversy over the authorship of the *Zohar*: some authorities say that it dates from the 2nd century when it may have been written by a mystic called Simeon ben Yochai, while others attribute it to its discoverer, Moses de Leon. Another important work is the *Sefer-hab-Bahir*, or Book of Bahir, which was probably written in the 6th century by Isaac the Blind. Supporters of the kabbalah insist, however, that it can be nothing less than divinely inspired. In the Book of Enoch the arcane wisdom is said to have been betrayed to mankind by the fallen angels, but a Talmudic tradition claims that God whispered it to Moses on Mount Sinai. According to this tradition its secrets were then imparted to seventy elders who thereafter transmitted them orally to their successors.

Thus the mystical content of the kabbalah has been translated into traditional Jewish concepts, and, more specifically, has been systematized largely according to a particular reading of the Pentateuch, the first five books of the Old Testament. This may have been a subterfuge on the part of the early kabbalists to make their teachings acceptable to rabbinical authority, although it is equally likely that as devout Jews they were only too eager to rest their philosophical theories on the bedrock of revelation. For this reason the text of the Pentateuch became in their eyes the exoteric form of the Torah, the law of God. Here zealous kabbalists searched for a symbolic account of the hidden processes of the divine life, the text itself being far less important than the concealed meaning which they tried to wrest from it by experimenting with the numerical value of its words and letters.* By these methods the same letters recurring in different combinations could, it was believed, be made to reproduce different aspects of the world, a fact that led one kabbalist to exclaim, 'In every word shine many lights.'

In contrast to its exoteric form, the esoteric Torah was regarded as a pre-existential being made up of the one great name of God.† This was the *torah kedumah*, or primordial Torah, whose creation was identical with the cosmogonic process that occurred when the divine name emerged under the appearance of light from God's invisible essence. For the kabbalist the world was not formed out of nothing, a *creatio ex nihilo*, but was instead an unfolding of the

---

* Three main cryptogrammatic methods were employed. (1) *Gematria*: this involved converting the letters of the Hebrew alphabet into their numerical equivalents and substituting another word of the same numerical total. In this way the words 'And lo three men' (Gen. xviii 2) could be reconstructed to read, 'These were Michael, Gabriel and Raphael.' The alignment of God, the Creator, with primordial man can also be justified by gematria since the numerical total value of God's name (YHVH) is the same as that of man (Adam). Kabbalistic scholars were greatly helped in their experiments by the fact that Hebrew has no vowels. (2) *Notarikon*: this was a method of forming sentences by taking every letter of a given word as the initial letter of another. Alternatively, the first or the final letter of each word in a particular sentence could be used to form a new word. Angelic names and divine appellations were usually 'discovered' in this way. (3) *Temura*: This was even more complicated than the two previous methods, and was fundamentally a means of deciphering the many divine messages believed to be buried in the sacred texts.

† In his *de vita contemplativa* Philo speaks of the Torah as a living being whose body is the literal text of the Pentateuch and whose soul is the occult meaning that underlies the written word. Among the Moslems there is an esoteric sect called the *batiniyya* who regard the Koran in exactly the same way. Similar claims are made about the Hindu Vedas which are said to have not only a literal meaning but another (*Devanagri*) which arises from their metre and intonation (*svara*).

potencies already within the *en sof*, the infinite God, who is beginningless and eternal. In His transcendence God would be totally incomprehensible were it not that His nature may be deduced from a knowledge of His attributes. We can declare therefore that by the finite act of creation God the infinite ceased to be a formal abstraction and manifested Himself as a dynamic unity marvellously rich in content. This means that creation was largely a theogonic process by which God emerged from His concealment in order to reveal Himself in His creation. The world in which we live can therefore be regarded as a world of divine being where the secret and the visible are wonderfully reconciled, just as creation itself was but the exoteric aspect of a mysterious process taking place within the godhead. When the kabbalists described these processes they often spoke of four realms, a sort of spiritual hierarchy consisting of *atsiluth*, the realm of divine emanation, *beriah*, the realm of creation, *yetsirah*, the realm of formation, and *asiyah*, the realm of activation. These realms, like the ten ineffable lights, were not successive but were held to exist simultaneously, being representative only of the manner in which the power of God materializes.

In kabbalistic terminology each of the divine emanations is called a *sefira* and together they make up the ten *sefiroth*. The word 'sefira' simply means a number or category. The sefiroth represent different aspects of the cosmic mind. They are manifested also in the forces that move the universe, and as we ourselves are a miniature of that universe they represent also the forces that move us. Here we return to the idea of the micro/macrocosm according to which the world and God are wholly contained and reflected in man. The complete man is thus the perfect man, the *Adam Kadmon*[1] or primordial being who is identifiable with God in His act of creation. This then is the aim of the magician when by the correct use of ritual he seeks to realize the magical nexus between himself and the cosmos.

For the sake of convenience the sefiroth are traditionally set out in a diagram known as the *Etz Hay-Yim* or Tree of Life (see p. 41). This is often referred to as the Great Glyph, and commonly described as an all-embracing pattern both of the universe and of man. In the *Sefer-hab-Bahir* we find the following passage: 'It is I who have planted this tree, so that the world may gaze at it in wonder. With it I have encompassed the All and have named it the All; all things depend on it and all emanate from it; all things have need of it, look upon it and yearn for it, and from it all souls must proceed.'² The All is present in the tree because its branches fully reflect the unity of our personality, the underlying pattern of the universe and the true nature of God. It is as if the whole of life were spread out before us in a way that is at once ingeniously simple and terrifyingly complex, a combination which is part of the perennial fascination of the kabbalah and which Eliphas Lévi once described in lyrical terms:

> On penetrating into the sanctuary of the kabbalah one is seized with admiration in the presence of a doctrine so logical, so simple and at the same time so absolute. The essential union of ideas and signs; the consecration of the most fundamental realities by primitive characters; the trinity of words, letters and numbers; a philosophy as simple as the alphabet, profound and infinite as the Word; theorems more complete and luminous than those of Pythagoras; a theology which may be summed up on the fingers; an infinite which can be held in the hollow of an infant's hand; ten figures and twenty-two letters, a triangle, a square and a circle. Such are the elements of the kabbalah.³

It follows that if we want to understand God, the universe and ourselves, we must learn the meaning of each of the sefiroth on the Tree of Life. This is not a gruelling exercise like learning irregular French verbs, and no one need be put off by the unfamiliar names. A great deal of the Hebrew terminology used by modern kabbalists is no more than a convention, just as Italian is still conventionally used in musical composition; despite the legatos and accelerandos, good music, like magic, is completely international. If you study the tree intuitively as well as intelligently, relating it to what you know of life and yourself, you will soon grasp its universal significance. In no time at all you will be able to fit your feelings, your experiences and all you see around you to the appropriate sefiroth. According to the enthusiasts you will then have found the answer to almost every question and be a little closer to the meaning of life.

A detailed explanation of the tree would fill a book and be a daunting challenge both to the writer and, because of its inevitable subjectivity, to the reader. Even then the explanation would probably be far from complete. The splendid thing about the Tree of Life, however, and, indeed, the entire kabbalah, is that the understanding of it is something that comes gradually from within yourself and is not the product of hard-learned lessons. There is a fine passage in the *Zohar* which describes the Torah as a beautiful maiden who lives alone in a secluded chamber of a great castle. From time to time she appears at the window so that her secret lover who waits outside may catch a glimpse of her. At last she begins to linger at the window thus enabling him to speak to her, but even then she keeps her face hidden behind a veil and when she replies it is in allegorical language. And then one day, just when the lover is despairing of ever getting to know her, she deigns to show her face and reveal to him the secrets she has hitherto kept in her heart. In this chapter we can do no more than lead you to the window where the maiden is waiting.

The first thing to be said about the Tree of Life is that it consists of three triangles and one final sefira called Malkuth situated at the bottom on its own. Although its true source is in heaven the tree is, as it were, 'rooted' in Malkuth. It is not surprising therefore that this sefira represents the earth. Here is the womb that contains all those things that make up the tree itself, just as there already exists inside the acorn everything needed to create the mighty oak. In Malkuth lie the forces which are manifest in all the other sefiroth and which, you will recall, are also the forces within ourselves. For the sefiroth are above all *forces* rather than things, and for that reason the tree should be thought of not as a 'map' of ourselves and the world, but as a diagrammatic presentation of the invisible and interrelated forces active in both.

If we look at the triangles on the tree we see that each contains two opposing forces while between them lies a third, the force of consciousness, which serves to balance them. This third force is the equilibrium which is so important in the doctrine of opposites. The sefiroth can be further classified by saying that those on the right of the tree, the Black Pillar or Pillar of Mercy, are male and therefore positive, while those on the left, the Silver Pillar or Pillar of Severity, are female and negative. From this it follows that the sefiroth in the middle, which reconcile the other two, must be bisexual. Because our minds are unable readily to conceive abstractions like 'force', each sefira has acquired its own mental image or symbolic personification, linked to which are further images and associations. These are simply the forms we have devised to help us understand and eventually use the cosmic forces they represent.

At the 'top' of the tree and at the apex of the triangle is the Sphere

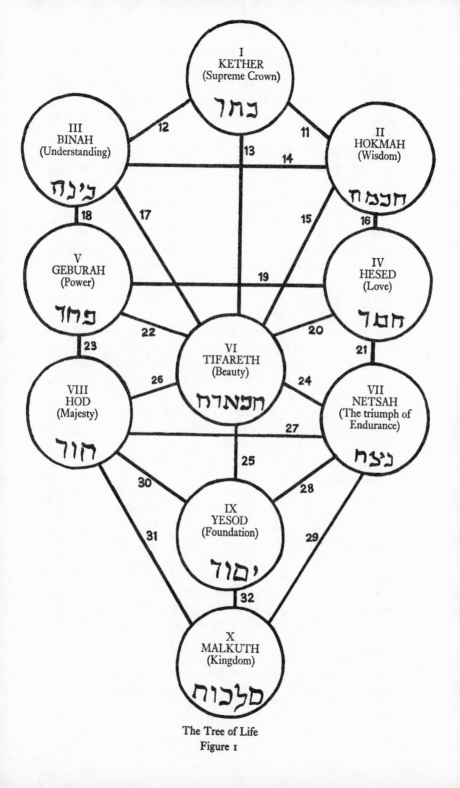

The Tree of Life
Figure 1

of Kether. The force behind this sefira is nothing less than the creative power of God, that initial emanation which produced the whole process of creation. By this token it is the sefira closest to the *en-sof*, the Eternal Infinite, which, though at present inconceivable by us, we know to be the unmoved Prime Mover of all movement and life.

Within the creative impulse were two principles, one active and the other passive. Male and female, they have become the twin forces of our universe. The active force Hokmah, on the right of the triangle, is the positive, dynamic energy that lies behind all movement, growth and change. Its opposite, Binah, is the passive principle, stable and unchanging, like the waters of a tranquil sea. We know, however, that once these dark waters are impregnated by the force of Hokmah, they will stir and bring forth life. Thus while Hokmah is the Father of the universe, Binah is the Great Mother, that passive wisdom whose ways are those of gentleness and whose paths are those of peace.

After the universal activity implicit in the first triangle we turn in the second to more homely things. For the sefiroth found here may be described in human terms as a father, mother and child. The first of these, Hesed, is the father, stern yet benevolent, just yet forgiving. His is the power that goes about calmly organizing things, ensuring that order emerges from chaos and that justice, peace and love prevail. On the left of the triangle is the opposite force, Geburah, which also represents authority, but this time that of the mother. This is the force that punishes, but does so only where punishment is merited. Even so, the energy of Geburah is essentially destructive, causing havoc, strife and war. In this way the actions of Hesed and Geburah complement each other and are observable in the manifold workings of nature where the established order succumbs to inevitable processes of destruction. Between the two, however, lies the redemptive sphere of Tifareth, held by tradition to be the sphere of the Sun. Here we see the urge to survive, the vital energy that impels life to continue regardless of setbacks. It may seldom realize its ambition to hold in perfect balance the forces that flank it, but it nevertheless ensures that progress results from their ceaseless interaction.

In the third triangle the child we encountered in Tifareth has attained adulthood. We are now able to perceive the two main forces that move him. The first, on the right of the triangle, is the male force, Netsah. Just as the child of Tifareth represented the urge to survive, so the mature Netsah is that same urge realized. For it is the endurance and continuation of Nature. In addition, it contains within itself all those things we think of when we use the word 'natural': it represents the senses and the passions, the world of instinct and primeval desires, our unreasoned reaction to the things that affect us.

As Netsah represents our natural proclivities, so Hod, its opposite, has to do with mental activity that is less dependent on sensory impulses. This is the realm of imagination and fantasy, abstraction and intellect. Whereas in the turmoil of Netsah we see the spontaneous activity of the mind, we behold in the repose of Hod the mind's own creativeness. Between the two, however, there exists a third force, Yesod, which contains the other two and much of itself besides. For in the mysterious depths of this sefira lie all those characteristics which combine to form our individual personalities.

Finally we return to Malkuth where, as children of the earth, we may stand looking up at the tree. Its source, it is true, is lost in the light of the eternal, but we need not despair of reaching that light. We are a part of it. Indeed, being a composite symbol of the universe, the tree can be used to help us draw closer to the fountainhead. We can use it too as our guide to the astral world whenever we choose to leave the sphere of Malkuth; for by recollecting the pattern of the tree we may safely go ahead and explore the astral without any risk of losing our way.

In some books the figure of a man is superimposed on the Tree of Life, as if to remind us that the microcosm he represents is an exact replica of the macrocosm. By studying himself, therefore, man can better understand the workings of nature and from this understanding learn something of God and the divine scheme of things. It is simply a matter of reasoning from the known to the unknown, the visible to the invisible, the human to the divine. But the conformity between the part and the whole has another consequence which is of vital importance in the practice of magic. This is the ancient belief that the one can directly affect the other since each is subject to the same laws. It is best summed up by the so-called Emerald Tablet of Hermes Trismegistus, reputed to have been a piece of emerald on which certain Phoenician characters were engraved. One tradition has it that this precious tablet was found by Abraham's wife, Sarah, in a cave where it was guarded

by the corpse of Hermes Trismegistus, grandson of Adam and archi-
tect of the pyramids. Another tradition names its discoverer as
Alexander the Great, while yet a third maintains that Hermes
Trismegistus, alias Tehuti, the Egyptian god of wisdom,* presented
the tablet to an alchemist, Maria Prophetissa, who is said by some
to have been Miriam, sister of Moses. Fortunately, readers familiar
with magical literature will not be put out by these dubious origins
which are, alas, an all-too-common feature of occultism. As for the
message on the tablet itself, the Latin version contains these words:
'*Verum est ... quod superius est sicut quod inferius et quod inferius est
sicut quod superius, ad perpetrando miracula rei unius.*' 'The truth is
that what is above is like what is below and what is below is like
what is above, to accomplish the miracles of the one thing.' The
'miracles' of magic are governed by the same principle, although
far from being miraculous, they are merely the results of applying
certain natural though occult laws.

For the magical adept the kabbalah and the Tree of Life are a
useful codification of these laws. However, on no account should the
novice magician feel that by studying the kabbalah he is turning
his back on other magical traditions. Magic, like the laws on which
it is based, is universal; the ju-ju man, the shaman and the kabbalist
are all using the same laws, though in different ways. Thus although
magic can assume protean forms, these are never more than the outward appearances of a consistent reality, just as the mechanics of
speech remain the same for all the wide variety of languages. When
a Western adept evokes the negative aspect of Geburah he is in
effect summoning the same destructive power as his colleague in
Madras who invokes the goddess Kali. The reason why in this
chapter we have singled out the kabbalah for special attention is that
its cosmology seems eminently reasonable, far more so than the
many rival theories which compete for our acceptance. In any case,
the kabbalah, while retaining its Jewish character, is itself an amal-
gam of several magical traditions, including the Greek, Gnostic and
Egyptian. For this reason it has become the most widely used

---

* Tehuti, who went about giving names to all created things, is also known as the
first man and so the name may itself be an alias of Adam. See on these points C. J.
Jung, *Collected Works*, vol. xii, *Psychology and Alchemy* (Routledge and Kegan Paul,
London, 1953), pp. 349–50. In his book *Alchemy Rediscovered and Restored* (Rider,
London, 1940), the modern alchemist, Archibald Cockren, draws attention to an old
tradition which places Hermes Trismegistus in the Egypt of Sesosris II who was one
of the pharaohs of the 12th Dynasty (*c.* 1900 B.C.).

magical system in the Western world. But there is nothing to stop you, if you wish to be eclectic, from consulting other traditions from time to time. It is only occultists with a vested interest in promoting their own pet system who recommend their readers to stick always to a particular one. You will find that the rituals given in this book have at least the merit of being a fairly representative selection.

We implied earlier that the Tree of Life could serve as a guide to the astral world. Traditionally this mysterious realm is divided into two parts, the upper and the lower astral. These expressions should not, however, lead us to think of a particular place situated somewhere beyond the world in which we live. It would be more correct to think of it as a supra-physical world that coexists with our own, but is, as it were, on a different wavelength. Because of this it can be said to infiltrate our own world. Thus when we speak of the upper and lower astral we have in mind differences of degree, not distance. It may become easier to grasp if explained in these terms: close to the earth the etheric atmosphere has a fairly high degree of density; that is why the astral fabric can so easily be moulded to form thought images. However, as we retreat from the world of matter towards another, which, for want of a better word, may be called that of pure spirit, the etheric atmosphere becomes progressively more refined until we reach the upper astral. But the refinement is not the result of ether diffusing through space; rather it is a slipping over on to a different wavelength. All these wavelengths, however, like the long, medium and short radio waves, coexist in the same space. The real difficulty in understanding all this is that our minds have been conditioned to think three-dimensionally so that time, distance and degree are generally conceived only in spatial terms.

Who or what inhabits the astral world? Well, for a start there are in the lower astral the etheric bodies of the recently dead. On the eternal principle of sympathetic attraction these at once find themselves after death in the company of people similar to themselves, many of whom may have been their friends and relations on earth. Here their own thoughts and those of their predecessors have moulded the ether into landscapes similar to those they knew in life; there are cities, mountains, streams and forests, just as there are on earth. That is why descriptions of the next world received through spiritualist mediums often bear an incredible resemblance to the English countryside on a sunny afternoon in June. The prevalence of such thought forms is forcibly indicated in Sir Oliver Lodge's famous book *Raymond*,[4] where the dead hero reports that in the spirit world a fine cigar can be his for the wishing. The lesson that emerges from all this is that after death our personalities remain very similar to what they were on earth, with the same likes and dislikes, the same weaknesses and limitations. Unfortunately, this does not prevent some of the recently dead from laying claim to deep wisdom and prognosticating whenever they feel inclined. Many of us have at some time or other encountered those spurious Red Indians who have a fondness for platitudes and broken English. Most of these seance-room visitors are harmless enough, provided one accepts them for what they are and judges any advice they offer by ordinary common-sense standards. I am afraid it has always been fashionable among occultists to denigrate the spiritualist movement, but such hostility smacks rather of the Turk who could brook no rival near the throne.* What some occultists tend to forget is that many celebrated magicians in the past frequently had recourse to necromancy which, unlike the innocent pleasures of table-turning, often had a sinister purpose behind it. For necromancy was primarily a method of divination and the spirits were summoned not to dispense milk-and-water sentiments but to answer specific questions, often concerning the whereabouts of hidden treasure. The answers obtained in this way were usually as ambiguous as those provided by the Red Hawks and Chu-chin-chows of the modern spiritualist seance. Not that this ever deterred the necromancers: Saul engaged the Witch of Endor to call up the shade of Samuel; Ulysses interrogated the spirit of Tiresius; and the famous Dr Dee, assisted by the mediumistic Edward Kelley, was wont to conjure up the dead in Elizabethan times. Closer to our own period we have Eliphas Lévi's picturesque account of how he persuaded the ghost of Apollonius of Tyana to materialize in nineteenth-century London.[5]

One of the difficulties about trying to communicate with the dead is that you risk contacting an astral 'corpse'. This is the astral shell left behind after the individual behind the personality has vacated

---

* Aleister Crowley's attacks on the spiritualists were, as might be expected, extremely virulent. In his *Magick in Theory and Practice* (first published privately by Crowley, reissued Castle Books, New York, 1961), he describes their putrescent auras, morbid natures and filthy minds, warning his readers that contact with such creatures is more deadly than syphilis. It is hard to believe that his tongue was not at least half-way to his cheek when he wrote such muck.

it to begin a new incarnation or to continue its spiritual progress in the astral world. For a time these astral corpses retain a fragment of their original personality, and they may return nostalgically to earth to haunt places associated with them in life or to manifest themselves at seances. The problem here is that it is not always easy to detect the difference between the still-inhabited astral body and the astral corpse. That is why there is little of value, apart from comfort to the bereaved, to be derived from trafficking with the departed. You will find yourself talking either to what is little more than a zombie or else to a perfectly ordinary human being – and there are plenty of human beings in this world without your having to seek company in the next.

If, however, you are determined to go ahead and try your luck at communicating with the dead there are two good ways of going about it. Admittedly, the first of these has recently fallen into disrepute among spiritualists, but it remains a good deal safer than sitting alone, as they currently advocate, with your mind left open to whatever spirit influences care to occupy it. This first method is the old-fashioned one that involves spreading bits of paper bearing the letters of the alphabet in a circle and placing an upturned glass or tumbler in the middle. In addition to the letters, the circle should contain the numbers 1 to 10, and two papers, one bearing the word 'yes' and the other 'no'. The glass you use should not be too light or long-stemmed as it may overturn too easily or, worse, break. On the other hand, do not select one that is too cumbersome. For this type of seance there should be at least one other sitter besides yourself. There is no need to dim the lights beforehand or have 'Abide with Me' wafting from a record-player in the corner. Such 'atmosphere' may send agreeable shivers down the sitters' backs, but it could just as easily scare away a nervous spirit. Each sitter should rest a finger lightly on the glass, which should then move across the table apparently of its own volition until it touches one of the letters. If you wish, and if it does not make you feel too foolish, you can begin the proceedings by asking aloud, 'Is there anybody there?' The glass should then either stand still, in which case there is no one present, or else glide smoothly to 'yes'. If it glides to 'no', there is clearly something very wrong somewhere. Once communication has been established you may continue to ask your questions and the glass will, it is hoped, provide you with suitable answers. Do try, however, not to ask silly questions of the sort that reduce the whole enterprise to the level of a silly parlour game. Remember that if there is a genuine intelligence impelling the glass to move beneath your fingers, then he or she is entitled to the same respect you would afford any other human being. If the glass moves only in an erratic fashion you may be in contact with an astral corpse or at best an illiterate personality. There is then no point in carrying on and it is time for all concerned to break contact by lifting their fingers off the glass and having a chat, a drink or a cigarette before trying again.

If you start getting messages, try from the beginning to ascertain the name of the communicating entity. Do not be fobbed off with some commonplace Christian name like John, but insist on the full name, and, if possible, try to discover when and where the character lived. Afterwards you will be able to check up whether such a person ever existed. But be very wary if offered a well-known identity like Cleopatra; the Serpent of the Nile is unlikely to drop in for a gossip with your little circle. Be equally wary of quick results that seem too good to be true; the chances are that one of the sitters is pushing the glass himself. A wise precaution against this sort of thing is not to arrange the letters of the circle in alphabetical order, but to jumble them up. This may not deter the joker, but it will at least make his job more difficult.

Another quite harmless spiritualistic diversion, which can turn out to be as revealing about your own subconscious as it is about conditions in the next world, is automatic writing. For this you can use the traditional ouija board, or a contraption known as a planchette. The latter is a small platform which is mounted on rollers and has a pencil stuck through its centre. The theory is that if you rest your fingers on the platform, spirit forces are able to move it and use the pencil to write out messages. A simpler and much less costly way of achieving the same result is to hold an ordinary pencil in your hand, its tip resting on a sheet of paper, and then wait until your hand starts moving of its own accord. To keep your mind occupied in the meantime you should run through the multiplication tables or recite whatever bits of poetry you remember. Any writing that appears in the first few attempts will probably consist only of meaningless combinations of letters and indecipherable squiggles. But it may encourage you to persevere if you bear in mind that some people have produced full-length novels through automatic writing. A few spiritualists even claim that Dickens,

Shaw and Shakespeare are at present controlling the ball-points of several suburban psychics.

On the whole, you would be well advised to avoid promiscuous psychic dabbling and leave the dead where they are. All that can be said in favour of communicating with them is that it fosters a matter-of-fact acceptance of the astral world which is more desirable than the sort of holy awe encouraged in some occult circles. Of course, the magician should never join the fools in rushing to yet uncharted regions, but he need not hold himself back. After all, the angels themselves do not fear to tread the astral; it is their natural environment. Moreover, it stands to reason that if we are to work with this plane of existence we must learn from the start to accept it as something as real in its own terms as the physical world we now inhabit. This does not mean that we can afford to shirk the task of finding out all we can about the astral world before venturing into it. With knowledge we shall be able to greet its inhabitants not as strangers but as friends.

We have already observed that the human mind is for ever creating thought images on the astral planes. Most of these lose their identity quite rapidly by dissolving into a general pattern which is the etheric aspect of a cosmic force. These patterns, together with other archetypical images, are among the thought forms most commonly encountered in the lower astral where they have the appearance of independent life. In reality, however, they draw what life they have from those aspects of the universal mind most closely resembling them. Even so, for all practical purposes it is best to overlook the mechanics and treat all thought forms as if they are real in themselves. Indeed, as many of them have been created by the pictorial imagination of whole racial and religious groups, they can be said to have acquired a formal reality of their own. Other forms, however, are merely the symbolic reality which astral forces may temporarily assume so that we can recognize them. As forces, of course, they existed long before any symbolic identification was attached to them. This is so in the case of those great sefirothic forces on the Tree of Life; each one is associated with a mental image, and in perceiving that image we contact the force of which it is the expression. Thus the traditional classification of the images allows us to understand the varied phenomena we shall meet when practising magic.

Most common of the forces active in the lower astral are the elemental powers. These are synthetic thought forms generated by every series of automatic reactions at work throughout the universe. According to occultists an angelic intelligence is usually responsible for the initial reaction, but this withdraws once it has set things in motion. Thereafter subsequent reactions gradually build up an elemental consciousness of their own. Sometimes these natural processes form a localized unit like a valley, wood or mountain and they then generate an elemental oversoul of their own. Such is the origin of those nature spirits which the ancients used to venerate and which in the East are known as *devas*, or shining ones. Many types of elemental exist, but the most familiar categorization involves the four primary elements of earth, air, fire and water. In alchemy the elementals belonging to each of these groups were known respectively as gnomes, sylphs, salamanders and undines, although these names were not meant to be taken too literally. Each group is ruled by one of the four archangels, Uriel (earth), Raphael (air), Michael (fire) and Gabriel (water). There is no doubt that in the past, magicians, like most of their contemporaries, believed that only these four basic elements existed, but although science has now rejected this fourfold classification, it nevertheless remains a convenient one. Modern occultists often attempt to justify its retention by arguing that it represents four types of molecular activity prevalent through the multiplicity of physical elements.

The elementals provide much of the energy on which we shall be drawing in order to effect our magic. In reality elementals are streams of life, although parts of each stream may occasionally appear to detach themselves and enjoy a temporary independence. This ability to detach themselves will be useful to us when we are negotiating with them, but we ought always to bear in mind that their independence is illusory. Nor should the word 'negotiate' be taken to mean that we shall ever start bargaining with elementals. To do so would be to imply that they are our equals, whereas they are in fact below us on the scale of spiritual evolution. Any intelligence they possess is dedicated solely to the achievement of whatever purpose lies behind the activity they represent, be it destruction or preservation, chaos or harmony. It is this single-mindedness that provides them with their strength. From it flow vast currents of cosmic energy which, given the right conditions, can be used to accomplish the seemingly impossible. Yet at the same time this is also their weakness; they rush inexorably and with blinkered vision towards a destination not of their own choosing. Nevertheless, we should not despise them when all they are doing is being true to their own nature. Nor should we ever consider making them our slaves, for to do so would be to challenge the authority of the archangels, also known as the Mighty Ones, who direct their activity. There is a traditional belief that because they are but creations of the created, elementals eventually cease to exist. As they develop, they gradually sense that they are doomed, and so look upon us to teach them how to acquire immortality. By coming into contact with human beings whose own survival, you will recall, is due to an ability to think conceptually, they hope to learn how to think for themselves and so establish an identity which is divorced from the relentless activity to which they are condemned. In return for this lesson the grateful elemental will perform favours for the adept who has helped it to master its destiny.

Apart from the elementals and their archangelic rulers, there are other astral beings which manifest themselves in nature. In the Hebrew tradition these are often depicted as angels, who are among the first creatures created by God and who serve as His messengers. Elsewhere they appear as *deva* kings (*Dhyan Chohans*) or pagan deities and to most of us they are also familiar as the gods and goddesses of classical antiquity. It is useful to study Greek mythology with this in mind, since the deities in its pantheon, like the spheres on the Tree of Life, are easily identifiable with facets of our personality and the forces at work around us. These, however, are all exalted beings who are rarely contacted directly. Thus when we summon a particular god or archangel, we do not expect that he himself will deign to appear, but that we shall somehow feel the power that flows from him. In occult language we say that we are 'attuning ourselves to his ray'.

Our social survey of the magical world has shown us that its denizens range from the great angelic aristocracy who move the planets to the minute sparks of consciousness within every tiny nucleoprotein. What occult tradition has done is ascribe to some of them a formal identity by which we can come into psychic contact with the force they represent. Some may appear to us as sylphs and others dryads, some as human beings, others animals. At first this diversity will seem confusing, but a knowledge of the Tree of Life and of the correspondences associated with it provides us with the code by which they may all be identified. For example, let us imagine that we are on an astral journey and, with the tree as our guide, intend visiting the region of Tifareth. As we proceed along one of the thirty-two paths we are suddenly confronted with two snakes, and this at once tells us that we have not yet reached our destination, for twin serpents are creatures of the neighbouring sefira, Hod. Our location will be confirmed if at the same time we observe a palm tree nearby, for this belongs to the planet Mercury in whose sphere Hod lies. If later in our journey we find ourselves passing a horse, we know we have wandered into the region of Geburah and shall have to retrace our steps to Hod. Thence we shall set off again along the twenty-sixth path that leads to Tifareth, where we can expect to see a golden landscape and, possibly, children playing among sunflowers. There will, of course, be other things to see, but small pointers like these can always be relied upon to guide the wise traveller. For the magician is no astral vagrant. He knows where he wants to go and knows where to seek the sign-posts that will get him there safely. A table of these correspondences is given on pp. 98 ff., and you would do well to familiarize yourself with it, since you are unlikely to have a copy of this book with you when you start flitting off to the astral planes.

Up to now our picture of these planes has been – apart from the snakes – all sweetness and light. Much of the region is quite pleasant; no one in his right mind would wish to have dealings with a dusty underworld peopled with chain-rattling corpses. Yet we saw earlier how all natural synthesis depends *per se* on an opposition of positive and negative factors. Both are encountered in the physical world and both exist in the astral as well. We shall have to learn therefore how to cope with both forces and to this end it is important that we first reconcile them in our own personality. The negative forces in the astral world originate in the primeval energy which was discharged throughout the cosmos before equilibrium had been established. Since then these forces have been clothed in forms conceived and nourished by the vicious thoughts of people here on earth. In magic, therefore, as so often in life, evil can be described as the product of excess. Once one of two opposing forces becomes the stronger, so creating tension, a dangerous unbalance ensues and that force is then said by kabbalists to be kliphothic. The magical adept does not ignore such forces, but tries to come to terms with them in order to accommodate them within his philosophy. He knows that when he evokes an astral force he must be prepared to reconcile its conflicting aspects, for before manifestation can take place the one must divide itself into its two complementary factors of action and reaction. Deliberately to concentrate on only one of these would be to evoke the kliphothic or unbalanced aspect of the force evoked, and this might have very dangerous consequences. The sad thing is that there will always be some for whom only the kliphothic holds any attraction and who will dedicate their rituals to the pursuit of it.

This leads us to the vexed question of white and black magic. Like most categorization, such a neat division of magic into good and bad is far too facile. After all, what some people judge to be good may appear evil in the eyes of others. As always, the difficulty lies in establishing objective criteria. Here the reader must be left to decide his own moral standards, although he would do well to remember that while he may use magic to pursue his own happiness, he must take care not to interfere with the happiness of others. To that extent it is the ritual intention which may be said to determine the colour of one's magic, and any ritual intended to cause harm is generally called black. But most occultists also label magic black or white according to the ingredients of the ritual: rituals that demand the spilling of blood, or involve sex, for example, are usually considered to be black.

This horror of sex is curious, and such prudishness is inconsistent with the complete acceptance of life which should be the goal of every magician. Sexual enjoyment has always been a part of magic, and if readers wish to go cavorting down the primrose path it would be presumptuous of this book to attempt to dissuade them; provided it does not disturb the astral fauna, what they get up to on the mossy banks is their own business. The trouble starts, however, when rituals based on sex and blood become an excuse for cruelty; sadism, in whatever guise, is an ugly thing and rites that pander to it are not only squalid but perilous too, for by a remorseless occult law all evil ultimately rebounds on the head of the evil-doer. In one short lifetime a magician could incur a karmic debt that it would take many lifetimes to loosen. Indeed, even in this life sooner or later a price is exacted: there is nothing more frightening than the occultist who has slept through the night of the demon and never dares to sleep again. Remember this and you will be unlikely to come to any harm in your dealings with the astral world and its numerous inhabitants.

3

A S THE READER may by now have realized, the first thing any aspiring occultist must do is cultivate an awareness of the magical universe and of his part in it. This does not mean, however, that we need to shut ourselves off from the real world or shun its pleasures. On the contrary, our interest in that world will grow as we learn to recognize in it the working of those same forces that also move us. To open our eyes to this new way of looking at things a brief salutation can be made three times a day to the Sun. By doing so we are acknowledging the vibrant life force that pervades the universe and is symbolically recharged by the daily presence of the Sun. It is a useful habit, for it not only reminds us of the non-corporeal aspect of life, which is all too easily forgotten in the hurly-burly of our everyday experiences, but also trains us to become aware of the passage of time, so that eventually we can measure it without having recourse to clocks and watches. This ability is essential when we are engaged in a magical operation or embark on a journey through the astral planes. But the main purpose of our salutation remains a devotional one.

Each morning the magician should make what some occultists call the 'matutinal invocation'. This sounds very impressive, as indeed it is meant to, but really is no more than a simple, often spontaneous, prayer. To perform it you must look towards the rising Sun, but if that is impracticable, you can get away with just turning to face the east. Now imagine the Sun pumping warm new life through the veins of the universe and through yourself. Picture its having done this since the formation of our planet and try in the space of a second to recapture that entire past. Choose from it, if you wish, a time and place with which to link your thoughts. Let it be a Celtic Sun you see, spilling golden over a soft green landscape, or an Egyptian Sun, the mighty Ra who watches his reflection in the mirror of the Nile.

The second invocation is made at noon each day, when again you should try through concentration to lose your present self in the splendour of the light. Now, when the Sun is at its peak, is the moment to steal a little of its power and draw it deep within your secret self.

The evening salutation should ideally be made while watching the Sun set. However, you may, if you prefer, choose any time in the evening that suits you, though in this case it is essential that you stick to the same time each day. Again you must turn towards the Sun and use your imagination to heighten the experience. You might, for example, be watching a sunset from the Parthenon in Athens, or else project yourself to some bleak cliff top and gaze upon a splendid Nordic Sun as it sinks into the sea.

What you actually say on these occasions is less important than what you feel. However, there will be times when, because you are weary, worried or busy, you may find it difficult to achieve the spiritual expansion which should accompany each salutation. The right words, spoken or unspoken, will then fail to spring up from within you and your thoughts will keep wandering back to mundane things. But do not lose heart if this happens. Even magicians have their off days.

There remains one caveat concerning the salutations. Because his mind is attuned to non-material modes of existence, the magician is liable to attract influences which he has not consciously summoned. That is why, although he trains his mind to be as receptive as possible, he endeavours always to keep it under control, allowing the astral world to intrude only when he wills it, and even then shutting out all unwelcome visitors. The last great blessing of the salutations is that they are a means of ensuring that only benefic influences surround you throughout the day as you go about your business in the world of men.

This constant awareness of the magical universe which every magician must cultivate is designed to bring home to us the fundamental unity of everything in nature. This was the great secret of the famous mystery schools at Eleusis and Alexandria. As you begin your search for the meaning of nature, however, you will gradually become aware that your conscious mind is only part of a marvellous realm which embraces both the personal subconscious and that part of you which is at one with the whole of material creation. It often happens that the novice magician begins to feel as if he is developing a magical persona quite distinct from his everyday personality. Certain occult books encourage such a belief and on occasion offer rituals designed to introduce the magician to his new-found magical self. Rather than acquire an *alter ego*, however, the adept enriches his own existing personality by encountering new ideas, many of which may have their origin in the treasure house of his unconscious. Jung has described this process as individuation and far from being the emergence of a new personality, it is, in alchemical terms, but the transmutation of the old. If, therefore, you find that your trivial worries seem to disappear when you turn your mind from mundane things to magic, do not start thinking that a more philosophical self has temporarily taken charge of you. The personality which rejoices in the wonderful unity of the cosmic scheme is no different from that which at other times frets over the household bills. The only difference lies in the things that occupy its attention. Be assured that in time the process of individuation within your psyche will reconcile all aspects of your personality (the totality of being) so that you learn to regard even the household bills with philosophical detachment.

Those occultists who argue the existence of a secondary magical personality are unable to accept that our everyday self is worthy of magic. The profound experiences arising from magical practice seem to them evidence of a superior personality which, like one's Sunday best, is kept in reserve for special occasions. Apart from making a schizophrenic of every aspiring magician, this attitude is wrong because it removes magic from the world of ordinary experience and makes it something that, like private vice, should be indulged in once in a while and on the quiet. How different this is from the attitude of the ancient world, where the mysteries played a part in everybody's life, and such centres as Eleusis and Delphi were common meeting-places.

When at last you become aware of the unity underlying the cosmos you will be able to appreciate that your magical work is capable of universal significance. This is because nothing acts independently in nature, but is subject to a general law of causation. In saying this we are not relying entirely on the 'as above, so below' principle of hermetic tradition, since the same view is propounded by science.

But this interdependence brings with it important moral consequences which we must now pause to consider, for if the universe
is governed by necessity, then men's actions are no less susceptible
to its influence. Both the scientist and the occultist regard man
as a constituent part of the material world, inextricably bound up
with the processes that govern it. Such determinism is inherent in
the concept of universal law, and it is implicit in the scientific view
of man as a physical organism equipped with five senses. Because
man relies on the information provided by his senses, his motivation
can truly be said to depend on whatever stimuli affect them. But
that is not all, for the union of mind and body means also that
physiological considerations, over which man has little or no control, play their part in deciding his behaviour. In the end his actions
may owe more to his cerebral structure or glandular secretions than
to what he fondly thinks is a rational evaluation of various possibilities. When, in addition, we take into account the known influence
of heredity and environment, we see that man is subject to an
intrinsic determinism which, in accordance with sound esoteric
principles, is simply a reflection of the pan-determinism around
him. When we add to this the astrological belief in planetary
influences we are clearly well on the way to reducing man to a
puppet bereft of all free-will.

This problem has taxed the minds of all the great moral philosophers. We must go back to the Epicureans to find a solution that
is consistent with what we now know of nature from modern science.
Epicurus believed that every object was composed of infinitesimal
atoms which were in motion all the time. Realizing, however, that
if these atoms all moved along an ordained path, then human atoms
must be equally determined and predictable, he was careful to
declare that atoms could on occasion swerve a little from the track
ordained for them by nature.[1] Those that deviated in this way were
exceptions, of course, and did nothing to upset the general rule. Yet
their very existence was enough to show that the fate of an atom
might sometimes depend on its own nature (one is tempted to say
inclination) rather than on factors outside itself. What was no more
than a useful theory for the Epicureans has fortunately been confirmed to some extent by twentieth-century physicists who have
discovered that the behaviour of some electrons is completely erratic
and unpredictable. Neither their position nor motion can be determined with any certainty. Like Epicurus' rebellious atoms, these

electrons appear to have the ability to decide their own careers for themselves.*

Now, what is natural to electrons may – or, rather, must – also be natural to man, so that in his physiological make-up there already exists a potential independence from the forces that lie outside him. This is borne out by observation, for we know that human conduct, like that of the electron, can never be predicted exactly. Even when we think we know all there is to know about a person's character or the circumstances affecting him, there remains an incalculable element. It is always possible that there is some reason for this which has somehow escaped our notice; but it may also be that although ideas are derived from sense impressions received from outside, man's conceptual faculty, his reason, enables him to correlate them in a highly personal way. Thus determinism by external causes is transformed into a sort of self-imposed determinism over which reason presides, reflecting on sense impressions and arranging them in its own peculiar order. Determinism is not evaded, since the material for reflection is provided by external causes and by information stored in the memory, but the mind's own contribution does mean that man is collaborating in his own destiny. The occultist would not stop here, but would extend man's collaboration in his own destiny to cover that greater destiny which arises from the processes of cause and effect at work throughout the universe. These are, after all, the practical bases of his magic. But his recognition of cosmic necessity does not mean that the poor occultist feels weighed down under the yoke of blind determinism. On the contrary, he is able to lend his conscious assent to the dynamic scheme of things and, thanks to his knowledge of ritual, is privileged to participate in it.

It is precisely this participation that we set out to achieve when we perform our thrice-daily salutation to the sun. This short ritual is the ideal means of relating ourselves to the universe we occupy and so understanding its workings. It enables us to appreciate man's place in the cosmic scheme intuitively – which, of course, is far less painful than a philosophical tussle with an issue like determinism. You may find that at first it is extremely difficult to retain a clear picture of the Greek, Celtic or whatever other type of sun you have

---

* These exceptions which testify to the occasional waywardness of nature may explain why ritual magic may sometimes fail no matter how scrupulously the instructions are followed.

chosen to visualize. But the technique of visualization is something you will gradually master, and indeed must master if you are to make any progress at all in magic. For in magical operations the ability to think constructively is more than an exercise in mental discipline; it is our only means of affecting the etheric atmosphere. It enables us to build our own thought forms, contact those already in existence and channel the elemental energy we need down on to the physical plane. In the next chapter we shall see how this is done.

4

THE SIMPLEST way of explaining what visualization involves in magic is to say that it is a pictorial rather than a verbal way of thinking. It is said that children think in pictorial terms, forming what psychologists would call eidetic images in their mind. What the occultist must do is recapture this ability which was natural to him before the shades of the prison house began to dim his imagination. But thought-building does not stop here, for in magic your mind must be trained to create images that seem real not only in visual terms, but in terms of all the other senses as well. Thus an imagined sprig of lavender must both 'look' and 'smell' real. Likewise if, when you have had sufficient experience, you decide to visualize a sea-shore, you must be able to 'hear' the waves beating on it, 'feel' the cool spray on your face and 'taste' the tang of brine around your lips. However, unless you are gifted with an uncommonly vivid imagination, this ability is one that can be acquired only through strenuous and, occasionally, wearisome practice. We in the West have always been inclined to shirk mental discipline, preferring to leave that sort of thing to the contemplative Orient where meditation is an integral part of daily life and a means to that mystical enlightenment which the Buddha managed to attain. The regular performance of the daily salutations will go some way to training your mind, but other exercises are necessary to complete the training.

When you decide to start your mental training you must set aside a few minutes each day for visualization practice. Fifteen minutes is quite long enough, and as little as five will do. It is far better to keep up five minutes each day than have much longer, but irregular, sessions. The morning has always been regarded as the best time for meditation, allegedly because the earth currents (whatever they may be) are waxing until noon and are on the wane between then and midnight. If you can, use some quiet room where you can meditate without being exposed to distracting influences. Make yourself as comfortable as possible. Some occultists can flop happily into a spectacular yogic *asana*, the well-known lotus posture being one of their favourites, but unless your limbs are extraordinarily supple you would be well advised to content yourself with sitting down normally. Choose a straight-backed armchair and rest your elbows on its arms, in the position in which Egyptian pharaohs are commonly depicted. It is sometimes recommended that one sit with hands clasped and feet crossed, in order, it is said, to keep the body circuit closed and so prevent any wastage of psychic energy. There is no harm in trying it if you want to.

Having settled in your chair you must now endeavour to liberate your body from all tension. To do this some experts suggest a thing called Moon Breathing which involves breathing through the left nostril and repeating the word 'Aum'. A more down-to-earth method is to start deliberately relaxing every muscle in your body from the tips of your toes to the top of your head. If with the best will in the world you still cannot relax, then lie flat on the floor and try there. At the same time close your eyes and picture yourself floating in a dark and silent void. After a few minutes like this, provided you have not dropped off to sleep in the meantime, you should be able to return to your chair and resume the relaxation process with fresh courage. When at last you do feel completely relaxed, avoid the temptation to start day-dreaming. Instead, will your brain and body to adopt a state of alertness. On the first few occasions this may cause you to tense up once more, in which case you must start again from the beginning. A wise precaution against this is to breathe very slowly and deeply while you are trying to relax, and then accelerate your breathing once you wish to effect the transition to a state of alertness. The quicker rhythm, while preserving your body from renewed tension, should induce the mental and nervous alertness you seek. At no time in your magical training, however, should you alter your breathing habits too drastically, since the increased oxygenization of your blood, though beneficial in the long run, can also have some alarming side effects if it occurs too suddenly.

The next step is to get down to image-building proper. Start by studying a simple two-dimensional diagram, and then with eyes closed form a mental reproduction of it. Do not be afraid to open your eyes to check the real thing against any portion of your mental picture that may be insufficiently clear, and keep on checking until the diagram held in your mind corresponds exactly with that drawn on the sheet of paper. Once you are able to perform this type of exercise without difficulty you are ready to graduate to three-dimensional objects. Again your aim should be to form a mental picture precisely like the original. You may find that it helps at first if you project your image of the object on to an imaginary lighted screen inside your mind. A variation of the exercise, which will test your powers of memory, is to look for a minute or so at some small objects arranged at random on a tray and then with eyes closed give a detailed description of each object. You may recall that this was the game described by Rudyard Kipling in his novel *Kim*. Another fascinating challenge, once you have become fairly expert at visualization, is mentally to examine the object visualized from several different points of view. Let us suppose that you have visualized an empty match-box. Your mind's eye sees the box exactly as it earlier presented itself to your physical eye. Now visualize the same match-box from various other angles – above, below, etc. Whatever the viewpoint, the match-box should be as clear and detailed as the original mental 'photograph', which in turn should be as clear and detailed as the match-box that was physically observed. From here some people are able to go one step further and actually transfer their consciousness to inside the match-box, or even visualize it from all points of view at the same time. If this proves to be beyond you at this stage, a slightly easier exercise is to project your consciousness to different parts of the room you are in, so that you get a completely different view from the one presented to your physical vision. You could possibly try this experiment next time you find yourself at a dull party or lecture. It may even help pass the time on a tedious journey, provided, of course, you are not in the driving seat.

In view of its importance in magic, colour must be visualized with special ease, and this too requires practice. Start by visualizing one of the primary colours, say red. For the purpose of this exercise do not visualize neat little rows of red pillar boxes or tins of red paint, simply flood your mind with the colour itself. When your mind is a sea of red, allow the colour to change slowly to orange. Again do not visualize orange *objects*, but the colour itself. When you have filled your mind with orange, let that colour change to yellow, then yellow to green, green to blue and so on. The absence of forms to visualize makes this one of the more difficult exercises to master.

There still remains the task of involving the other senses in your thought-building. Fortunately, some of the visualization exercises can be adapted for this purpose. Smell and taste, for example, may be reproduced by visualizing suitable images – a good hot curry is an excellent one to start with. You can then go on to develop the sense of touch by imagining yourself soaking up the warm sunshine on a Mediterranean beach. As for hearing, a useful way to begin is to strike a tuning fork and then continue the note in your mind for as long as possible. From here you can progress to more ambitious things.

Up to now your image-building will have been entirely subjective, and as such scarcely differs from the type of concentration taught in many schools of meditation. The secret of magical visualization, however, is that the chosen image is not just locked away inside the mind, but is 'projected' into the real world. This 'projection' is a knack which, like learning to swim, will be acquired all of a sudden, but you should not attempt it until you have perfected subjective visualization. When you are ready, open your eyes while still retaining your mental picture in all its detail. Eventually you will discover that because of a subtle collusion between your mind and your vision, you are able to 'see' the mental picture just as if it were a part of your normal physical surroundings. One thing to guard against, however, especially in the first flush of success, is the tendency for such mental images to impose themselves on your everyday vision without your willing them to do so. Resist this firmly. Throughout your magical training you should allow things to happen only when you wish them to. Involuntary hallucinations belong to the realm of mental illness, not magic.

By the time you can objectify mental images of such clarity that they appear to possess an empirical reality of their own, you will be well advanced on the way to magical attainment. Exercises are always a chore, but in this case they are very necessary if you are later to derive any benefit from your magical operations. But, of course, magic would scarcely be magic if it did not provide some little assistance to lighten the burden. What it offers, however, is not a short cut but merely a crutch to help you along what can, at times, seem an arduous path.

A great deal of help can be obtained by performing a short and simple rite known as the kabbalistic cross. This has nothing at all to do with the cross of Calvary or the Christian devotion known as the sign of the cross. The glyph of the cross is much older than Christianity and was held sacred by ancient civilizations as far apart as Egypt and Mexico, where it was adored as a symbol of, among other deities, Tlaloc, the god of rain, and Quetzalcoatl, lord of the four winds. In Scandinavia, too, long before the birth of Christ, a cross was used to mark the burial places of dead kings and heroes. Indeed, its adoption as a symbol by the Christian church occurred quite late in our era. Before then the monogram ✗ had been favoured.

To make the kabbalistic cross, stand upright and visualize a splendid cloud of light above your head. This is the ketheric light that crowns the Tree of Glory against which you can, if you like, imagine yourself to be standing. Now, raise your right hand to touch the light and, drawing some of it down towards you, place your middle finger on your forehead, saying the word 'Ateh'. With the light still cascading upon you, move your finger to your solar plexus and say 'Malkuth'. As you do so picture more light surging up from the earth beneath you so that a band of light now extends from your head to your feet. Next, touch your right shoulder and say 'Ve Geburah' and then, with your finger still trailing a stream of white light, touch your left shoulder and say 'Ve Gedulah'. The form of the cross is now complete, and folding your hands you may speak the final words which are 'Le Olahm, Amen'. It is not absolutely essential to use these Hebrew expressions rather than their English equivalent, but constant usage over the centuries has endowed them with a special efficacy, much of which is due to the acoustic vibrations that occur when they are spoken aloud. The effect of such vibrations is discussed in Chapter 5. What the words themselves mean is: Thou art (Ateh), The Kingdom (Malkuth) And the Power (Ve Geburah) And the Glory (Ve Gedulah) Unto all the ages (Le Olahm). Amen.

While your hands are still clasped in an attitude of prayer, imagine the four branches of the visualized cross stretching outwards through space, and yourself growing with them to a tremendous size. If it makes things easier, shut your eyes and imagine that you are poised over the universe with the stars at your feet. A few seconds of this vertiginous contemplation will be enough and you should gently let your body contract to its normal physical dimensions. We shall be using the kabbalistic cross as a preliminary to many magical operations, so it is as well to learn how to do it properly. It should never become a formalistic touching of head, chest and shoulders accompanied by the appropriate words.

The astral light which you channel into your body when making the cross will assist you greatly in your visualization exercises. It will also help if you imagine, while still surrounded or, rather, transfused by the ketheric radiance, that you hold in your right hand a gleaming sword pointing upwards. This is the Sword of Power, your Excalibur, and it is your symbolic defence against evil and aggression. Now stretch the sword out horizontally and draw a circle all around you. As you do so, imagine a jet of gold and silver fire emanating from the tip of the sword, so that by turning full circle you have in effect surrounded yourself with a fiery barrier. This will serve to exclude those alien psychic forces that might interfere with your meditation. For remember that the power of thought is such that your symbolic gesture has created an etheric barrier which is no less real for not being physical. After all this effort you should feel relaxed enough to sit down and commence your visualization practice.

At this point, when your visualization is still little more than an academic exercise, we ought perhaps to decide once and for all what is the true nature of the forms you will be visualizing when eventually you begin your magical work. It will help if we at once plant our feet firmly on the ground and assert that the visualized images, though apparently real in themselves, are in fact no more than representations of an imperceptible reality. We shall find that the best argument in favour of this concealed reality comes from practical experience, where results alone count. These results will demonstrate that while the forms themselves may have no phenomenal existence, they nevertheless have an extrinsic value of their own. In this respect they can be compared with a pound note, which derives its worth not from the paper on which it is printed, but from what it represents in terms of credit with the Bank of England. The same is true of the seemingly concrete shapes we shall visualize when we contact the astral world. By treating these as if they enjoyed an objective existence outside our consciousness, we are able to take advantage of the specialized forces they represent. For practical purposes, therefore, it is as unnecessary to question their immediate validity as it is to doubt the credit promised by the chief cashier of the Bank of England on every pound note we handle.

But even if the results obtained enable us to postulate the reality behind the astral forms, not everyone will be convinced. In any case there is always the risk that the results obtained in the early days of your magical career will be too meagre to inspire much confidence in the astral forms you are using, and without confidence it is unlikely that the results will ever improve. Before we discuss the nature of these forms, we must first concede that the astral world is incompatible with the old-fashioned materialistic viewpoint which accepts matter as the sole criterion of reality. Fortunately few materialists nowadays would go this far anyway, and most have already abandoned their former simple faith in 'matter' as something characterized by mass and occupation of space. Instead, modern physics is having to contend with wonders like non-causal effects, irreducible uncertainty and a thing which, for want of a better word, has been dubbed 'anti-matter'. Compared with these the astral planes are indeed simple stuff. Even so, it remains a fact that these planes, like much else in the universe, are as yet inaccessible both to our senses and to the most refined scientific instruments. Yet to infer from this that they do not exist would be to adopt the premise that reality depends for its existence on our awareness of it. This is clearly untenable.

The trouble with the astral world is not its unreality, since the results of magic prove that it is real enough, but its inaccessibility to our senses. But telepathy has already shown that the human mind is not entirely dependent on the senses for the information it receives. I know that telepathy is fast becoming a peg on which to hang all sorts of occult hats, but the most we are doing here is inferring from it that the mind can in certain circumstances receive direct impressions from agents outside itself. This faculty, call it extra-sensory perception, psi or anything you like, is what enables us to become aware of the astral world. The mechanics of this awareness are best explained if we think of the mind as a mirror in which images are reflected. Most of these images are due to the reaction of one or more of our sense organs, but it is still the mind that does most of the work. This is what Aristotle meant when he declared that the words 'I see' really mean 'I have seen', for the mind has in this case intervened to sort out whatever impressions were made on the optic nerve. Because of this the mind can be described as the surface on which is reflected the reality known to us by experience. Like the celebrated Lady of Shalott we behold the outside world in a looking-glass and like Tennyson's heroine we need only change the angle of the glass for it to reflect new and hitherto unsuspected things. This is exactly what visualization is intended to achieve. It is the tilting of our mental mirror to accommodate new images derived from the astral world.

When our mind perceives these images they appear to be as solid and three-dimensional as any received via the senses. But no one is naive enough nowadays to believe that lions, snakes and knights in armour populate the astral planes. We see such things because our subconscious has translated the non-pictorial impressions it has directly received into objective forms recognizable by the mind. It does this because the mind would otherwise be incapable of appreciating them, so accustomed is it to receiving only sensory impressions. It is the old adage: '*Nihil in intellectu est quod non prius in sensu erat.*' To this extent, any magical image we visualize may be said to be subjective. It is, after all, our subconscious that has created it for us. On the other hand, the image is at the same time a reflection of something else, and so may be said to have an objective existence as well. Thus when we subjectively visualize an astral form we make an image which has as its subject an objective astral force. We may say that we are accepting at one and the same time both the subjectivity of the object and the objectivity of the subject.

All that remains to be considered is the appearance of the forms themselves. The attribution of particular forms to different cosmic principles occurred very early in the history of mankind. In that time which witnessed the dawn of magic it seemed only reasonable to anthropomorphize the forces discernible behind natural phenomena. These traditional personifications survive to this day and bear the stamp of their primitive origin. The pity is that the rather *simpliste* psychology behind them has tended to obscure the merits of the system. Yet its very antiquity is also its strength. For the traditional forms have by now become a part of what Jung would call the 'collective unconscious'. As this collective unconscious is by definition something much larger than the individual unconscious, it follows that at some point the forms we visualize merge into larger forms which have an existence outside ourselves. These are what the Jungians would call a racial memory, although occultists prefer to describe them as etheric thought forms. Because of them the forms we visualize are only partly self-induced, since they take on the appearance of astral forms already in existence. We may say in conclusion, therefore, that although any astral lions, snakes or knights in armour we may visualize are not quite the real thing, they are certainly as near as dammit.

BEFORE GOING on to look at some of the rituals used in magic, it is worth while pausing to consider what ritual is and what exactly it is meant to achieve. The word itself is enough to put some people off, and I must confess that it took me a long time to get used to the idea that ritual could serve any useful purpose. A Nonconformist upbringing made me jib at the pomp and circumstance surrounding some church services, and having been taught that splendid vestments brought one no nearer to God I took the view that the money spent on such things could be put to better uses. Nor am I even now completely reconciled to all forms of ceremonial. Too often they seem to have been designed only to dazzle the masses and pander to the vanity of the participants.

But, of course, ritual is much more than just an excuse for dressing up and swinging the occasional incense burner. All religious worship, however simple, becomes ritualistic once it follows a formal, pre-arranged pattern. There is nothing wrong in this. Without such a pattern, communal worship would lack all cohesion, and that is why even Quaker meetings tend to fit themselves within a definite framework. However, ritual is not only a safeguard against what we might call liturgical anarchy, it serves also to concentrate the thoughts of the individuals present on a common object of devotion. Many rituals do this by re-creating in symbolic fashion one of the sacred mysteries of a particular religion. For example, the Roman Catholic Mass, which is a dramatic re-enactment of the sacrifice on Calvary, seeks to ensure that every worshipper fixes his undivided attention on the crucifixion of Christ so as to understand better the central mystery of his faith.

To this extent ritual may be said to have a psychological motive, but there is another, more important, reason for its performance. On one level the Catholic Mass is the re-enactment of a historical event, but at a certain point the play-acting merges with the sublime reality it is striving to imitate. This happens when the priest speaks the words of consecration over the host, after which the appearance of bread disguises the actual crucified body of Christ. From then on the ritual assumes an awesome sacramental meaning by becoming the outward and visible sign of an inward divine grace.

These two aspects of ritual, the psychological and the sacramental, are not confined to Christianity; they recur in pagan worship all over the world, and, apparently, throughout history. Rituals are conducted in two stages: first, the worshipper attunes himself to the sacred mystery being performed and then, usually as the climax, the presence of a particular deity is invoked. Magic ritual is no exception, and so kabbalistic rites may be described as the finite embodiment of all the mystical content of the Tree of Life. The adept's slightest gesture can thus extend through all the worlds of being into the depths of the Godhead, and any words he whispers will echo throughout the length and breadth of the universe.

In magic the immediate psychological benefits of ritual arise from the fact that every object in range of the adept's senses has a symbolic connection with the idea behind the ceremony. This symbolism may not always be apparent, but you may be assured that having evolved over hundreds, nay thousands, of years, it is already well known to those deeper levels of your mind that are in communion with the collective unconscious. Indeed, we know that all the symbols used in magic have their powerful astral counterparts which, you will recall, are but the appearance of the force they represent. Form, sound, colour and movement, all are pressed into the service of magic, as also is incense which through the sense of smell can appeal to whatever part of the subconscious we wish to arouse. In short, everything involved in the rite will have been carefully chosen with a view to its effect on the mind of the magician.

At this point we should mention that apart from all the material means to induce the required states of consciousness, some occultists also advocate the use of sex and drugs. Sex we shall discuss later, and as for drugs, all we need say is that the ones generally recommended are of the kind which produces visions rather than euphoria; hashish used to be a favourite before LSD and Mexican mushrooms

became fashionable. This is not the place to discuss the wisdom of
drug-taking, although clearly the excessive use of drugs, as of anything else, can cause serious harm. It has recently been suggested
that the so-called 'soft' drugs are really no more unhealthy than
alcohol or tobacco, but you should never forget that in most countries it is still illegal to possess them. Fortunately, as far as magic is
concerned, drugs are useful only in certain advanced visualization
work and they certainly have no part to play in any practical work
undertaken on one's own. The reason for this is that narcotics
inevitably reduce one's conscious control of the will, and without
that control the chances of success in magic become exceedingly
remote. It was Aleister Crowley, himself no stranger to drugs, who
once summed up magic as 'the Science and Art of causing Change
to occur in conformity with the Will'. Disregard the part played by
the will, and the intended changes will either not occur or will turn
out quite differently. In any case, some magic ritual is so complicated
that the adept needs all his wits about him to do the job properly.
There is so much exorcising, consecrating, asperging, fumigating
and perfuming to be done that he would find no time to puff a reefer
even if he wanted to.

And where does all this phrenetic activity take place? The author
of the *Key of Solomon* (who most certainly was not Solomon),*
instructs us to seek out

> places that lie concealed, distant and removed from the haunts
> of men. For that reason desolate and unfrequented regions are
> most appropriate, such as the borders of lakes, forests, dark
> and sombre places, old and deserted houses, whither men
> scarce ever come; mountains, caves and grottos; gardens, woods
> and orchards; but best of all are cross roads and the spot where
> four paths conjoin in the depth and blackness of the night.

Mercifully the pseudo-Solomon has the good sense to tell us later
that our own rooms, if suitably consecrated, will do at a pinch.

---

* Back-dating and imputed authorship are common to most magical textbooks which,
at various times, have been ascribed to, *inter alios*, Adam, Abel, Moses, Noah, Elijah
and, of course, Hermes Trismegistus. Solomon's great reputation always rendered him
as attractive to magicians as he later became to Freemasons. In the 13th century Roger
Bacon was already bewailing the number of books attributed to that proverbially wise
monarch. Of these, however, the *Key of Solomon* is by far the best known and has
influenced magicians from the 14th century onwards.

In an ideal world the room used for magic would be devoted solely to that purpose. But just as a scientist could experiment over the kitchen sink if he were denied a laboratory, so the occultist can make do with his bedroom, living-room or study if he must. Naturally the everyday associations of such a room may be distracting to begin with, but a little mental discipline will enable anyone to overcome these difficulties. Methods of consecrating the room are described later and these, together with a locked door, should keep out all undesirable influences, whether astral or mundane. Even so, you will find that some rites are best performed at special places, which is why our contemporary Druids troop all the way to Stonehenge for their traditional pre-dawn observances.

Certain magical weapons are also needed for ritual work. Occultists have always insisted that these must be virgin, which means that they should be used for no other purpose save magic. There is also a tradition that they should be bought without haggling, although another more extreme tradition insists that far from buying his equipment, the really dedicated magician will forge his own. It is my opinion that provided the tools you use are 'demagnetized' and thereafter employed only for magic, there is no real harm in using the ready-made article. With a little imagination even the humblest kitchen knife can seem like the most ornate sword. This does not mean, of course, that there is nothing to be gained from fashioning your own ritual tools whenever possible. The greater the trouble you take over this, the more your personality becomes associated with the instrument you are making. So, if you can manage it, try at least to carve your own hazel wand or construct your own incense burner. It will be well worth the effort.

Earlier we observed that most ritual has a sacramental function. In this respect it merely copies nature which, being nothing less than God made manifest, is possibly the supreme sacrament through which the highest spiritual forces are mediated. In the same way, because it too is the outward sign of an inner meaning, magic ritual is endowed with its own intrinsic sacredness. By its performance there occurs *ipso facto* a mystical reunion between appearance and reality. The prescribed ceremonial may therefore be repeated by anyone with exactly the same results, for its effectiveness lies in the rite and not in the personality of the celebrant. The results, in other words, occur *ex opere operato*, or by virtue of the action, and not *ex opere operantis*, or by virtue of the agent's acting. Nevertheless the agent clearly has an important role to play if the action he is performing is to release its self-contained force. If things were otherwise it would be rather like giving a screwdriver and length of wire to an aborigine who knew nothing about electricity and expecting him to mend a fuse. He would have all the things needed to restore the power except the essential knowledge of what to do with them. Likewise, in the celebration of the Mass the unconsecrated host remains a wafer of unleavened bread until the priest pronounces the words '*Hoc est enim corpus meum*' above it. Each of the magic rituals that has been handed down to us similarly depends on the conscious participation of the magician who must see to it that he does the right things in the right order at the right time. He too must speak the appropriate words if he is to convert the accidental appearance of the things around him into the substantive reality they are supposed to represent.

Words are important in magic because they are regarded not just as a means of communication but as an intrinsic part of the thing they name. They can therefore be accepted as a substitute for that thing because they contain its essence. From this it follows that to know the name of someone is to have power over them, and we have all read stories in which someone, be it Rumpelstiltskin or the angel that wrestled with Jacob, is reluctant to reveal his name to a possible adversary. A knowledge of the names of angels, spirits and demons has always been highly prized by magicians,* but to the kabbalists the greatest name of all is undoubtedly the divine name since it ensouls the power of God. Already in the Old Testament there was such awe surrounding this name that several harmless synonyms were commonly used. Among them were *El, Elohim, Tzabaoth* and *Adonai*, many of which recur throughout magical literature. The real and personal name of God, however, was composed of the four Hebrew letters YHVH (Yod, Hē, Vau, Hē), and as Hebrew has no vowels this has been translated as both Yahveh and Jehovah. The word YHVH itself is thought to mean 'he is', and you will recall that when God addressed Moses from the burning bush He identified himself with the words, 'I am that I am.' Because the divine name was so revered by the Israelites it was scarcely ever uttered by them,

---

* Iamblichus (250–325 A.D.) teaches in his *Mysteries of the Egyptians, Chaldeans and Assyrians* that the names culled from ancient religious systems like those of Egypt and Assyria have an inherent magic virtue. This is due not only to the antiquity of the languages they are drawn from but to their origin in popular theology.

with the result that no one now has any idea of its correct pronunciation.* So fearful were people of using the actual name that they
chose instead to refer to it obliquely as the Tetragrammaton, or
'four-lettered name', a word which soon accumulated its own store
of magical power.

The confusion of identity between an object and its name
probably has its origins far back in prehistory when speech first
began. The Book of Genesis even tells us that one of God's first tasks
was to name everything He had created, as if that put the finishing
touches to His handiwork.† The old story may have a grain of truth
in it, for experience teaches us that all our conscious mental activity
is verbal. This is a notion that linguistic philosophers are still ex-
ploring, but whereas most of them would dispute the close relationship between the name and the thing named which magic claims,
few would deny that a creative thought, perhaps even a barely
formulated impulse, needs always to express itself in the form of
words. Sensing the truth of this, magic has equated the divine self-
awareness that resulted in creation with God's discovery of his own
identity, or 'name'. That name, so ineffably majestic that no human
tongue dared speak it, becomes therefore the sacred word that
brought the whole universe into being. It is the eternal Logos that
dwells with God, the mighty Tetragrammaton of the Jews, the Tehuti
of the Egyptians and the creative word of a hundred other cultures.

Inseparable from magical speculation about words is the theory
of vibrations, which supposes that certain sounds have a powerful
acoustic impact on both the physical and astral worlds. That
vibrations do in fact govern sound is confirmed by physics which
teach us that sound originates when molecules begin to vibrate and
trigger off a wave formed by the sympathetic vibration of neighbouring molecules. In the same way sounds can only be heard when
air causes our eardrum to vibrate in such a way that it excites the
terminals of the main auditory nerve. Since the fifth century B.C.
when Pythagoras began to study sound by plucking at a one-stringed
harp, science has developed specialized techniques for measuring
its pressure, velocity, frequency and intensity. We know, for
example, that certain high-frequency sounds, no matter how intense,
remain inaudible to the human ear. Like beams of light these ultra-

* Aleister Crowley could not resist claiming that he alone knew how to pronounce
this great name which, once spoken, would rend the universe asunder.

† The Hebrew verb 'to name' is in fact the same as the verb 'to give form'.

sonic sounds streak through the air around us. It is possible, too, that if sound is the product of atmospheric disturbance, then the rotation of the planets may create a celestial, albeit ultrasonic, music like that imagined by Pythagoras, although as so much of space is a vacuum, these planetary harmonies are unlikely to travel far. It is certain that because sound vibrations, whether audible or not, are in reality propagated motion, and motion implies energy, then currents of kinetic energy are generated by every sound we make. Presumably some of this energy is lost quite quickly in the form of heat, but even so there are some vibrations still energetic enough to affect physical objects. It is well known that a certain note played on the violin has shattered glass, or bridges capable of supporting huge weights have collapsed under a company of soldiers marching in step. There is also the Biblical account of the walls of Jericho crumbling at the sound of a fanfare of trumpets. Like the physical world, the astral planes can in some circumstances be affected by sound, so that verbal magic may be said to derive its power not only from the idea contained in certain words, but from the peculiar vibrations these words create when spoken.

Similar vibrations are alleged to be caused by numbers, and between them and names a close relationship has long been adduced by occultists. Indeed, names are frequently reduced to numerical values, each of which is said to have a special vibration that distinguishes it from all others. Mysterious numbers abound in most religious and magical traditions, seven, ten and twelve being almost universal favourites. Once again it is Pythagoras who provides magicians with most of their lore about numbers. He and many other Greek philosophers felt sure that in the science of numerology, inherited, it was believed, from the Egyptians, they had discovered a way to identify the pattern on which nature was modelled.[1] According to them, all things were numerically expressible and had come into being when the limited, represented by the odd numbers, emerged from the unlimited, represented by the evens. Since then this dualism has persisted throughout the universe. The view of Pythagoras was that numbers were composed of geometric figures arranged in various ways, but magicians have gone further than this and ascribed to them an eternal, formless existence that naturally preceded their discovery by man. From here most magical authors go on to rhapsodize about numerical vibrations which they like describing in terms of light waves, musical rhythms and divine harmonies, their language betraying that poetical enthusiasm which is a congenital weakness of the occult breed.

Whatever doubts you may have about the mystical significance of numbers, it is unwise to ignore any instructions you find about their use in ritual. The same holds true of any other advice you find, for you will soon discover that results are hard to come by once you start tampering with the recommended procedures. And, after all, it is results we are after in practical magic. Without these our ritual would be no different from the antics of the Freemasons or the Royal Antediluvian Order of Buffaloes.

Needless to say, the type of results you get in magic will depend on the purpose of your ritual. In the early days it would be unreasonable to expect objective phenomena to occur, so you should not feel too disappointed if Lucifer and all the fallen angels fail to turn up despite your most fervent conjurations. On the other hand, you should avoid becoming one of those timid occultists who dabble in ritual only for the feeling of exhilaration and the peace of mind it often brings. Satisfying though these mental states may be, they have nothing in common with the lasting, tangible benefits that can be obtained through the use of magic. The first thing you must always do therefore is decide what exactly you want your ritual to achieve. This is important because it is the intention behind your ritual that will vivify it and bring it to fruition. This is why the old kabbalists were so fond of describing the intention or, as they called it, the *kavvanah*, as the soul which animated the body of every rite. It is thanks to the *kavvanah* that each small step prescribed by ritual is guided through the worlds of creation, the *beriah*, to the appropriate aspect of the Godhead. In other words, the intention is what transforms each ritual into a mystical adventure where for a few brief seconds the initiate can become the Adam Kadmon and so realize the macrocosm within himself.

Once the ritual intention is clear in your mind, consult the Table of Intentions (see pp. 96 ff.) and see what sort of rite is appropriate. Let us assume by way of example that you are lovelorn, and that the table has recommended that you undertake a rite of Venus. A glance at the Table of Correspondences will at once inform you what symbolism is needed for such a rite. These details have then to be incorporated in the master ritual which is described on pp. 122 ff. In the case of a Venusian rite you will see from the advice given on the timing of rituals that it should take place on a Friday, since that

day is ruled by Venus. There are also instructions on how to determine the most propitious hour, and this again will be that traditionally ruled by the planet. Returning to the correspondences,
green you will find is the colour used in Venusian rites, and copper
the appropriate metal for as many as possible of the ceremonial
instruments. Copper's tendency to turn green is one reason for its
supposed affinity with Venus; it is also suggested that this derives
from the ancient practice of using polished copper to make mirrors.
Another possible explanation is that Aphrodite is reported to have
emerged from the sea just off the island of Cyprus, which in the
ancient world was a major source of copper. The combination of
green and copper should be continued, if possible, in any jewellery
worn by the adept; emeralds set in copper, for example, would be
an ideal adornment. As for scents, those with Venusian associations
include ambergris, musk, benzoin, myrtle, rose and sandalwood.
Finally, we learn from the table that the sacrificial creatures might
be a dove, a sparrow or a swan, although modern occultists agree
that you may dispense with the sacrifice, if you wish.

These small details are not dragged in just to make the whole thing
more complicated, although the energy spent trying to get everything right will be of considerable value to the operation. The aim, as
we have said, is to alert that part of your mind traditionally held to
belong to the third heaven or realm of Venus. Once this fragment
of your subconscious has responded, it immediately links up with
its macrocosmic equivalent. The ritual then becomes 'live', and
every word and gesture is informed with the power of universal love.
In order to recognize the presence of this power, however, the
adept's mind must already be filled with a corresponding emotion;
you will gain nothing from magic if you set about it with the cool
detachment of a scientist. A high degree of personal involvement is
required, and unless you experience the appropriate emotion, be it
love or pity, hate or anger, you will find that magic is as difficult as
persuading a china hen to lay eggs. To perform a rite of Venus
satisfactorily, therefore, you would need to cultivate those extremes
of joy and sadness felt by people in love. There are no half measures,
and it becomes almost literally a case of '*Vénus toute entière à sa proie
attachée.*' If your imagination fails to transport you to the required
heights of emotion, a useful technique is the old Couéist trick of
reciting a suitable litany which serves to focus the attention on a
desired result. The result is a self-induced emotion, which means

that the tides of astral power flowing into you will remain subject to your will, and at any given moment can be directed towards the attainment of your ritual intention.

The climax to all magical ritual occurs when the adept draws into himself the astral force he has evoked so as to project it towards a chosen object. To do this he must surrender his complete being to the astral force which is waiting to possess it, and this he does by cultivating a state of mind or, rather, madness, akin to the divine frenzy of the Bacchantes. There are various ways of doing this, and the adept must choose the one that suits him personally. The usual method is intense concentration, but some magicians resort to sex. As this is one of the things that has given magic a bad name, let us put the record straight before we go any further. By drawing attention to the sexual element in magic we risk bestowing on it an importance it does not deserve. However, the subject must be dealt with pretty thoroughly, if only because of the strong feelings it arouses in those who think that magicians spend their weekends deflowering young virgins in chilly, candle-lit crypts.

Sex has played a part in magic since the very earliest times. Among primitive communities where strength depended on numbers, the sexual act was necessary to the survival of the tribe. But survival depended on a great many other factors as well, including, once agriculture had been discovered, good crops. It cannot have been long, therefore, before the earth's fecundity came to be regarded in sexual terms, with every winter seen as a period of gestation prior to the rebirth of spring. Herein lay the beginnings of religious belief; the earliest cultures were matriarchal in character, and people worshipped an earth mother who was looked upon with awe and affection as a sort of munificent providence. That the earth was capable of producing new life was something men knew from experience, but instead of grasping that her fertility was an indispensable part of the seasonal cycle, they thought it depended on prayer and sacrifice. The sacrificial victim seems usually to have been a young person whose character and appearance made him or her a worthy offering to the Supernal Mother. It was also realized that without sexual impregnation the earth, like any other female, was incapable of producing anything. To ensure good crops recourse was had to a form of sympathetic magic* whereby a man and a woman,

---

* This already worked in hunting. One of the earliest cave drawings in Europe, at

one of whom might be a member of the priesthood, copulated in order to symbolize the earth's impregnation. In some cultures the object was to encourage the appropriate deities, the male and female principles of nature, to do likewise, but among others it is likely that given the converse of the 'as above, so below' principle, ritual copulation was thought be be sufficient in itself.

Gradually, primitive societies adopted an increasingly patriarchal character. The deity they worshipped became a sky father who, unlike the earth mother he had usurped, was extremely jealous of his privileges and authority. The reason for this may be that as men proceeded to understand and conquer their environment they felt guilty about assuming responsibilities they had hitherto been content to leave to the gods. They would have learned, for example, that a good harvest depended more on agricultural planning than on the earth's inherent fertility. The only thing about which they could do nothing was the weather, and this again must have directed their attention from the earth to the sky. The form of their worship also changed, and the old fertility rituals gradually gave way to expiatory rites intended to avert the wrath of a stern father god up above. This seems to have coincided with a fundamental change in their ethical outlook which, psychologists tell us, arose because the deity assumed the characteristics of Laius, the jealous father of Oedipus. Ever fearful of being supplanted by his precocious children on earth, the sky father sulked, bitter and resentful, behind the clouds.* The sinfulness of these children, like that of Oedipus, manifested itself sexually, and so the cure prescribed by religious morality was sexual repression. In this way sin came to be identified above all with sexuality and only to a lesser extent with various forms of anti-social behaviour. Sex typified man's rebellion against God, the disobedience of Adam. Virtue, on the other hand, was identified with submission to authority, asceticism and a sense of utter

Saint-Girons, Ariège, France, shows a man dressed in animal skins who would probably be pursued by his fellows in a ritual enactment of the successful hunt they hoped to have later. Cave paintings discovered in South Africa similarly depict men wearing animal heads and taking part in a ritual dance.

* The change is reflected also in the type of sacrifice offered. Whereas the earth mother received a victim chosen for his or her worthiness, the sky father was offered a criminal or a scapegoat who bore on his shoulders the sins of all the people. The sacrifice thus became the symbolic murder of the precocious child, by which it was hoped to satisfy the jealousy of the paternal deity.

unworthiness. Soon the sexual act, accepted as something entirely natural during the matriarchal period, had become constricted by a multitude of taboos.

In the Western world our attitude to sex has been largely determined by Christianity, which inherited an existing set of do's and dont's, mostly the latter, from Judaism. The Christian Church always regarded sex as an evil, but a necessary evil, and realized that a compromise would have to be made. Sexual activity was permissible only when confined to the marital bed, and even there its procreative function, and nothing else, was to be uppermost in the minds of the couple. However, because sex was so devilishly enjoyable in itself, a further compromise had to be made and sex became an officially approved way in which the spouses might express their love for each other. But not even ecclesiastical approval could rid the leopard of its spots and there still lingered the old feeling that sex meant nasty goings-on in that private region *inter faecem et urinam*, which both repelled and fascinated St Augustine. Nor did sex lose its link with reproduction, which had been so important to a small tribe like the Israelites. The modern controversy over birth control is a survival of this, as is the blanket condemnation of any sexual activity which thwarts the generative processes.

Like his pagan ancestors and most contemporary liberal thinkers, the magician accepts sex as a natural activity devoid of theological implications. This does not mean that magicians are a lecherous breed; on the contrary, there are grounds for supposing that the rejection of taboos may reduce the genital appetite which, like most appetites, seems to prefer forbidden fruit. Yet it is probably true that people for whom sex is something to be enjoyed as and when the opportunity arises do get a chance to gratify their appetites more often than their guilt-ridden fellow citizens. This, of course, is enough to warrant the disapprobation of the latter who unconsciously envy other people their indulgence in something they themselves have renounced through fear. The object of repressed desires can often evoke feelings of rage or loathing, which explains why sexual freedom has been condemned as blasphemous presumption, and a threat to established religion and the moral health of the community. The upholders of sexual 'morality', who condemn pagan worship because of the sexual licence it condoned, equally condemn any form of occultism involving sex. In 1969 a bishop writing in *The Times* about parapsychology was most careful to dissociate his own pious brand from the 'obscene occultism' which he claimed was rampant in England.[2]

Although sex does play a part in magic, it is not indispensable. Like drugs and mantric recitation it is one of several ways of achieving that complete involvement which is the climax of all ritual. When later you read the description of the master ritual, you will see how the final 'divine frenzy' resembles sexual ecstasy with the outpouring of power coinciding with orgasm. This is not sexual indulgence for its own sake, although the incidental enjoyment is nothing to be ashamed of. The fact is that by its very nature sex is the closest we can get to imitating, however imperfectly, the creative power of God. In its way it is a mystical realization of the One which contains all things, for sex becomes the conjunction of the masculine and feminine, the symbolic fusion of two opposites, just as the central pillar on the Tree of Life reconciles the male and female pillars on either side. If, however, you are long past it, too shy or just do not fancy the idea, you can keep off sex and still practise magic. What you must not do, however, is see the mark of the beast on anyone whose views differ from your own.

We have said that sex imitates the power of God. Occult (or 'esoteric') tradition goes further and insists that sex also releases its own form of power which can then be used in magic to reinforce or propel the elemental power evoked by ritual. Certainly, if all thinking processes generate a form of electro-magnetic energy, then the intensity of feeling that accompanies the sexual act must release its own very special force. In occultism, therefore, ritual sex is thought to possess an intrinsic value in addition to its symbolic and psychological purposes.

It is difficult to provide any scientific justification for this theory, although the reason may be that scientists have not yet bothered to consider its validity. The only exception is the late Dr Wilhelm Reich whose findings, though admittedly rejected by most of his colleagues, merit our attention because they seem to confirm the esoteric view.

Wilhelm Reich began his career as Freud's chief assistant in Vienna, but they parted company after a disagreement over the cause of the morbid anxiety they had detected in so many of their patients. Freud believed that this anxiety sprang from frustrated libido, but Reich blamed the absence from the sexual act of what he called true orgasm. By true orgasm he meant that final ecstatic shiver which he had observed in copulating animals. Reich endeavoured to find a physiological basis for his theories by measuring the electrical potency of people's erotogenic zones before, during and after sex. His oscillographs and infra-red apparatus provided him with what he considered to be definite proof that sexual impulses were bio-electrical by nature. His greatest breakthrough came when he discovered that units of energy, which he later called orgones, were always produced when orgasm took place. These orgones were, he claimed, particles of an elementary cosmic energy whose existence could be registered by geiger counters, measured by electroscopes and even reproduced on photographic plates. So sure was he of their physical existence that he later asserted that orgones were blue in colour, like the sky whence they came.

According to Reich the orgiastic free-for-alls that were a feature of pagan religion had a serious orgone-producing purpose behind them. More important to him as a psychologist, however, was the therapeutic effect which orgasm had on those taking part. Towards the end of his career Dr Reich had come to see himself as the Messiah of the new sexual millennium. The unremitting hostility of his detractors probably drove him to make exaggerated claims which hardly encouraged his scientific colleagues to take his work seriously but there are now signs of a revival of interest in his work and we may soon know whether orgones really exist.[3] If they do, there can certainly be no dearth of them in our permissive society.

Because the magician, like Dr Reich, accepts sex as something natural, he can also accept deviations from what is generally regarded as normal sexual behaviour.* Normal is in any case the wrong word, since it is a relative term to which the egoistic majority attributes universal significance. This does not mean that heterosexual occultists suddenly lose interest in the opposite sex, or that their homosexual colleagues abjure their own. There is scope for all within the magic circle. You will often hear it suggested, however, that the most competent magician will be bisexual, since in this way

---

* The danger in accepting that all in nature is natural and therefore permissible is obvious. Such thinking can lead to the approval of murder, or any other crime, on the grounds that the perpetrator is merely following his natural inclinations. This, of course, is the moral nihilism in which de Sade revelled. To prevent it one needs a commonsense ethical standard like that suggested when we discussed 'white' and 'black' magic: each person has the right to act naturally provided his action harms no one else. This, I know, is a simplistic view of personal morality but as a rough and ready guide to conduct there is much to be said in its favour.

he can combine within himself both the male and female principles, the theory being that although God is customarily referred to in masculine terms, He must, as the sum total of all things, be feminine as well. This female element in God is known in kabbalistic literature as the *Shekhinah* which literally translated means the 'in-dwelling' of God, that is, His omnipresence and His active manifestation in the world. (For that reason it is often identified with the sphere of Malkuth.) In the *Sefer-hab-Bahir* the *Shekhinah* is depicted as a semi-independent feminine aspect of God that has somehow or other been separated from the divine source. Some of the kabbalistic rituals of this period are concerned therefore with effecting a reunion of the two. In early Christian theology the Holy Ghost, the Comforter, was likewise thought of in female terms, when its role was curiously similar to that of the *Shekhinah*. More recently the cult of the Virgin Mary gained ground because it made up for the absence of any overtly female aspect in the Trinity, although the devotion owed to the Mother of God is inferior to the worship due only to God. We can understand therefore why the bisexual man or woman is judged to be a truer image of the Creator than the exclusively heterosexual or homosexual. However, one's sexual proclivities are rarely of one's own choosing, so the main thing is to stick to what is natural to you and get on with it.

If you decide to fit sex into the master ritual and are working alone, the experience will, of course, have to be auto-erotic.* In that case you should, if the correspondences allow, try to visualize the possessing entity in appropriately sexual terms. This will increase your emotional involvement in what you are doing and simultaneously contribute to the store of power building up around you. If you have an assistant working with you, your partnership can, if you both wish it, be extended to the sexual act† and indeed,

---

* Onanism and nocturnal emissions were believed by the Jews to be brought about by Lilith, the First Eve (she was sacked for wanting equal rights for women) and Queen of Demons, who, with her cohorts, sought to procure bodies for themselves out of the seed spilled by human beings. This led to the belief that every act of 'impurity', whether deliberate or accidental, engendered foul demons. Sometimes the devilish instigators of these acts were seen as incubi and succubi, both of which are described fully in accounts of the witch trials.

† Magical partnerships do not always have a sexual content. Some alchemists, for example, prefer to work with a *soror mystica*, with whom they enjoy a platonic relationship or sacred marriage (the *hieros gamos*). Nor does group work invariably culminate in a pan-sexual debauch. On the contrary, the proceedings of most magical lodges are as eminently respectable as a royal investiture.

on the basis that the more sex there is, the greater the power, you can eventually branch out into sex *à trois*, *à quatre* or indeed into as many permutations as can be fitted comfortably within the circle.

Despite this encouragement, however, you should avoid falling into the bad habit of esoteric lechery. Unlike those immature sensation-seekers who occasionally use magic to heighten their sexual pleasure, the real adept views the sexual content of his rituals as subordinate to their main magical purpose. It is a means to an end and not the end itself. You should examine your motives closely before you make up your mind to combine sex with your magical activity. If you are just looking for an excuse for sex, forget the magic and have the sex without the garnish. The pity is that many people turn to magic, and especially to what they fondly believe is 'black' magic, in the hope of indulging a ravenous libido. Despite the magic circle and the kabbalistic jargon, all they are really enjoying is a conventional orgy in unconventional surroundings. They would achieve the same result if they were to hire a circus ring for their diversions.

Because sex in magic is so often associated with that old bogey called the Black Mass, we had better digress a little and consider this strange ritual. From the start it must be emphasized that as the Black Mass is meant to be a grotesque parody of the Roman Catholic Mass, it can have no significance except to Roman Catholics. Common sense tells us that unless someone believes in the efficacy of a 'White' Mass, he cannot believe in its Black equivalent. Thus when at the climax of a Black Mass the consecrated host is insulted by priest and onlookers, the blasphemy is evident only to people who already believe that the host is nothing less than the body of Christ.

The French novelist J.-K. Huysmans has left a memorable description of the satanic Mass in his novel *Là-bas*. As Huysmans is known to have dabbled in occultism, it is likely that he once attended one of the Black Masses which, it seems, were a favourite attraction in *fin de siècle* Paris. The general idea behind the ceremony is to perform the opposite of what happens in the Catholic Mass. To this end every detail of the latter has been modified, from the opening '*Asperges me, Domine, urina*' to the final '*qui flagitiose libidinaris per saecula saeculorum*'. The proceedings are, however, a great deal more inventive than one might imagine from the hoary reports of the Lord's Prayer recited backwards, the exaltation of evil in place of virtue and the inevitable black candles (which, incidentally, do not defy physical law by burning upside down, as popular fiction supposes).[4] Ideally, the celebrant of a Black Mass should be a priest of the Catholic Church, but it seems that in our present secular age an ordinary lay person will do almost as well provided he can get hold of a consecrated wafer. The important thing is that he must be naked, as must the young woman whose body serves as his altar. Towards the end of the ceremony the host is reviled by all present, and the ritual culminates with the sacrifice of a chicken or, rarer nowadays, a newly baptized infant, whose blood is poured into a chalice held between the woman's thighs. A scatological perversion of the communion then becomes the precursor to a general orgy in which the entire congregation takes part.

What this deliberate nastiness has to do with traditional magic ritual is unclear, although in some of these Masses the priest will dedicate the ceremony to the realization of a particular intention. Thus we have the well-known story of Mme de Montespan who in the seventeenth century subsidized innumerable Black Masses in an endeavour to retain the affection of Louis XIV. Some time previously her distinguished compatriot Gilles de Rais had tried by the same means to restore his waning fortunes. However, modern devotees of the Black Mass are probably keener to gratify their *nostalgie de la boue* than to win either love or riches. Their interests are certainly very different from those of most modern occultists, and the two are lumped together only by careless reporters and affronted clergymen. No doubt if you are prepared to pay for the privilege you may still witness a Black Mass in any of the European capitals, but these are little more than squalid side-shows like the 'exhibitions' put on for foreign tourists in Tangier, Cairo and Panama City. Lucifer, it would appear, is poorly served by his followers.

Among those who are accused of celebrating the Black Mass are modern witches. The improbability of this particular accusation is shown up by the witches' belief that their religion ante-dates Christianity, so that any version of the Catholic Mass, Black, White or Technicolored, would therefore have no part to play in it. It may be, of course, that some witch covens have mocked Christianity or insulted its devotional objects, but the aim of such behaviour would be to demonstrate their allegiance to a separate religion of their own.

A possible explanation of the link between witchcraft and the Black Mass is the tradition, carefully nurtured by the ecclesiastical authorities, that the god the witches worshipped was the Devil or Old Nick himself. What exactly they worshipped is now largely a matter of conjecture, but anthropologists suggest that their deities were a god and goddess who symbolized the male and female principles of nature. Because the male principle was represented by a goat-like figure, the Church soon had the bright idea of attributing horns and cloven hooves to its arch-fiend Satan. In this way the old pagan god became the devil of the new religion and his worship could be condemned.

The great impetus to modern witchcraft was undoubtedly given by the late Dr Margaret Murray, in whose books the cult is presented as the ancient religion of our continent.[5] Not all anthropologists agree with Dr Murray's conclusions, but the witches and would-be witches were greatly encouraged. Later the more articulate dignitaries of the movement began to produce their own books,[6] and these, like the many books on druidism published in the last century, enjoyed widespread popularity. Their back-to-nature philosophy appealed to people who felt ill at ease in a highly mechanized age. Few noticed, however, that the revelations made in them were no more capable of verification than the extravagant theories of the druid revivalists.

According to the witches, their rituals employ 'age-old' methods to build up magical power which is then used to achieve an end. This, of course, is exactly what the ritual magician does, although unlike him the witches work *outside* the circle. A certain amount of imprecision enters their writing when they start discussing the nature of the power they use: sometimes it is said to be the combined willpower of the thirteen who make up the coven; sometimes it is a power inherent in the human body; sometimes it is the product of divine intervention at the climax of the rite. Probably it contains a little of each, although the one thing most witches are agreed upon is that their ritual power, whatever its source, emanates from the bodies of those taking part. For that reason nudity is observed by most covens, although not by some, who argue, sensibly enough, that if the power they produce can travel to any destination they choose, then it will certainly penetrate their clothing. This power is sometimes likened by them to the 'odic' force which von Reichenbach claimed was liberally discharged by all living bodies. Other apologists point to the doubtful proofs of radiesthesia to show that during their rituals the witches' bodies radiate a special power.

It is often said that this power is generated most strongly by the sexual regions, which takes us back to Dr Reich and his research into the bio-electrical output of the erotogenic zones.

The witches hold weekly or monthly meetings called *esbats** at which the ordinary business of their coven is conducted and some magic worked. More important are the sabbats, of which Hallowe'en and May Eve are the most well known, the others being February Eve, August Eve and each of the solstices and equinoxes. During the magical part of the ceremony the high priestess generally stands inside the circle, while her fellow witches, making six couples, dance around her chanting and singing. Sometimes the partners dance back to back, and in one coven on the Isle of Man the high priestess used to whip the couples as they spun around. It is not clear, however, whether this was one of the 'age-old' ritual methods or a personal kink of the retired civil servant who organized the proceedings. At the height of all this activity the cone of power that has gradually built up within the circle is dispatched to effect its business and the exhausted couples at once collapse in careless abandon. There then follows some light refreshment known as cakes and ale, after which the duly fortified witches may indulge in a little free love, always provided there is still some power left in their sexual parts.

The common feature of witchcraft, the Black Mass and magic is the sexual element. Other movements with more or less occult connections are free from this. No one doubts, for example, that in the darkness of the seance room, spiritualists care for anything save the pleasures of the next world, although ectoplasmic forms presumably offer necrophiliac possibilities.† Nor are the Theosophists thought of as other than high-minded seekers after truth.‡ Such purity does not go unenvied by some occultists who, in print at

---

* The word may have an etymological connection with the Old French *esbahir*, which meant to enjoy oneself. It also bears a resemblance to sabbat, the etymology of which is sometimes traced to the Thracian god Sabazius, as well as the Hebrew word *Shabbath*.

† The 'spirit' of Katie King, which may or may not have been the medium Florrie Cook in her shift, was renowned for the hugs and kisses she bestowed on gentlemen sitters. The reader is sure to be intrigued by Trevor H. Hall's masterly account of these carryings-on in *The Spiritualists* (Duckworth, London, 1962).

‡ Apart, that is, from the late 'Bishop' Leadbeater, whose fondness for adolescent boys caused a flutter in the Theosophical dovecotes. For further details see A. H. Nethercot, *The Last Four Lives of Annie Besant* (Hart-Davis, London, 1963).

least, pretend that ritual sex is either non-existent in this enlightened Aquarian Age or has been practised only by Aleister Crowley who, in addition, took drugs, tortured cats and ruined poor Victor Neuburg.

Crowley is the great *bête noire* (or 666, as he would put it) of twentieth-century occultism. His fellow magicians have damned him for publishing so many of their secrets, but as that has not stopped them following the example he set, his really unforgivable crime may be that the books he wrote are rather better than their own efforts. No mean poet either, he is the Oscar Wilde of magic, although the latter's liking for stable-lads pales to insignificance beside Crowley's voracious appetite for sex, drugs and cruelty. No one was more active than Crowley himself in perpetuating the legend of his own beastliness, but even allowing for a great deal of exaggeration, there remains enough that is unsavoury about the man and the things he got up to. However, behind all the posturing there was an almost encyclopedic knowledge of hermetic lore, much of which fortunately found its way into his writings. Even so, none of these is suitable for beginners, for they all demand a certain basic knowledge if one is to extract anything of value from them. It is therefore wise to wait until you find an experienced guide to accompany you before you embark on Crowley's work. The consequences of following some of his ritual instructions could be disastrous.

Crowley – though he lived to the age of seventy-two – paid dearly for his ritual excesses. His physical deterioration is evident from the photographs of him taken towards the end of his life. However, it would be foolish to conclude that this is the inevitable result of using sex in magic. In Crowley's case it was due to his deliberate flouting of all the rules conducive to good health. Anyone, magician or not, who indulges almost continuously over several years in hashish, fasting, self-mutilation and pan-sexuality is bound at the very least to end up with bags under his eyes. But to imply, as some writers do, that the same effects are caused by occasional ritual sex is not unlike warning adolescent boys that masturbation leads to blindness.

Finally, let me stress again that sex need play no part at all in your magical work, if you do not want it to. Excellent results can be achieved without it. Indeed, some people find that however good their intentions, they become so involved in the sexual part of the ritual that they forget the main purpose behind it. As a result, all the ritual preparation goes by the board and any astral force accumulated is promptly squandered. The lesson seems to be that if you enjoy your ritual sex too much, keep off it, just as other people have to if they happen to dislike sex or have no chance to try it out. The fact is that every ritual is potentially powerful, and what sex does is increase the magician's personal involvement in his rite so that its full potential can be realized. In addition, sex generates its own 'natural' power which supplements the rite's 'supernatural' power. The words 'natural' and 'supernatural' are used here to describe a power which in the first case is of physical origin and in the second of astral origin, though manifesting itself on the physical plane; neither form of power is, of course, any more natural than the other. What all this teaches us is that rituals are effective without sex, although the chances of success may be marginally enhanced by its inclusion.*

So here you are, ready at last to get down to business. Or, to put it in the more dignified language of occult literature, you have reached the Pylon Gate that stands on the threshold of the etheric. According to some experts this is the moment when, if you are really ready to proceed, an enlightened person will show himself and help you along. For those who promise to be flyers in the occult movement this person may belong to an esoteric oligarchy known as the Masters. A great deal of controversy has surrounded these august gentlemen ever since the early days when a Master named Koot Hoomi began posting letters to the endearing Mme Blavatsky, co-founder of the Theosophical Society. The theory seems to be that Masters are superior human beings who, though exempted from further earthly incarnations, have chosen to defer their spiritual evolution so as to return here to help us. A group of them is rumoured to be living in the Himalayas, whence they emerge from time to time to do missionary work among us mortals. The Masters are said to look just like ordinary human beings, and to occupy a physical body; this is how in 1851 Mme Blavatsky was able to bump into one of their number during the celebrations in Kensington Gardens. Some occultists, however, deny that the Masters are genuine flesh-and-blood creatures; instead, they believe them to be exalted

* The magician's penchant for anthropomorphizing the forces he summons is evident even where sex is concerned. Sex is traditionally, if somewhat unoriginally, associated with the Great God Pan. In classical mythology Pan represented those wild and unpredictable impulses which take hold of us without warning and deafen us to the voice of reason. Aleister Crowley had a special liking for the horned and shaggy goat-man and his famous 'Hymn to Pan' was included in the service which preceded his cremation.

spiritual beings who may on rare occasions assume bodily form through a mysterious process known as *kriyashakti*. An impressive-looking Asiatic calling himself the Thibetan used to materialize like this in the home of a well-known lady occultist called Alice A. Bailey. Yet another group of occultists claims with equal confidence that even temporary materialization is far beneath the dignity of the Masters, who prefer to supervise events on earth without ever leaving the astral planes. I understand that there is at least one occult fraternity in California which maintains that flying saucers are the means of transportation invented by a group of Masters, who commute regularly between Earth and Venus. You will have gathered that there are grounds for suspending one's belief in the Great White Brotherhood, as the Masters are collectively called, until one of them introduces himself to you. If they are as enlightened as they are claimed to be, they will not be offended by your scepticism.

The likelihood is that if you do meet someone who can help you with your magical training, he or she will be an ordinary person like yourself. And if you are fortunate enough to meet such a person, it will be when you least expect it. The true adept will never advertise his presence in advance. For that reason it is always best to fight shy of mystery-mongers and the sycophantic coteries that gather round them. Obviously it is reassuring to belong to a group of people with common interests, but too often the esoteric groups who parade their credentials in the occult magazines will, when you really get to know them, fail dismally to live up to their promises. And remember too that a closer acquaintance with them will cost you money. In this unhappy age there is usually a cash desk outside the adytum. Not all groups, I hasten to add, are like this, but the exceptions are hard to find. I know only too well that the path to high magic can be a very lonely one, but it is far better to tread it alone than in unsuitable company. Sooner or later and quite by chance you will meet the right person or group, and then you will be glad that you waited. For Rudolf Steiner it was a stroll in the Black Forest that brought him face to face with his mentor, and your own encounter may be equally unexpected and, I hope, auspicious. So do not feel despondent if so far your only travelling companion is this book. The path before you is well lit: as one of the Graeco-Egyptian magical papyri[7] puts it:

Open your eyes and you will see that the door has been

opened and the world of the gods lies within; and your spirit, rejoicing in this vision, will find itself drawn onwards and up-wards. Now pause awhile and draw the divine essence into yourself, your eyes fixed upon the light. And, when you are ready, say 'Approach Lord'. With these words, the light will shine on you and as you gaze into its centre, you will behold a god, very young and exquisitely formed. His hair will be like the sun and his tunic as white as snow.

That god is within yourself. To discover him is to know that you are not – and never have been – completely alone.

PART TWO

MAGICAL PRACTICE

6

THE NEXT two chapters are intended to give you your first taste of practical magic. Afterwards we shall go on to study other ways of putting your magical knowledge to use. I am afraid that after all the theorizing in the earlier part of this book, it may come as an anticlimax to find yourself now having to mess about with planets, zodiacal signs and other astrological trivia. The terminology of magic is unfortunate, but most of it is used only because no one has yet taken the trouble to invent anything better. What you should bear in mind is that behind the slightly shop-soiled nomenclature there hides a reality as vital, fresh and relevant today as it was at the beginning of time.

Another problem is that the rituals given below, though they properly belong to high magic, are pretty elementary stuff. I do not want to sound like a salesman who declines at the last minute to deliver the goods, but there is no point in setting you advanced tasks at this stage. Such work demands a great deal of experience and understanding. Magic, like playing the violin, is something you have to work at; unless you learn first to cope with the scales and simple pieces, you will never tackle the great sonatas. Even so, you may be assured that there is enough here to keep you happy, and certainly much more than has ever previously found its way into print.

THE INTENTION AND THE CORRESPONDENCES

Earlier we saw that magic was a means of effecting changes in conformity with the will. The first step is to work out what sort of changes you wish to effect. To assist you in this respect a special Table of Intentions has been drawn up (pp. 96–8). This lists a series of possible motives for wanting to use magic and then, in the second column, tells you what category of rite is appropriate. For convenience these rites are classified under various planetary names. When consulting the table you should make a note also of any supplementary remarks and of the number found in the third column, although the significance of this number will not emerge until later.

The next step is to examine the three Tables of Correspondences (pp. 98–101). These are your key to the mysteries, for here at your fingertips you have a comprehensive exposition of occult symbolism. You will observe that the first column of each table reproduces the planetary classifications found in the Table of Intentions. Once you have identified whichever of these you want, you have only to read across the other columns to discover all the hermetic correspondences. These, or as many of them as possible, must then be incorporated in the master ritual which is given on pp. 122 ff. and which supplies all the ingredients needed to give your ritual that sacramental quality we discussed in the previous chapter. For good measure there are also two tables of zodiacal correspondences (pp. 101, 104), which list the symbolism connected with the twelve signs of the zodiac. These will come in useful when you start experimenting with your own ritual construction.

Table of Intentions

Intention	Rite	Degree	Remarks
Ambition, general	Jupiter	2	
Astral World, travel in	Moon	1	See also Chapter 8
knowledge of	Saturn	2	
Beauty, to acquire	Venus	1	See also Chapter 12
Business, success in	Mercury	1 or 2	Burn an incense of benzoin and cinnamon
Career, success in	Jupiter	1 or 2	
Commerce, success in	Mercury	1 or 2	
Discord, to cause	Mars	2	Perform when Moon is waning

Intention	Rite	Degree	Remarks
Examination, to study for	Saturn	2	An incense of cinnamon and mace or mastic is conducive to study
to succeed in	Mercury	2	
Friendship, to disrupt	Mars	2	Perform when Moon is waning
to foster	Venus or Sun	2	
to obtain	Jupiter or Sun	2	
Future, to learn	Mercury	1	See also Chapter 10
Health, to obtain	Jupiter or Sun	2	See also Chapter 12
Harmony, to create	Sun	2	
Home, anything connected with	Saturn	2	A new house should be fumigated with an incense of camphor, myrtle and either nutmeg or aloes wood. The home comes under the astrological sign of Virgo.
Honours, to acquire worldly	Jupiter	2	Special incense required of benzoin, pepperwort, cloves and aloes wood
Influence, to influence people	Mercury	2	
Journey, to ensure a good or safe	Moon	2	
Knowledge, esoteric	Saturn	1	See R. Fludd, in Appendix 3
Love, to obtain	Venus	1	See also Chapter 12
Luck, to obtain	Sun or Jupiter	2	See also Chapter 9
Lust, to gratify	Venus	1	
Military success	Mars	1 or 2	
Money, to acquire	Sun	2	
Patronage, to obtain	Sun	2	
Peace, to create	Sun	1 or 2	

Intention	Rite	Degree	Remarks
Pleasure, to ensure	Venus	2	
Property, to recover lost	Sun	2	
Reconciliation, to achieve	Moon	2	
Theatre, success in	Mercury	2	
Travel, safety in	Moon	2	
War, to prevent	Sun or Moon	1	
to cause	Mars	1	Perform when Moon is waning
Wealth, to obtain	Jupiter	2	
Youth, to regain	Sun	1	See also Chapter 12

Tables of Correspondences

Table 1

This first table consists mainly of the physical details which you will bring into your ritual so as to link your subconscious with the astral world.

Planet	Colour	Plant	Metal	Gem*	Perfumes†
Sun	Orange	Sunflower, heliotrope, chicory	Gold	Topaz, diamond	Aloes wood, saffron, cinnamon, myrrh, cloves
Moon	Violet	Hazel, almond, peony	Silver	Crystal, pearl, quartz	Camphor, jasmine, frankincense, white sandalwood
Mercury	Yellow	Vervain, palm, cinquefoil	Quick-silver	Agate, opal	Cinnamon, mace, cloves, narcissus, storax

* Ideally, the gems used in ritual work should be set in the appropriate planetary metal, but they may, *faute de mieux*, be worn generally with gold or silver.

† Some of the perfumes listed are incenses, others liquid scents. If it is impossible to obtain the correct incense, it is ritually permissible to burn frankincense which is easily obtainable from any church-supply shop.

Planet	Colour	Plant	Metal	Gem*	Perfumes*
Venus	Emerald green	Rose, myrtle, fennel, vervain, maidenhair	Copper	Emerald, turquoise	Ambergris, sandalwood, musk, benzoin, pink rose, myrtle
Mars	Scarlet	Absinth, rue, lambstongue	Iron	Ruby	Benzoin, sulphur, tobacco
Jupiter	Blue	Narcissus, oak, poplar, agrimony	Tin	Amethyst, sapphire	Nutmeg, cinnamon, cloves, aloes wood, balm
Saturn	Indigo	Ash, yew, cypress, houseleek	Lead	Onyx, sapphire	Civet, musk, alum

Element	Colour	Plant
Earth	Russet, green	Red poppy, thrift
Fire	Orange, scarlet	Nettle
Air	Pale yellow	Aspen, mistletoe
Water	Deep blue	All water plants

Tables 2 and 3

These tables supply further information and list those things you will have to visualize during the course of your ritual. You will recollect that a cosmic force is contacted by visualizing its traditional form. In the body of the master ritual you will find instructions telling you when to visualize the appropriate planetary creatures, spirits and sefirothic forms. The names of these planetary spirits vary from one magical tradition to the next. The so-called 'Olympic' names are listed in the following table, with their kabbalistic equivalents in brackets.

Again, try not to be put off by the banality of some of the objects listed. There is no need to take them too seriously: it would be a poor magician who saw nothing funny in the lunar goose and astral crocodile which are solemnly mentioned overleaf:

* See notes on p. 98.

Table 2

Planet	Associated Greek or Roman God	Symbolic Creature	Planetary Spirit	Description of Planetary Spirit
Sun	Adonis, Apollo	Lion, Sparrow-hawk	Och (Sorath)	A king holding a sceptre, a cockerel, a roaring lion
Moon	Diana*	Dog	Phul (Schael)	An archer astride a doe, a goose, a huntress with bow and arrow
Mercury	Hermes, Mercury	Swallow, ibis, ape	Ophiel (Taphthar-tharath)	A king astride a bear, a handsome youth, a magpie, a dog
Venus	Aphrodite, Venus	Dove, sparrow, swan	Hagith (Kedemiel)	Young girls, a dove, a camel
Mars	Ares, Mars	Horse, wolf, bear	Phaleg (Bartzabel)	Man dressed in armour, a king astride a lion with a severed head in one hand and an unsheathed sword in the other, a stag, a horse
Jupiter	Poseidon, Zeus, Jupiter	Eagle	Bethor (Hismael)	Eagle, lion, dragon, bull, peacock, sword
Saturn	Cybele, Rhea, Persephone	Crocodile	Aratron (Zazel)	Bearded king riding a dragon, elderly bearded man, crow, dragon, people clad in black

Element			Elemental King	
Earth	—	—	Gheb	—
Fire	—	Lion	Djin	—
Air	—	Man, eagle	Paralda	—
Water	—	Snake, scorpion	Necksa	—

* In classical mythology the Moon is linked with Diana only when it is actually in

Table 3

Planet	Sefira	Symbolic Creature	Sefirothic Form	Archangel	Guardian Angels
Sun	Tifareth	Lion, child, phoenix	A king, a sacrificial god, an infant	Raphael	Shinanim
Moon	Yesod	Elephant	A handsome nude man	Gabriel	Ishim
Mercury	Hod	Two snakes	An hermaphrodite	Michael	Benei Elohim
Venus	Netsah	Lynx	A beautiful nude woman	Haniel	Tarsishim
Mars	Geburah	Basilisk	A warrior driving a chariot	Chamael	Seraphim
Jupiter	Hesed	Unicorn	A king seated on a throne	Zadkiel	Chasmalim
Saturn	Binah	Woman	A mature woman	Zaphael	Aralim
Earth	Malkuth	Sphinx	A young woman, crowned and sitting on a throne	Sandalphon	Cherubim
—	Kether	—	A venerable bearded king in profile	Metatron	Holy living creatures
—	Hokmah	Man	A bearded man	Ratziel	Auphanim

Zodiacal Tables*

These tables are mainly for reference, but with experience you will be able to enrich your ritual with some of the correspondences listed in them.

the sky; before it rises and after it sets, Hecate is its goddess. Selene and its Roman equivalent, Luna, are personifications of the Moon, which at other times is known as Phoebe and Astarte. Occultists have a special affection for the Egyptian Moon goddess, Isis, wife of Osiris and mother of Horus.

* Given that the basis of hermetic theory is the 'as above, so below' principle of the

Table 4

Sign	Metal	Gem	Colour	Plant
Aries	Iron	Ruby, red jasper	Scarlet	Geranium, sage
Taurus	Copper	Topaz, emerald	Red, orange	Mallow, vervain, clover
Gemini	Quicksilver	Alexandrite, onyx	Orange	Orchid, gladiolus
Cancer	Silver	Emerald, turquoise	Amber	Lotus, comfrey
Leo	Gold	Opal, zirkon	Greenish yellow	Sunflower, cyclamen
Virgo	Quicksilver	Diamond, chrysolite	Yellowish green	Snowdrop, lily, narcissus
Libra	Copper	Chrysolite, jade	Emerald green	Aloe
Scorpio	Iron	Cornelian, malachite	Greenish blue	Cactus, hounds-tongue
Sagittarius	Tin	Carbuncle, sapphire	Blue	Rush, pimpernel
Capricorn	Lead	Black opal, tourmaline	Indigo	Thistle, sorrel
Aquarius*	Lead	Aquamarine, lapis lazuli	Violet	Absinth, fennel, buttercup
Pisces*	Tin	Pearl, amethyst	Crimson	Opium, birthwort

Emerald Tablet, and that all things in nature are known to be interdependent, we need look no further for a justification of astrology. However, readers who are interested will find more information in the introduction to R. C. Davidson's excellent textbook on this subject, *Astrology* (Arco Books, London, 1963).

* Astrologers had long completed their system before the discovery of Uranus (1781) and Neptune (1846). There is now general agreement that these planets have some affinity with Aquarius and Pisces respectively and so uranium and neptunium are sometimes put forward as metals also sympathetic with these signs. To the chagrin of everyone a further planet, Pluto, was discovered in 1930 and it has, after some hesitation, been assigned to Scorpio, thus making plutonium an alternative metal to the traditional iron of that sign.

Table 5

Special attention should be paid to the details given in the third and fourth columns which are important if your ritual intention is to promote good health or cure disease. The optimum time to perform such a rite is when the Sun, Jupiter or the ruling planet of the patient's natal sign is in the sign that rules the part of the body in which you are interested.* Thus a rite to cure impotence would take place when the Sun, Jupiter or the victim's ruling planet was in Scorpio, the plant on your altar would be a cactus (an alternative to the Jupiterian plants which would normally be used); the main Jupiterian colour (violet) would also be joined by the Scorpion shade of greenish blue. Always use your initiative to include as many correspondences as possible in your ritual work.

Sign	Symbolic Creatures	Part of Body	Bodily System	Harmonious Signs for Business, Marriage
Aries	Ram, owl	Head	Cerebral	Sagittarius, Leo
Taurus	Bull	Neck	—	Capricorn, Virgo, Cancer
Gemini	Magpie, hybrids	Hands, arms, lungs	Nervous Pulmonary	Aquarius, Libra
Cancer	Crab, turtle	Breast, stomach	Digestive	Pisces, Scorpio, Taurus
Leo	Lion	Heart, spine, arms, wrists	Cardiac	Sagittarius, Aries
Virgo	Virgin, anchorite	Abdomen, hands, intestines	Alimentary	Capricorn, Taurus
Libra	Elephant, tortoise	Lower back, kidneys	Renal	Aquarius, Gemini
Scorpio	Scorpion, wolf, turtle, lobster	Pelvis, sex organs	Generative	Cancer, Pisces
Sagittarius	Centaur, dog, horse	Hips, thighs, liver	Hepatic	Aries, Leo

* Further advice on all this will be given in Chapter 12.

Sign	Symbolic Creatures	Part of Body	Bodily System	Harmonious Signs for Business, Marriage
Capricorn	Goat, donkey	Knees, bones, skin	Bony	Taurus, Virgo, Libra
Aquarius	Eagle, peacock, man	Ankles	Circulatory	Libra, Gemini, Aries
Pisces	Fish, dolphin	Feet	Lymphatic Hepatic	Cancer, Scorpio, Virgo

THE TIME

So far all you have done is note what type of ritual you need and which set of correspondences it involves. Before you can go any further you will want to ascertain whether the time is right for its performance.

The Tattvic Tides

The most propitious seasons for magical work are spring and summer, but this need not preclude such work during autumn and winter; you may simply find that a little extra effort is required. Spring and summer are traditionally favoured because the correct Tattvic tides are then believed to be flowing. Five, or possibly seven, in number, the Tattvas are held by Hindus to be the forces from which our universe is made. The incidence of the cosmic currents they produce is thought to coincide with the solstices and equinoxes. They are set out below, the dates given being relevant to the northern hemisphere.

1. *Prithivi Tattva*   December 23rd to March 21st
2. *Taijas Tattva*   March 21st to June 21st
3. *Vayu Tattva*   June 21st to September 23rd
4. *Apas Tattva*   September 23rd to December 23rd

I must admit that I have never taken the Tattvic tides too seriously. More important by far is the lunar cycle.

The Lunar Cycle

Nowadays it is very tempting to scoff whenever people start

talking about the Moon's influence on terrestrial affairs. In the space age we all know that the Moon is only a chunk of dead rock. But the fact remains that even if the Moon's physical structure is devoid of mystery, much about its influence has yet to be explained. The word lunatic, as we know, was coined by the Romans because of the adverse effect the Moon was believed to have on the mentally unbalanced; it is interesting that this belief has been confirmed by the experience of psychiatric workers who have discovered a correlation between the lunar cycle and the electro-magnetic activity of the human brain. A similar correlation has also been discovered by scientists studying metabolic changes in both animals and plants.[1] The latter may well offer a scientific justification for the old farming tradition that corn planted at Full Moon is bound to fare badly.* Some of the latest research into the Moon's influence has taken place in Italy, where chemists working under Professor Piccardi in Florence have found a connection between the Moon's phases and the rate at which certain chemicals dissolve.[2] Add to these examples the Moon's well-known influence on tides and female rhythms and you are presented with evidence that, whatever else they may be, lunar influences are not all moonshine.

Some modern occultists have attempted to explain the Moon's influence in terms of electro-dynamics, arguing that throughout nature there is an electrical rhythm which coincides with the Moon's cycle. An older, more poetic tradition tells us that all nature waxes and wanes with the Moon. The appearance of the New Moon is taken as a sign of renewal, when every living object is able to draw in fresh strength. The trend is reversed once Full Moon is reached; from then on, the Moon begins to withdraw its strength in order to pour it forth again later, and our own powers are sympathetically depleted. In accordance with this tradition, most magical work is performed when the Moon is waxing, although 'black' magic, with its works of discord and hatred, is more suited to the waning Moon which seems in some way to assure its success. Always remember

* For those who are interested, lettuces should be planted under the New Moon when they will grow to be full and tender; potatoes should be dug when the Moon is waning; and fruit should only be picked when the Moon is waxing. The Moon-conscious gardener will also take care to plant flower seeds during the Moon's first quarter and, for extra fragrance, when the Moon is in Libra. He will know too that cucumbers fare best if planted when the Moon is in Scorpio and waxing. Fishermen, incidentally, would do well to bear in mind that bigger catches are likely immediately after the Full Moon or, better still, when the Moon is in either Pisces or Cancer.

that any enterprise undertaken when the Sun and Moon are in conjunction is doomed to failure, so keep an eye out for any eclipses predicted in your diary when you start planning rituals.

Planetary Exaltations

The lunar cycle is not the only form of celestial guidance available to the conscientious magician. Another is provided by the ancient doctrine that some planets are 'exalted' when found in certain signs of the zodiac. In astrological terms[3] this simply means that the principle associated with a particular planet expresses itself more freely when that planet is traversing the zodiacal sign most sympathetic to it. From this magicians have deduced quite sensibly that a ritual is likely to be more successful if its performance coincides with the exaltation of the planet that governs it. Thus a rite of Venus would have its chances of success enhanced considerably if it were performed when Venus was passing through Pisces. Some magicians go on to suggest that if no convenient exaltation is in sight, you should arrange to hold your ritual while the Sun is occupying whichever sign exalts the ritual planet. On this basis a rite of Venus would take place some time between February 18th and March 21st when the Sun is in Pisces. However, it is unlikely that you will ever find your ritual intentions corresponding so neatly with the zodiacal calendar.

Details of the signs in which different planets are exalted are given below. You will see that there are also signs in which the same planets are said to be 'depressed', because here their natural self-expression is inhibited. This is something else to be taken into account in timing your ritual. You would, for example, try to avoid performing a rite of Venus when that planet is in Virgo. On the other hand, because it is the great benefic and never 'depressed', it would not matter at all if the Sun happened to be in Virgo or anywhere else.

Planet	Exaltation	Depression
Sun	Aries	—
Moon	Taurus	Scorpio
Mercury	Virgo	Pisces
Venus	Pisces	Virgo
Mars	Capricorn	Cancer
Jupiter	Cancer	Capricorn
Saturn	Libra	Aries

Planetary Rulerships

In addition to being exalted in certain signs, planets also enjoy the rulership of others. This astrological doctrine can again be adapted for magical purposes. All you need do is see which sign is ruled by the ritual planet, and then arrange everything for a time when the Sun or, better still, the planet itself, is passing through that sign. If we once more take a rite of Venus as our example, we can see by looking at the list below that it should be performed when Venus is in Libra or Taurus* or, alternatively, when the Sun is in either of these signs.

Note, however, that in the sign opposite to that which it rules a planet is said to have its 'fall'. Here, as in its 'depression', that planet will be unable to express itself fully, thus making your ritual intention slightly harder to realize. Astrologically the Sun has its fall in Aquarius, but this has no bearing on the practice of magic.

Planet	Rulership	Fall
Sun	Leo	—
Moon	Cancer	Capricorn
Mercury	Virgo and Gemini	Pisces and Sagittarius
Venus	Libra and Taurus	Aries and Scorpio
Mars	Scorpio and Aries	Taurus and Libra
Jupiter	Sagittarius and Pisces	Gemini and Virgo
Saturn	Capricorn and Aquarius	Cancer and Leo
Uranus	Aquarius	Leo
Neptune	Pisces	Virgo
Pluto	Scorpio	Taurus

You will observe that this list affords you slightly more scope than the previous one, but once again you need not throw in your hand if the heavens still refuse to arrange themselves to suit your purpose. Most rituals are intended to meet immediate needs and so leave little opportunity for lengthy preparation. The best thing to do in these circumstances is to see whether there is a time that is astrologically auspicious in the near future and, if there is, to postpone your ritual until then. If you are unable to find such a time, then just carry on regardless. When we select a propitious time for the

---

* Readers who are already familiar with astrology may care to know that the results obtained from the ritual will often differ subtly according to the actual sign adopted. The consequences of a Venusian rite might thus express themselves in either Libran terms (i.e. harmoniously) or Taurean terms (i.e. possessively). This is a field which merits further investigation.

performance of a ritual, our object is to make sure that any short-comings on our part will be compensated by the planetary influences whose help we have enlisted. Fortunately, should these influences be unobtainable by virtue of exaltations, rulerships and affinities, we can still go some way towards attracting them by selecting the day and/or hour traditionally ruled by the ritual planet.

Planetary Days and Hours

The planetary days are easily memorized, but a little more work is needed to calculate the appropriate hours. Even so, it is not difficult, since all you need do is to look up the hours of sunrise and sunset for any particular day and then work out for yourself which is the first hour, second hour and so on. The following table will then tell you which planet rules each of these hours.

Table of Hours

	Sunday	Monday	Tuesday	Wednesday	Thursday	Friday	Saturday
Planetary ruler	Sun	Moon	Mars	Mercury	Jupiter	Venus	Saturn
Sunrise							
1st hour	Sun	Moon	Mars	Mercury	Jupiter	Venus	Saturn
2nd hour	Venus	Saturn	Sun	Moon	Mars	Mercury	Jupiter
3rd hour	Mercury	Jupiter	Venus	Saturn	Sun	Moon	Mars
4th hour	Moon	Mars	Mercury	Jupiter	Venus	Saturn	Sun
5th hour	Saturn	Sun	Moon	Mars	Mercury	Jupiter	Venus
6th hour	Jupiter	Venus	Saturn	Sun	Moon	Mars	Mercury
7th hour	Mars	Mercury	Jupiter	Venus	Saturn	Sun	Moon

Repeat the series for those hours still remaining until sunset.

	Sunday	Monday	Tuesday	Wednesday	Thursday	Friday	Saturday
Planetary ruler	Sun	Moon	Mars	Mercury	Jupiter	Venus	Saturn
Sunset							
1st hour	Jupiter	Venus	Saturn	Sun	Moon	Mars	Mercury

	Sunday	Monday	Tuesday	Wednesday	Thursday	Friday	Saturday
Planetary ruler	Sun	Moon	Mars	Mercury	Jupiter	Venus	Saturn
Sunset							
2nd hour	Mars	Mercury	Jupiter	Venus	Saturn	Sun	Moon
3rd hour	Sun	Moon	Mars	Mercury	Jupiter	Venus	Saturn
4th hour	Venus	Saturn	Sun	Moon	Mars	Mercury	Jupiter
5th hour	Mercury	Jupiter	Venus	Saturn	Sun	Moon	Mars
6th hour	Moon	Mars	Mercury	Jupiter	Venus	Saturn	Sun
7th hour	Saturn	Sun	Moon	Mars	Mercury	Jupiter	Venus

Repeat the series for those hours still remaining until sunrise.

Having explained how to time your ritual to the best advantage, we can now proceed to consider what further preparatory work is required.

THE PLACE

The preparation of the place involves assembling all the materials in the room where the rite is to be performed. The walls should be adorned with drapery of whatever colour has been recommended in the Table of Correspondences, but if such extravagance is beyond your means a cloth of the correct shade covering the altar will be sufficient. The altar itself may consist of an ordinary table or chest, but it must be large enough to accommodate all the necessary ritual implements. If you intend taking your magic seriously you will sooner or later have to construct a proper altar of your own or have one made to suit your individual requirements. Contemporary magicians seem to have a penchant for cube-shaped altars painted black inside and white without, these colours representing the material and astral worlds. Such altars are a recent invention and their use is a matter of taste.

We shall assume that you have already cleared all furniture from the centre of the room so as to provide ample space for the circle in which you will be working. With an ordinary compass you must now locate the four cardinal points and place on the floor the symbols of the elemental kings who govern them. These are:

North

This is the station of Earth ($\triangledown$) and is ruled by Uriel. Its symbol may be a rock, a handful of sand or just a clod of earth. Whichever of these objects you select, it is an advantage to obtain it from a sacred site, ideally one connected with the Ancient Mysteries.* However, it is not always possible to cart back buckets of soil from Delphi or Eleusis, and it would be sheer vandalism to start chipping pieces off the Great Pyramid or the boulders of Stonehenge. I know of one magician who swears by a small rock he lifted from a cromlech in north Wales, while another regularly uses soil from a dolmen in Brittany. Until you have an opportunity of getting something on these lines yourself, you must make do with the best you can. Anything gathered from the spot where two paths cross is said to be particularly effective, and that should not be too difficult to manage.

South

The station of Fire ($\triangle$) is ruled by Michael, and a candle or votive light will be quite adequate here. If, of course, you are determined to do things in grand style, you can purchase a beeswax candle from any church-supply shop. In Chinese magic, red jade (*chang*) is widely used as the symbol of Fire.

West

Here we have the station of Water ($\triangledown$) which is ruled by Gabriel. A glass of consecrated water is required. To perform

---

* The adept will have a special affection for the shrines revered by his ancestors. Again and again he will be drawn to them, since they are his point of contact with an age-old esoteric tradition. The elemental guardians of such places will be sure to welcome his interest after so many years of neglect and desuetude. At the same time he can attune his mind to the astral memory of the holy mysteries once enacted there. A pilgrimage to one of these shrines, if accompanied by a suitable act of devotion to the local deity (*genius loci*), will bestow great blessings on his subsequent magical work. A most useful reference book for the European magician who wishes to discover the location of former religious monuments is the *Recueil général des bas-reliefs, statues et bustes de la Gaule romaine*, itself a monumental work, by Emile Espérandieux. First published in Paris in 1910, the original or later editions should be available in most good libraries.

the consecration you need only add a pinch of salt, the emblem of eternity, to a glass of rainwater and, while making the sign of the pentagram over it, say aloud: *I exorcise Thee, O Creature of the Water*. There is a far lengthier incantation in Latin, if you prefer it. It goes like this:

*Te exorcizo per Dei omnipotentis virtutem qui regnat per saecula saeculorum. In nominibus Mertalliae, Musaliae, Dophaliae, Nemaliae, Zitanseiae, Goldaphairae, Dedulsairae, Gheninaireae, Geogropheirae, Cedahi, Gilthar, Godieth, Ezoliel, Musil, Grassil, Tamen, Puri, Godu, Hoznoth, Astroth, Tzabaoth, Adonai, Agla, On, El, Tetragrammaton, Shema, Ariston, Anaphaxeton, Segilaton, Primeuraton, Amen.**

East

The last station belongs to Raphael, who rules Air. The object generally used to represent that element is a sprig of mistletoe, which is particularly appropriate because of its alleged druidic connection with the Sun, itself a symbol of Raphael. A card bearing one of the esoteric symbols of Air ($\triangle$) (O) or the Sun's astrological symbol ($\odot$) will do as an alternative if you perversely decide to embark on your magical career when mistletoe berries are out of season.

The Circle

The circle on whose periphery the elemental symbols are placed may be drawn in chalk or, as Eliphas Lévi advised, made of strips of doe-skin. Less trouble is a circle made of string or cotton. It is important that the two ends be left undone until the magician is ready to step into the circle. Once inside he can then tie up the ends and so close the circle. Still less trouble is a circle that is visualized by the magician but has no ordinary physical existence. In the early days, however, it is far wiser and more reassuring to have

---

* Readers will recognize some of the divine synonyms among these barbarous names. If the water is to be used for washing, the magician has to invoke another batch of angels and demons: Imanael, Arnamon, Imato, Memeon, Vaphoion, Gardon, Existon, Zagverium, Zarmesiton, Tilecon and Tixmion. Even if there are no astral beings to lay claim to all these names, their mere recitation is, it is claimed, useful since it produces acoustic vibrations which astrally charge the salt-water solution. The psychological effect on the magician's mind is also important.

something tangible around you. There is a cautionary tale involving Aleister Crowley and Victor Neuburg who once decided to summon up the demon Choronzon in the Sahara Desert. When neither was looking, the fiend threw sand over part of the circle they had drawn, leapt inside and began to wrestle with the astonished Neuburg.

The curious thing is that the circle is scarcely mentioned at all in any of the extant Graeco-Egyptian magical papyri. Instead, the magician is told to depend for protection on amulets worn on his person. On the whole, I think a circle may well be a great deal safer than a battery of charms and talismans.

In many *grimoires* the magician is urged to reinforce his circle by writing various names of power along its circumference. If you feel nervous, you may care to do this, although in my opinion it is unnecessary except in certain highly advanced and dangerous operations which do not concern us here. These names are mostly culled from the various forms of the Tetragrammaton and should be written in chalk on the ground or, which is probably more convenient, on cards which can then be placed at strategic points along the inner edge of the circle. Three favourite names for this purpose are Shaddai El Chai, Tetragrammaton and Ararita.

The Triangle of Art

This is a triangle delineated at an eastern point outside the magic circle. Its main purpose is to confine any elemental or angelic being that has been conjured to visible appearance. It is extremely unlikely that you will be troubled by a physical visitation of this nature, but to be on the safe side it is as well to make up the triangle before you begin any magical operation. It has the added advantage of providing you with a convenient focusing-point for your visualization; any astral form that manifests itself will then be psychically observable within the triangle and nowhere else. Like the circle, the triangle may be formed with chalk, string or cotton. If, however, there is reason to suspect that the force you wish to contact may be boisterous, like that involved in a rite of Mars, for example, or if you persist in pursuing the kliphothic aspect of any force, then take the precaution of tracing a *second* triangle in salt inside the first as this will reinforce the barrier. It is said that the Chinese used to form this second triangle out of scarlet peony petals since that flower was believed to keep demons in thrall.* Once again words of power may be written or placed along the sides of the triangle as in the following example.

Figure 2

The Altar

This is situated inside the circle and faces due east, whence all light comes. In magic with a nefarious or kliphothic purpose the altar faces north,† with north and east exchanging places throughout the remainder of the ritual. On top of the altar will rest a cloth of the appropriate ritual colour, and some of the following *objets de magie*.

---

* This may be why Theophrastus tells us in his *Enquiry into Plants* that peonies gathered by night are a certain cure for epilepsy. The petals and roots of this plant are to be found among the ingredients of many herbal nostrums.

† Cf. Jer. i 14: 'Out of the north an evil shall break forth upon all the inhabitants of the land.' Traditionally the east is the side of God, the west that of man, the south that of good spirits and the north that of demons. In Zoroastranism Angra Mainyu, the deadly deva of devas, came from the regions of the north, a point worth noting since Mme Blavatsky, discussing the Persian tradition in her *Secret Doctrine* (Theosophical Publishing House, Adyar, 1962, p. 399), wrongly describes the north as the provenance of 'every beneficent (astral and cosmic) action'.

The five infernal kings of the north were Sitrael, Palanthan, Thamaar, Falaur and Sitrami.

The Ritual Sword

The true magical sword is a rare and costly item. Those that do turn up from time to time are made of various planetary metals or, for general purposes, of tempered steel. On them are inscribed or painted an assortment of names of power. If you have to make do with an ordinary sword or large knife, then you can adapt it for magical use by having engraved or painted on the blade whatever names of power you fancy. Many magicians possess replicas of the famous trident of Paracelsus (figure 3) which, they claim, bestows considerable power on whoever is wielding it.

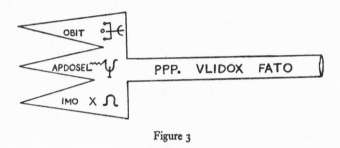

Figure 3

The Wand

The wand performs much the same function as a wireless aerial, since it serves to conduct etheric vibrations on to the plane of dense matter. Although it is itself a part of the physical world it is capable of reaching out and arresting the supra-physical forces that charge the air around it. Traditionally the wand, like that used by water diviners, is made of a hazel branch cut from the parent tree with one stroke of the knife in spring or summer. The tips of the wand may then be stopped with metal caps similar to the ferrules of walking-sticks. These should ideally be of the appropriate ritual metal, but lead is generally held to be a satisfactory alternative. When not in use the wand should be wrapped in a silk cloth of any colour save brown or black.

I have seen wands made of other woods besides hazel. Ash seems to be a favourite in Scandinavian countries, where it is identified with Yggdrasil, the fabulous tree that binds together heaven, earth and hell. Oak also is used by magicians, because of its druidic connections; the branch must be cut between April 10th and May 26th since the tree usually bursts into leaf some time between these dates.

The Incense Burner

In an earlier chapter we briefly discussed the psychological value of incense. It has in addition another purpose. There is a magical tradition that incense enables 'spirits' to assume a tangible form. This was borne out in the late 'twenties when Stella C. was delighting the Society for Psychical Research with her physical mediumship. Incense was burned during her seances because, according to the late Harry Price, the medium liked the smell – as apparently did the spirits, for they excelled themselves.

Nowadays incense burners can be purchased quite cheaply, but it is far better to make your own. All you need for this is a small bowl and a tile, or piece of asbestos, on which to rest it. If possible the bowl should be of the metal shown in the Table of Correspondences, but this is not always practicable; you will not, for example, want to be distracted in the middle of a solemn Saturnine rite by the sight of your leaden incense burner melting away. Earthenware bowls will serve quite adequately, and no one's resources are likely to be strained in getting hold of an old flower-pot. Whatever bowl you decide to use, it should be filled with sand or shingle to a depth of some three inches. On top of this you place some pieces of charcoal, taking care to leave the surface of the sand uneven so that air can circulate under the charcoal (figure 4). To start the thing off, all you have to do is sprinkle a few drops of spirit on the charcoal and apply a lighted match to it. It will then burn for a few minutes

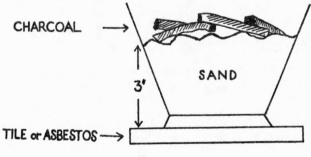

CHARCOAL →

SAND

3'

TILE or ASBESTOS →

Figure 4

with a blue flame before it settles down to smoulder with a red-hot glow. A little incense scattered on these embers will give off aromatic vapours as it burns. Easier to cope with are sticks of incense which can be stood in the sand and allowed to burn away. The difficulty is that the type of incense you need may not always be manufactured in stick form. Church-supply shops will be able to provide you with some incenses, and at least one specialist supplier regularly advertises in the occult magazines.

The Correspondence Chart

Until you are completely familiar with the correspondences, it is prudent to keep near you a card on which they have been copied. This can be referred to as the need arises. Where colours are mentioned, you will find it helpful to have these painted on the card instead of being written out by name.

The Tree of Life

A copy of the glorious tree, suitably coloured,* should also be on hand for easy reference. Once you are at work inside the circle you will be unable to step outside it to consult a textbook whenever your memory fails you.

The Ritual Card

This is the programme of your ritual, and the occasional glance will remind you what is to be done next. To prepare your card, copy out the master ritual and expand this wherever necessary by adding the extra details culled from the Tables of Correspondences and elsewhere.

The Pentacle

This Solomonic symbol is reputed to make a profound impression on such creatures as elemental spirits. You can either fashion

---

* The sefirothic colours vary slightly according to each plane of manifestation (*atsiluth*, *beriah*, *yetsirah* or *asiyah*). For present purposes, however, it will be sufficient to use the sefirothic equivalents of the planetary colours shown in the Tables of Correspondences. Not mentioned there are *Kether* (brilliant white) and *Hokmah* (slate grey).

one out of wood or draw one on a stiff white card which should be placed in an upright frame. Keep the pentacle covered by a cloth of coloured, but not black, silk until such time as you need to use it. There exist graphic accounts of how magicians used to ward off demons by waving pentacles before them just as a lion-tamer might wave his whip under the noses of his charges.

The Gong or Gavel

In the rituals provided you will find that the adept is frequently instructed to strike a gong or gavel a certain number of times. This is done for two reasons. The first is simply to keep the celebrant's mind on the job, since during ritual work it is all too easy to drift off into a dreamy state which is both unproductive and dangerous. A few timely knocks will prevent this. The second reason is that the knocks are a means of establishing contact with the appropriate astral forces. This can be achieved subjectively by way of the operator's subconscious, or objectively by way of the sonic vibrations that are generated. In either case it is the *number* of knocks which is of paramount importance, since each series will correspond with a particular plane of manifested existence.

The Crystal

This is merely an aid to visualization, and its use is a matter of choice. Some people find it easier to 'project' their images into the crystal, or else they find that an occasional glance into it will reveal to them the form they have been attempting to visualize. In both cases the phenomenon is subjective: there is nothing physically visible inside the crystal itself.

The Candles

Apart from providing illumination these symbolize the flame of understanding which burns in the magician's heart (v. 2 Esd. xiv 25). They also heighten his awareness of those strange and wonderful things that come not by day but 'By starlight and by candlelight and dreamlight'.[4]

The Sacrificial Knife

Ritual sacrifice is rarely practised in magic, or at least magicians rarely admit that it is. However, they have always laid great store by it, knowing that much power is released when blood is spilled. This power (*kama*) lends itself particularly to materialization work, for it enables astral forms to assume bodily appearance within the Triangle of Art. The use of incense is probably just as effective in this respect, so whether or not you decide to perform a sacrifice will finally depend on your temperament. I hope you decide against it. If you must indulge in blood-letting, you can always nick your arm with the sacrificial knife and let your own gore provide the vital energy you seek. Incidentally, one *grimoire* suggests that by cracking open an egg, the sensitive magician can obtain the same benefits as his more unfeeling brethren get from killing birds or small animals.

The Flowers

It is always agreeable to have a few flowers on the altar to remind you of the beauties of nature. However, do not overdo this; it is better to have just one bloom than to clutter up the altar with a large bouquet. If they happen to be available, the plants or flowers mentioned in the Table of Correspondences are the ones to get. These will then have a symbolic as well as aesthetic function.

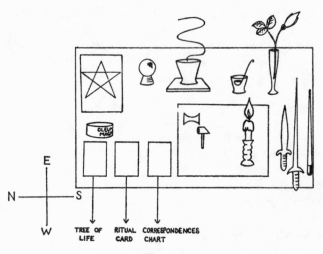

Figure 5

The Oleum Magicale

Magical unguents are applied before and sometimes during ritual work. The psychological impact of their distinctive smell is perhaps secondary to the curious effect which their application has on the nervous and circulatory systems of the body. Further details of their composition and manufacture will be found in Appendix 1.

Other objects may be included if a particular ritual demands them. Those shown in figure 5 are what would usually be found on an altar used in ceremonial magic of the Western/kabbalistic tradition. You will find, however, that the Egyptian master ritual given on pp. 134 ff. dispenses with a few of these objects, although it does substitute some others of its own. When everything has been laid out on the altar the adept may, if he wishes, consecrate it by saying the following words over it: 'Dolmaley, Lameck, Cadat, Pancia, Velous, Merroë, Lamideck, Caldurech, Anereton, Metatron: Most Pure Angels, be the guardians of these instruments, they are needed for many things.'

All is then ready for the ritual itself.

T

WO MASTER rituals have been provided in this chapter.
Both are short and relatively simple. The first, following
the most commonly accepted Western magical tradition, is
based on the kabbalah, while the second owes its inspiration
to ancient Egypt. It is the kabbalistic rite which can most conveniently be used with the tables previously given, since both are
based on the same esoteric tradition. However, those readers who
do not feel completely at ease in the wonderful world of the sefiroth
can quite happily exchange it for the more primitive splendour of
the Egyptian rite.

The rituals of magic may generally be divided into three categories, only two of which need concern us here. The third category
is by far the most advanced and for that reason is rarely undertaken
on one's own. It demands, above all, a very close rapport with certain
astral entities known as Group Forms. These are immensely powerful beings who on occasion can assume human shape, when they
will co-operate with the other participants in a ceremony that com-
bines the spiritually elevated with the wildest dreams of wanton-
ness. Experience of such ritual, if you are fortunate enough to get it,
will not come until you are fully adept* at the other two. I am afraid
therefore that you will have to contain your patience yet awhile.

* We have already used the noun adept in this book to signify magician and we shall
continue to do so throughout these rituals. As the word implies a high degree of proficiency it should not really be used in this general way. However, repeated use of the
word magician can get very tedious, while such alternatives as thaumaturge or sorcerer
are either precious or inappropriate.

Members of the Hermetic Order of the Golden Dawn who were active at the turn
of the century confined the term adept to those among them who belonged to an Inner
Order, the R.R.A.C. (*Rosae Rubeae et Aureae Crucis*). Above this was a still more
exalted order, the A.A. (*Argenteum Astrum*) which had no mortal members. Instead

The two remaining categories are, for the purpose of this section, referred to as first- and second-grade rituals. Those of the first grade are only slightly more difficult because to be really effective they demand a little extra preparation. Some venerable textbooks exhort the magician who is about to embark on them to fast, keep chaste, keep silent and let his mind dwell on the ritual intention for several days on end. They then go on to list enough preliminary ablutions and anointings to drive the most dedicated occultist into the ranks of the Anabaptists.

Unhappily one cannot do away with all these observances, for no matter how ridiculous some of them may seem, they do have some psychological effect which will later enhance the magician's performance. Before all rituals numbered 1 in the Table of Intentions, therefore, you are advised to:

1. Keep off sex and solid food for twelve hours.

2. Drink only water for the first six of these hours and thereafter a glass of wine whenever you feel thirsty.

3. Have no sleep at all during this time.

4. Talk to no one during the hour immediately preceding the rite and, if possible, keep silent during the full twelve hours.

5. One hour before the rite is due to begin have a bath, shower or good wash. Afterwards anoint yourself liberally with a magical oil and, if available, one of the scents listed in the Table of Correspondences.

it was manned by Secret Chiefs who resemble the Masters of the Theosophical Society. For those who have an ambition to set up a magical lodge of their own, here are the grades adopted by the Golden Dawn. Each was associated with two complementary sefiroth on the Tree of Life. They had also a corresponding planetary significance:

Astrum Argenteum	Rosae Rubeae et Aureae Crucis	Golden Dawn
Ipsissimus	Adeptus exemptus	Philosophus
Magus	Adeptus major	Practicus
Magister Templi	Adeptus minor	Zelator
		Neophyte
		Probationer

6. Put on whatever ritual vestments you intend to wear.*

You are now ready to put on any ritual jewellery you may have before proceeding to the ritual chamber. From here on, the instructions given apply equally to rituals of either degree. Needless to say, any or all of the preliminaries to Grade 1 rituals, especially the anointing and the donning of vestments, may also be adopted for rituals of the second grade, but whereas they would in that case be optional, they remain essential for those of the first grade.

THE KABBALISTIC MASTER RITUAL

Once in the ritual chamber, you should set about preparing the altar, lighting candles and incense. The cardinal points have then to be located and the elemental symbols placed thereon. Your next task will be to make out the Triangle of Art in the east and, when that is completed, the magic circle itself, leaving, of course, a gap to afford you access inside. At last, when everything is ready, extinguish all lights except the altar candle and the elemental flame, step inside the circle and immediately close it by knotting or over-lapping the two loose ends. The rite is about to begin.

* Newcomers to occultism, nurtured as many of them are on Hammer films and Dennis Wheatley novels, often expect that they will have to dress up for magic, usually in something half-way between a toga and a jazzed-up version of a monk's habit. Many readers will be pleased to know therefore that dress is in fact optional. In private, ritual vestments are often more of an embarrassment than a blessing, unless you happen to be one of those people who enjoys dressing up. Most occultists defend the use of special robes on the grounds that our everyday clothing soaks up all sorts of etheric influences which, they argue, can have a deleterious effect on magical work. There is no doubt that astral hygiene is sometimes important, but this need not turn one into a faddist. I would suggest therefore that you need not worry unduly if you have no special clothing to wear for the occasion. It would, after all, be a poor type of ritual that depended on sartorial formality for its success.

Where ritual vestments are necessary is in all group work. Not only do they add to the ceremonial but their symbolic colouring increases the psychological impact which the ritual must make on the subconscious levels of the mind. Again, the decision as to what is worn can be left to the group or its leader, and provided the robes accord with the correspondences they can be as simple or elaborate as imagination or dress sense allows. A word of warning, however: some occultists insist that ritual vestments should have no buckles, buttons or hooks on them. This may spring from the old Roman law which forbade the priest of Jupiter (*Flamen Dialis*) from wearing knots or rings about his clothing. Personally I see nothing wrong with them.

The Rite*

The Purification of the Place

This is an essential preliminary to kabbalistic ritual work since it serves to banish
all undesirable influences from the room.
The adept begins by facing due east† and
solemnly formulating the kabbalistic cross.

When this has been completed he remains where he is and uses the ritual sword
to trace an astral pentagram in the air
before him. There are two ways of going
about this, one for the evocation of astral
forces, the other for their dismissal. The

*Ritus***

Purificatio Loci
Regio orientalis

Ateh‡

Ve Gedulah | Le Olahm Amen | Ve Geburah

Malkuth

---

* Ritual instructions are given, sometimes in diagrammatic form, on the right-hand
side of the page and described or enlarged upon on the left. You will see too that the
words spoken by the magician are in Latin and you may wonder why this should be so.
Let it be admitted at once therefore that English is a perfectly satisfactory alternative,
and may be used if you prefer it. The reason why this particular ritual contains a great
deal of Latin is that its formulations were first consolidated during the Renaissance,
when many scholars quite unjustly scorned the vulgar tongue and resorted instead to
Greek or Latin. Some people may argue that it is unnecessary for us now to continue
what was originally just a humanist fad, but there are good reasons for retaining the
Latin. One is that it lends a dignity to the proceedings which would be absent if English
were used, however elevated its style. Another reason is that while Latin is admittedly
an international language only among certain scholars, it nevertheless gives the rite an
appearance of universality. Of course, it would be foolish of any magician to stand inside
a circle muttering words about which he knew nothing, but it is hoped that the commentary will explain fully what is being said and done. Perhaps in the end the use of
Latin is no more than an affectation in keeping with the occult tradition of making
things as complicated as possible. But by now its use is something that has been made
respectable, if not hallowed, by time.

Those unsure of their Latin pronunciation may care to remember that the consonants
c and *g* are always hard as in *c*at or *g*oat. As for the vowel sounds, they are normally the
same as those in the words in brackets: *a* (b*a*t), *e* (g*e*t), *i* or *j* (s*ee*), *o* (t*oe*), *u* (c*oo*l). The
v in Latin is pronounced as if it were a *w*. Remember too that every letter in a Latin
word is pronounced.

† In rites which have a malevolent intention, and so involve the kliphothic aspect of
the forces evoked, the adept must turn to the north. Throughout the rest of the ritual
north then changes places with east and any formulations are altered accordingly. In
addition, he must strike his gong or gavel eleven times whenever seven or ten strokes
are recommended in the text. Such rites are often dedicated to a demon named Peolphan.

‡ The words to be spoken by the adept are those which are *not* italicized.

distinction is of doubtful value and one version only will be given here. For this the adept uses the full sweep of his arm, beginning at the bottom left-hand corner of the pentagram (i.e. from a point some-where half-way between his left knee and hip) and proceeding to the apex which will be at a point above his head. From here he lowers his sword to the penta-gram's bottom right-hand corner so that what he has traced is an inverted V. With-out pausing here he proceeds straight up to the pentagram's top left-hand corner whence he continues horizontally to its right-hand equivalent. Finally he moves the sword down to the bottom left-hand corner from which he began. The pro-gression is thus:

With each movement of the sword he visualizes himself drawing a line of pure white light, so that by the time he has finished, a gleaming pentagram is sus-pended over the eastern station. His next task will be to vivify this shape by pointing his wand towards its centre and pronounc-ing the word YHVH (Yod-Hē-Vau-Hē). As he utters this most holy name, he imagines the pentagram shimmering with newly infused energy.

Oriens (east)

Yod-Hē-Vau-Hē

A similar pentagram must then be traced in exactly the same way over each of the other cardinal points and charged in every case with the appropriate words, which are given opposite.

The function of these pentagrams is to create astral barriers capable of withstanding assault from any direction. They also form points of contact with the elemental world. For this reason the adept has next to visualize and greet the four elemental kings who will be stationed there. By his visualization he also creates the etheric likeness of these great beings on the periphery of his circle.

Once more the adept begins by turning towards the east, where he visualizes the Archangel Raphael (pronounced *Rǎfǎhěl*) standing on a purple hilltop, his pale yellow garments billowing in the breeze. Having spoken the words of greeting, he next visualizes behind him the Archangel Gabriel (*Gǎbrěěl*) dressed in blue and surrounded by cascading torrents of water. On his right the figure of Michael (*Měkahěl*), clad in scarlet and bearing aloft a red-hot sword, appears to the adept's psychic vision while at last, on his left, he visualizes Uriel (*Awrěěl*), archangel of Earth, standing against a fertile landscape whose greens and browns are the colours of his cloak.*

The adept now proceeds to visualize a lambent six-pointed star above his head, its interlaced triangles anticipating the

Australis (south)
Adonai Tzabaoth
Occidens (west)
Eh-Ei-Hé
Borealis (north)
Agla

Before commencing his visualization of the Archangelic Guardians the adept speaks the following words:

Huc per inane advoco angelos sanctos terrarum, aerisque, marisque et liquidi simul ignis qui me custodiant, foveant, protegant et defendant in hoc circulo.

The visualized archangels are addressed as follows:

Oriens
Salve Raphael cuius spiritus est aura e montibus orta et vestis aurata sicus solis lumina.

Occidens
Salve Gabriel cuius nomine tremunt nymphae subter undas ludentes.

Australis
Salve Michael, quanto splendidior quam ignes sempiterni est tua majestas.

Borealis
Salve Uriel, nam tellus et omnia viva regno tuo pergaudent.

---

* These images, together with their complementary colours, are most important. The adept must therefore reflect on them constantly during his magical training so as to be able to bring them effortlessly to mind when he commences ritual work.

fusion of his temporal self with the eternal forces he hopes to evoke.*

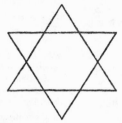

Non accedet ad me malum cuiuscemodi quoniam angeli sancti custodiunt me ubicumque sum.

With these words the adept proclaims his confidence in the angelic protection he has invoked.

Occidens

Ateh

Ve Gedulah | Le Olahm Amen | Ve Geburah

Malkuth

This part of the ritual – known as the 'Banishing Ritual of the Lesser Pentagram' – is concluded by a second formulation of the kabbalistic cross during which the adept faces west, his back to the altar.

Turning to the east again he focuses his attention on the Tree of Life, for he is ready to move from Malkuth, the sphere of Earth, to Yesod, which is the silver gateway to the astral world. Yesod is the sphere of the moon, and the name of Gabriel will be the one he gives on approaching the ishim who guard the gate. This password will be enough, and having uttered it he imagines that a blue-and-silver curtain is parting to allow him access to the wonderland beyond.

These words serve as the adept's passport to the astral world:

Excubitores, in nomine Gabrieli, Fas mihi tangere limina illa.

While still on the threshold of the astral kingdom the adept humbly acknowledges his ignorance of the sublime mysteries which surround him. He recites his confession three times and follows this with three series of seven knocks with the gavel.†

The following confession is recited three times:
Nescio quis sim
Nescio unde veniam
Nescio quo eam
   Quaero
Sed quid nescio.

* The six-pointed star or hexagram is generally taken to symbolize the aspiration of the lower self (△) towards the higher (▽) or, alternatively, spirit reflected in matter. The pentagram, too, has a symbolic connection with man, as it is a symbol of evolution; it represents man endowed with reason and so raised above the beasts. Readers will have seen Leonardo da Vinci's famous drawing where the figure of a man is superimposed on a pentagram enclosed within a circle.

† Each stroke is represented by ▓.

Before going further he must attend to the incense on his altar and anoint himself ready for the journey he is about to undertake. The magical oil is rubbed on the forehead, the inside of each wrist and under the chin. Oil must also be applied to the base of the spine if the adept plans a sexual climax to his rite.*

Now that he is fully prepared he may step out on to the sphere of Yesod where he visualizes the Yesodic correspondences in his crystal or outside the circle.

Silently he informs the elemental intelligences which sefira he intends to work with. This will, of course, be the one shown alongside the ritual planet in the second Table of Correspondences.

Mentally he proceeds towards his destination along the sefirothic paths of the tree. As he goes he visualizes all the forms, colours, etc., he would expect to encounter *en route*. He will be helped in this by the information extracted from the Tables of Correspondences and recorded on his ritual card. As he approaches each sefira he constrains its angelic guardians to admit him in the name of the appropriate sefirothic angel.

When at last he reaches his destination and satisfies the guardians at its door, he strikes the gong or gavel ten times. As he

These words accompany each anointing:

Odoratis unguentis me unguo.
Exsultat cor, fervent sensus.
Membris venit vigor habilis
Et purificatus sum.

On leaving Yesod the adept comments on the wonders that lie before him:

Hanc regionem felix aggredior
Sub pedibusque miracula miror.
Fervet mens, exsultat cor
Et inter stellas progredior.

Dis immortalibus volentibus qui inter ignes sempiternos habitant, precor a spirituis sanctis ut progrediam ad [sefira]. Ducite me, O spiritus, per locos tenebrosos, sedes vestras.

Divum praecepta secutus sto
Ante alta ostia
Tremens ibi video
Divum simulacra,
Sed nomen N. loquor
Et confidenter ingredior.

---

* Located at the base of the spine is one of the Tantrist *chakras*, or psychic centres, of the human body. In this particular one (*mulhadhara*) dwells Kundalini, or the Serpent Fire, which, when awakened, will ascend to the head where its vivification of the pineal gland can bring spiritual enlightenment and, it is said, the memory of past lives. More relevant in our present context, however, is Kundalini's connection with sexual energy and its enhancing effect on one's enjoyment of the sexual act. Observed clairvoyantly the Serpent Fire, once activated, is a vertical blue jet emitting red flames from one side and yellow from the other. In men and female homosexuals the red flames are on the left (*ida*), the yellow on the right (*pingala*), but in women and male homosexuals it is the other way round.

does he visualizes the sefirothic form materializing in the Triangle of Art. This form may then be allowed to assume whatever other shapes it chooses, although the adept makes sure that every two minutes or so he bids it resume the shape originally visualized. The gong is struck the same number of times as that attributed to the particular sefira on the Tree of Life. If the form refuses to obey, it must be commanded to do so in the name of the seven archangels or, if necessary, in the name of God Himself. However, if all else fails the pentacle may be unveiled and used to force the unruly form into submission.

Although the form is obliged to remain outside the circle, the force it represents can flow into the circle. There it masses itself near the cardinal point most sympathetic to it, where it is psychically visible as a swirling cloud of vapour. The theory is that communication with the entity outside the circle enables it to surrender its power to one of the elemental archangels who will then permit it to flow into the circle through the pentagrammatic gate constructed earlier.

When he is ready, the adept can dismiss the sefirothic form, after which he gives three sets of three knocks.

The next occupant of the triangle will be one of the planetary forms which should be visualized in the ordinary way. Once the form has been built up, it will assume an individuality of its own and there is no reason why the adept should not converse with it if he feels so disposed. But on no

To bid the form return to its original shape the adept should point his sword at it and speak thus:

Te nunc transforma in
    formam veram
Quod eludet species
mentem meam.

A rebellious entity can be constrained by the following words:

Mihi te est aequum
    parere
In angelorum septem
    nomine
Michael, Gabriel,
    Raphael, Uriel,
Chamael, Haniel atque
Zadkiel.

Pointing his sword at the manifested form the adept commands it to depart:

Monstrum e locis
    emissum summis
Abi nunc ex oculis meis.

account is he to be inveigled into leaving the circle or admitting the form into it. The temptation to do one of these things will be very great indeed since a favourite trick of such forms is to appeal to the magician's good nature. And they can be exceedingly persuasive. Equally dangerous is their ability to assume the appearance of what, for the adept, is the most sexually desirable person imaginable. If this happens the adept must, like St Anthony in the desert, resist all blandishments and will the form back to its original shape.

During his ritual the adept may find that the walls of the room in which he is working appear to dissolve into the most pleasing landscapes. He may even find that as he strolls along the sefirothic paths the landscape changes without his willing it, while the sefirothic correspondences present themselves of their own accord. This is a fascinating experience and one you may be lucky enough to enjoy quite early in your career. On the other hand, some magicians have to wait years before their inner eye can perceive spontaneously the beauties of the astral world.

Planetary forms are controlled by the judicious use of divine names, and the following words are usually effective:

Meae artis non
  immemor
Et nomen Dei lente
  loquor
Yod-Hē-Vau-Hē*
Tzabaoth
Transforma te in formam veram.

Fresh incense should be burned as the climax to the rite approaches. These words are spoken:

In ignem iacto unguenta pretiosa, et mira somnio. Nam fumos somniferos exhalat ignis et quae erant somnia vera facta sunt.

By now the adept has visualized the required forms and, it is hoped, contacted their astral equivalents. In addition, the force behind these forms will have been admitted into the circle. At this point we come to the most important part of the ritual. Everything that has gone before was merely a preparation for the impending moment when, to revive our earlier comparison with electricity, we shall flick the switch that lets in the cosmic power.

* Each sefira is associated with a particular divine appellation which may be substituted here. Thus if the adept were working with Tifareth, the name Tetragrammaton – Aloah-Va-Daath – would be appropriate. The other names, with their related sefiroth in brackets, are: Eheihé (*Kether*), Yod-Hē-Vau-Hē (*Hokmah*), Yod-Hē-Vau-Hē Elohim (*Binah*), El (*Hesed*), Elohim Gabor (*Geburah*), Yod-Hē-Vau-Hē Tzabaoth (*Netsah*), Elohim Tzabaoth (*Hod*), Shaddai-El-Chai (*Yesod*), Adonai Malekh (*Malkuth*).

This is something no book can teach; the assembled correspondences, the visualization and all the other ritual details can do no more than help the adept find the switch, and as that switch is situated inside himself, he alone can turn it on. To do so he must temporarily lose his reason, for it is reason which bars the doors of the conscious mind where the astral world lies waiting. The way to open these doors is to assume a state of unreason similar to the divine frenzy of the Bacchantes. Like their delirium the aim of such unreason will be to receive the deity that is being invoked.

The method adopted to induce this frenzy will be the one which the adept's experience has shown him to be the best. The Bacchantes, you may recall, got drunk and then beat one another with vine fronds, but this will certainly not be to everyone's taste. There is no doubt that alcohol – and drugs too for that matter – are the surest means of breaking down mental barriers, but, as we have said, they do tend to weaken the will while they are about it. This is why drugs, though often used in group ritual, are not something to be tried in magical work where inadequate supervision is available.

Some magicians cultivate the sweet madness by reciting one word over and over again. The adept begins by heaping incense on the charcoal and then, kneeling before the altar, he starts his verbal repetition or mantra. Any word will do for this purpose; it may be one of the words of power, an euphonius word of the adept's own invention or even a keyword associated with his ritual motive, a crude example being the word 'money' in a ritual intended to procure wealth. While engaged in this, the adept imagines that the god-form or the most congenial of the planetary or sefirothic forms is materializing behind his back. He visualizes this in as much detail as possible. Slowly, as the altar candles flicker, he will sense with a sureness which precludes all doubt that the visualized form is in fact towering inside the circle behind him. On no account must he turn his head to look at whatever is there; any temptation to do so must be sternly resisted: the form may be unbearably hideous or else possess a beauty that may literally be fatal. In the meantime the adept should endeavour to continue his mantra, although by now his heart will no doubt be beating furiously. Whatever else happens he must not move, even when he senses that the form is so close as to be almost touching him. Above all he must not panic, but should comfort himself with the thought that he is safe enough provided he stays where he is. At last – and he will certainly know when – the god-form will take control of him. To begin with, the adept will feel an exquisite giddiness somewhere at the base of his skull and quickly convulsing the whole of his body. As this happens, and while the power is surging into him, he forces himself to visualize the thing he wants his magic to accomplish, and wills its success. He must put all he has into this and, like our friends the Bacchantes, must whip himself into a veritable frenzy. It is at this point that the force evoked will be expelled to realize the ritual intention.

As he feels the force overflowing inside him the adept, while still visualizing the realized magical intention, bids it go forth to fulfil his wishes.

The discharge of the force evoked may be accompanied by the following words:

Effusus labor. Defuncta vita
Fiat nunc voluntas mea.

To encourage the force evoked to reach its destination and there achieve a desired result, it is sometimes advisable for the adept to establish a link between himself and his target. If a person is involved this link may be an article of clothing or something still more personal such as a lock of hair or nail clippings. The adept decides whether such a link is appropriate to his particular ritual intention and, if so, whether it is practicable.

From now on no further incense should be added to the burner.

Once the force has left him the adept will find that he is overcome by a delicious feeling of exhaustion. The mystical union, the *Razar Rabba*, is over and he is himself again.

For some magicians the dislocation of reason coincides with the moment of sacrifice.* Others perform this sacrifice before proceeding to the climax of the rite, arguing that the vital energy discharged

When all power is spent the adept should turn to the west, kneel and whisper:

Refectus particeps ritus sacri, scio desiderium animae ac voluntatem labiorum meorum perfecta esse.

---

* The sacrificial victim will rarely be the creature listed in the Table of Correspondences; when this is impracticable a dove or white cockerel may be used instead.

by the victim's blood assists the possessing entity to appear inside the circle.*

Traditionally the victim's throat is cut and the warm blood allowed to gush into a chalice of the appropriate planetary metal. Those for whom the oblation coincides with the climax to the rite generally visualize the god-form behind them in the usual way, but possession then occurs as the magician drinks from the chalice or, if he is squeamish, plunges his hands into the blood it contains.† At the same time the intention is visualized and willed in the normal manner.

Sacrificial acts are cruel, messy and, above all, unnecessary. More common, fortunately, is the use of sex to attain the desired climax. The outburst of power is effected at the same time as orgasm is reached, with possession occurring a few seconds before. It should be stressed that the sexual act, while enjoyable in itself, must at all times remain subordinate to its magical purpose. It is closer to a *hieros gamos* than a satyricon.

Although the ritual climax has come and gone there are still some things to be done before the work is finished. For a start he must return to the sphere of Malkuth, retracing his earlier steps and, at each sefira he passes, thanking the appropriate archangel and his servitors for their hospitality. Thanks are due also to the

These words should coincide with the actual moment of sacrifice:

Rubrum a iugulo
   demitto cruorem
Ut tibi supplex donem
   honorem.

These are the words of thanks:

Sumpto caeleste auxilio
   vobis,
N. et Nn. gratias
   humiliter ago.

To dismiss the assembled forces, the adept walks around the circle holding the veiled pentacle and uttering the following words:

In Dei sancto nomine
Gratias ago sine fraude
Umbris omnibus tenui-
   bus
Et lucem claram ferenti-
   bus.
Hoc templo vos dimitto
Abite nunc opere facto.

---

* Cf. '... blood, being a vital fluid, contains a large proportion of ectoplasm, or etheric substance. When shed, this ectoplasm rapidly separates from the congealing blood and thus becomes available for materializations.' Dion Fortune, *Sane Occultism* (Aquarian Press, London, 1967), pp. 132–3.

† Blood-drinking and ritual cannibalism were common among primitive peoples, who believed that the virtues of the victim could be acquired in this gruesome way. Before we scoff at such practices it is salutary to recall that recent research has shown that if a flat-worm (*planarium*) that has been conditioned to act in a certain way is fed

THE MASTER RITUALS 133

elemental forces which have been evoked in the course of the rite. These must then be thanked and dismissed, as must all the other forces which gather uninvited whenever magic is performed. Such forces are attracted to the magic circle like moths to a candle, and although generally harmless must still be ordered back to wherever they came from. Failure to do this can sometimes have unpleasant consequences since these forces will linger on, causing all sorts of mischief from playing at poltergeists to violent psychic assault.* Lest this sound too medieval it must again be stressed that the personification of these forces is no more than a convention to render them more intelligible. Although as a result they may appear to us in traditional forms, they remain natural forces working behind and through the commonplace world of form.

Next, the adept graciously thanks the four archangels whose respective 'rays' were contacted earlier when he visualized their anthropomorphic forms. He turns to each compass point to address them individually in turn.

The adept faces each of the cardinal points in turn (east, north, south, west). With hands folded and head bowed he speaks the following words:

Ab incurso malevolorum me protexisti et munera ferentes venisti. Praesta, quaero, rex (orientis, borealis, australis, occidentis) ut custodiae munerumque causa gratias tibi agens, beneficia etiam majora sumam.

to an untrained worm, the latter will behave as if it has inherited the knowledge of the victim. Similar results have been obtained when laboratory rats conditioned to respond to certain light stimuli were killed and their brain fluid injected into untrained rats. Within six hours the latter had inherited the light preferences of the trained animals (see Brian Tiplady, 'The Chemistry of Memory', *New Scientist* [June 25th, 1970], p. 626). What works for rats and flat-worms may also work for the magician who in drinking the blood of a creature associated with a particular god is, as it were, partaking of the god himself.

* The symptoms of psychic assault range from a vague malaise to the most terrifying hallucinations. Only a competent magician can drive out the obsessing entity, although a long stint of psychoanalysis may teach your mind to come to terms with it and so perform its own exorcism. Many occultists believe that a substantial proportion of the patients in mental hospitals are victims of obsession. Their theory is that the patient has no control over his subconscious, which as a result opens its gates to all the astral flotsam and jetsam waiting to get inside. There may be a few cases where this is the cause of dementia, but it would be wrong to revert to so medieval a view to explain madness in general.

Finally the ceremony is concluded with a formulation of the kabbalistic cross when the adept faces west.

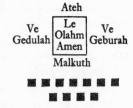

Seven or ten strokes of the gong or gavel mark the closing of the whole operation, with an extra four knocks if a little extra 'luck' is needed.*

Since it is the exoteric aspect of a mystery, no printed ritual can reveal the true beauty and meaning it conceals. Essentially it is a dramatic confrontation between man and the cosmos, and as such it demands to be enacted, just as the plays of Shakespeare, though they admittedly make fine reading, are meant to be performed. You must live the ritual in order to understand it. You must make it a part of yourself. To this end there is nothing to prevent you introducing into it any other details which may appeal to you. Some of these you can obtain from books of magic, others from your own imagination. Provided the basic structure remains the same the rite can only be enriched by these additions.

THE EGYPTIAN MASTER RITUAL

The inclusion of this Egyptian ritual must not be taken to mean that the writer is one of those occultists who regard Egypt as the seat of all wonder and magic. That religious mystery was a part of everyday life in ancient Egypt and that, like all such mysteries, it often enshrined great spiritual truths is beyond dispute. Herodotus was probably speaking the truth when he said that the Egyptians were the most religious people in the world. But the fact remains that much of their religion was as primitive and superstitious as that found anywhere else on the dark continent, and only by the eighteenth dynasty do we encounter religious writings of any appreciable merit. This, and the groundless enthusiasm of some Egyptophiles, have led a few experts to deny that there were any 'mysteries' worth mentioning in the valley of the Nile. However, such a view is as extreme and untenable as its opposite which detects an occult significance in every brick that makes up the Great Pyramid.

---

* Four is the number of Jupiter who, like the Sun, is a great benefic. The final four knocks may be little more than a piece of harmless superstition.

The prevalence of magic throughout ancient Egypt may be inferred from the apparent absence from its language of any word for magician. This suggests that whereas religious practice was the prerogative of an established priesthood, magic* was something available to all men, enabling them to assume in life, as they would in death, the divinity of Osiris. It is interesting to note also that Indian esotericists have long claimed that their knowledge came originally from Egypt.

The origin of the Egyptian ritual given below is unknown. Certain lines in it are reminiscent of the *Book of the Dead*, but an examination of the Papyrus of Ani shows that none has actually been lifted from the text, although many of the words and expressions used are to be found there. An esoteric tradition, based more on imagination than scholarship, claims that the rite is an adaptation made at Alexandria of a much earlier one derived from genuine Egyptian sources. The story goes that this rite later fell into the hands of one of the Gnostic sects flourishing in the eastern Mediterranean where it managed somehow to avoid both Christian and Semitic accretions. Brought into Europe during the time of the crusades, nothing is known of its subsequent history during the turbulent centuries that followed, but there are grounds for supposing that it was known in its present form to occultists in the eighteenth century. It may even have been the ritual used in the Egyptian Lodge which Cagliostro established in France and which is thought to have included Casanova among its members. At about this time the rite, or variants of it, is said to have come into the possession of several occult and Rosicrucian societies, but at no time before does it seem to have been made public. My own opinion is that the version we now have is a synthetic rite, composed of ritual elements gathered from several different sources. All these elements seem authentic, however, and none the less efficacious for having been arranged in their present form. The plain truth is that apart from certain funeral observances, our knowledge of the rituals used by the ancient Egyptians is pretty fragmentary, although some attempt has been made to reconstruct them.[2]

The details given below are thought to date from the illustrious eighteenth dynasty, but there is good reason to suppose that they

---

* The Egyptian word for magic is *heka*, which is thought to be connected etymologically with Hecate, goddess of witchcraft.

may go back as far as the fifth and sixth dynasties, that is, to a period some three thousand years before the birth of Christ. The text accompanying the hieroglyphics* is intended to provide some idea of their linguistic equivalent, but the correct pronunciation of the words given is largely a matter for conjecture. Even so, the Egyptian – and not the English translation – should be spoken by the adept. For this reason a short guide to pronunciation is tentatively offered below, based on both magical tradition and the views of Egyptologists. There is certainly no guarantee that what you will find here is representative of what was spoken at the Court of Unas, Pepi or the mighty Men-kau-Ra.

Vowels. These are sounded long or short as in the English examples. Long vowels are generally surmounted by a dot or, less commonly, a dash.

a	p*a*t
à or ā	p*a*lm
e	g*e*t
ė or ē	b*ea*r
i	f*i*t
ī	f*ee*t
o	n*o*t
ȯ or ō	m*o*re
u	p*u*t
u̇ or ū	h*oo*f

Consonants. Only those that differ from English are noted.

---

* These would have been arranged in perpendicular rows, but have been set out horizontally for our present purpose.

χ   equivalent of Greek χ and sounded like ch in Scottish word, loch

ḍ   as th in English this

g   always hard, as in English go

ḥ   aspirated, but tending to resemble χ, though not as strong. Rather like German (but not Swiss German) ch

ḳ   a difficult staccato sound mid-way between χ and ḥ

ṭ   as th in English thin

The symbol ' after certain letters indicates a break which occurs mainly in words where the same letter is repeated, e.g. *t'ta'at* (the divine chiefs).

Stress. As a general rule all syllables are stressed equally. An exception will arise, however, if a long vowel (˙ or ‾) in a word otherwise composed of short vowels imposes its own stress on a syllable, e.g. *mātennu* (roads).

The Timing of the Egyptian Ritual

The time of performance may be astrologically determined in exactly the same way as for kabbalistic rituals. The planetary, but not the sefirothic, correspondences may then be introduced in the ordinary way. However, as the Egyptian master ritual is primarily a solar rite, it is much less dependent on the astrological time-table. One of its greatest beauties is that it may be performed on any day and in any season provided it is not within twenty-four hours before or after a full solar eclipse. Two other considerations should be borne in mind: first, the ritual must be performed at dawn, midday or sunset *and at no other time*; second, works of discord, destruction or death must *never* be undertaken at dawn or midday. Such negative operations have to be confined to sunset, just as kabbalistic rites of a similar nature are conducted only when the Moon is waning. This does not, of course, mean that constructive ritual work cannot also be performed at sunset if that hour happens to be the most convenient.

The Place

Since it is an all-purpose solar ritual, the colours associated with it are white and gold, and the adept must ensure that these are conspicuously represented. The altar will face east if the ritual takes place at dawn, south if at midday and west if at sunset. Although no physical circle is required, the four elemental points, though important only in late Egyptian magic, may be marked out as in the previous ritual. The archangelic beings will not, however, be invoked in this instance. More correct, perhaps, is the tradition of placing a flower at each cardinal point while beseeching the favour of the elemental guardian under its Egyptian aspect. Details of this are given in the commentary which again accompanies the ritual text.

As for the ritual instruments upon the altar, there will be no need for the pentacle, Tree of Life, and sword, and if possible an ivory wand should be substituted for the wooden one. Some occultists also place on the altar any object that will serve to link the celebrant's mind with ancient Egypt. This can be anything from a genuine relic to a photograph of the temple at Abu Simbel. In addition the adept should also have in front of him a small bowl of milk, to which has been added a teaspoonful of honey, a bowl of water* and a posy of aromatic herbs such as mint, marjoram or rosemary.

The pre-ritual observances are similar to those already given for the Grade 1 and Grade 2 operations. It is particularly important that the adept should complete the necessary preliminary work before the actual moment of dawn, midday or sunset. This demands good timing.

Again, the success of the ritual depends ultimately on the adept's ability to realize its full magical potential. Read objectively, the Egyptian ritual, like all others, appears to consist only of certain pretty formulations. But it was never meant to be read objectively. It is up to you to discover through personal experience its esoteric value. You may be sure that once your heart and mind become linked through it with the Akashic memory of Egyptian civilization, you will find here a richness and power far beyond your wildest expectations.

---

* There should really be lotus petals ( ) floating on the water, but this is a luxury few occidental magicians can afford.

Egyptian Rite

Consecration of the Circle

The adept (*Reh-het*) picks up the wand and, holding it thumb uppermost to show his mastery over nature, draws a circle around his working area. At the same time he visualizes the protective barrier thus created.

As has been pointed out earlier, the Graeco-Egyptian papyri make no mention of the magic circle and the adept may do without one if he wishes. In that case, however, he should wear an Egyptian amulet (see chapter on talismanic magic). Regardless of whether or not a circle is drawn, the appropriate words must be spoken in order to ensure protection.

Ån seχem - sen åm -

å

Let the Shining Ones not have

χu

power over me

The Purification

The adept dips his finger in the water and touching his forehead declares himself ritually purified.

Turå - nå

I have purified myself and

ab - k   åu

my heart is filled with joy

The Anointing

The adept anoints his forehead and wrists with *oleum magicale* no. 3, thus making himself worthy to receive the great Sun god. The base of the spine should also be anointed if the serpent power (Kundalini) needs to be aroused for a sexual climax to the rite.

Urhu

hekennu

Having anointed myself with unguents

ma - å - kua

I have made myself strong

The Incensing

Incense was valued by the ancient Egyptians since it was regarded as the ideal offering to the pantheon on high. The word itself, *snutri*, means literally 'that

Ar - nå en ţen

I bring to you

which makes divine'. Any incense will do for this purpose, but you may care to know that an Egyptian recipe specifies the following ingredients: camphor, juice of laurel leaves, salt, white resin and sulphur. Most appropriate of all, however, is Kyphi, an incense compounded from resin, galangal root, mastic, myrrh, juniper berries and honey.

Whenever the adept places more incense on the burner in the course of the ritual, he solemnly informs the god of his pious intention.

The Four Points

The adept picks up four flowers and proceeds to the eastern point, where he places one of the blooms before going on to do the same thing at each of the other points. As he does so he respectfully dedicates his offering to the elemental gods.

If the ritual intention is kliphothic, or malevolent, the adept must begin with the north as he would in a kabbalistic rite.

The Dedication

The adept returns to the altar where he requests the blessing of Khentamentiu. This name is most appropriate on the lips of European magicians since the god's name means 'Leader of all Westerners'. Originally a local deity, he later became associated with Osiris. Indeed, the great god of the dead is sometimes referred to as Osiris-Khentamentiu. Because the magician regards himself as Osiris for ritual purposes, the co-operation of Khentamentiu is particularly desirable.

For kliphothic intentions the name of Seth (Set) is generally substituted for

bet   neter -

senther.

perfume and incense,
O Glorious One

Ertáu en sen neter-
senther

Let me place incense

her set ánet-ḥrá - ḳ

on this Fire as homage
to Thee

East: Ánet-ḥrá-ḳ Tefnet
All homage to Tefnet
(Water)

North: Ánet-ḥrá-ḳ Geb
All homage to Geb
(Earth)

South: Ánet-ḥrá-ḳ Atum
All homage to Atum
(Fire)

West: Ánet-ḥrá-ḳ Shu
All homage to Shu (Air)

Ṭebḥu - á   neter
            χentamentiu

I supplicate thee
Khentamentiu (This is
recited twelve times)

that of Khentamentiu. Seth, the slayer of Horus, has rightly or wrongly become the patron of 'black' rituals based on the Egyptian tradition.

The Attendance

The adept now waits for the sun to rise, reach its zenith or set, depending on the time of his ritual.* As he waits he recites a litany which will attune his mind to the Egyptian forms of the cosmic forces he hopes to utilize. Any of the major deities may be selected for this purpose and their names can be preceded by a suitable expression such as 'Hail N.', 'All homage to N.' or 'I adore N.' The examples given opposite will serve as a basis on which to build.

★ 𓀀   Ra, I adore thee
Tua Rå

𓀀 𓁹   À   Anset
Hail   Isis

𓀀𓏤𓂉𓂝   Anet - ḥra - ḳ   Teḥuti
All homage to   Thoth

Alternatively the adept may incant the following, which is an Egyptian formula containing the magically transformed names of the gods Osiris and Seth:

O Mamuram-Kahab
O Oualbpaga
O Kammara
O Kamalo
O Karhenmou
O Amagaaa

For those who prefer something less polytheistic there is a devotional litany (opposite) which is equally appropriate. It would be reassuring to think that the Egyptians recognized only one Supreme Being whom they worshipped under

𓀀𓏤   Tua neter
I adore God

𓍢   neb pet
Lord of Heaven

𓍢   neb ta
Lord of Earth

* If unable to observe the Sun's appearance, the adept should have a watch on his altar which will tell him when the precise moment, which he can discover from any newspaper, is reached. The solar positions are likely to be given in GMT so that an adjustment may be needed to determine the local equivalent.

various aspects, each represented by a different god or goddess. However, there is no real evidence of this. The only sign of monotheism was the worship of Aton, the sun's disc,* which flourished under the aegis of Ikhnaton during the reign of Amenhotep III. Afterwards the country seems to have reverted to polytheism.

suten mâât
King of Righteousness

neb ḥ eḥ
Lord of Eternity

heq t'etta
Prince of Everlasting Life

neter anχ
God of Life

ȧn ḥeḥ
Builder of Eternity

The Arrival of the God

The following ritual proclamations differ according to whether the rite is performed at dawn, midday or sunset. The following symbols will therefore be used to show which is appropriate to each:

   dawn

   midday

   sunset

As the Sun appears above the horizon the adept visualizes the god-form Khopri (Khepera) who is depicted as a

---

* Aton is depicted as the Sun holding the symbol of life (⚕). The famous Aton hymn was composed by Ikhnaton (King Amenhotep IV). It has close parallels with Psalm 104:

> When thou settest in the western rim of heaven
> The earth is clothed in darkness like the dead ...
> The lion cometh forth from his lair
> The serpents hiss. Darkness reigns ...
>
> The earth is bright when thou risest once more ...
> The two lands rejoice in daily festival
> Refreshed and standing on their feet ...
> Then throughout the world men work.
>
> How manifold are all thy works!
> They are hidden from our gaze.
> Oh, thou sole god, whose powers are unequalled,
> Thou didst create the earth according to thy will, being alone:
> Men, all creatures, large and small,
> All things that live upon the earth.

man with the head of a beetle.* This insect is a suitable emblem because in ancient times it was believed to be self-begotten and so became a symbol of life emerging from inertness.‡ To this belief we owe the thousands of scarabs that turn up in Egyptian tombs.

☼   The midday belongs to Ra, undisputed ruler of the Hathoric§ sky, whom the adept addresses as the Lord of Rays. He is the visible emblem of God and his appearance marked the beginning of time. In the pyramid texts the soul is said to make its way after death to Ra's abode in heaven where it is assured of eternal bliss.

In his setting Ra is adored under the aspect of Tem (Tmu). As such he has always represented the death of Osiris and his subsequent departure to the next world.‖ But this departure is a triumphal

A   Kheperå†
Hail   Khopri

Ut'a hen neter pen seps
who now approaches
in divine splendour

A   Rå   neb   satetu
Hail Ra   Lord   of Rays

Neter anχ   neb mert
Thou art the God of Life,
Lord of Love

hra – nebu   anχ
All people   live

pest   –   ḳ
[when] thou shinest

A   Tem
Hail   Tmu

---

* The rising Sun is also depicted as Ra-Horakhti or Ra of the Two Horizons when he sometimes appears as the hawk-headed god Horus.

† The combination *kh* is pronounced as χ.

‡ The idea that insects are self-begotten was a very common one in the ancient world. In the fourth book of the *Georgics* Virgil tells us that bees materialize from the putrid blood of slaughtered cattle. He goes on to say that Egyptian apiarists often obtained their bees in this way (*Georgics* iv. 295 ff.). Auto-genesis was accepted by some biologists as late as the eighteenth century.

§ Hathor, or the Vault of Heaven, means 'The House of Horus', as can be inferred from its glyph ▨.

‖ Once it has set, the sun's hieroglyphic emblem is the same as that of Osiris (⌐▨). In later texts Osiris is also associated with the moon, who by reflecting sunlight becomes the sun's representative during the night.

one, a 'Coming forth by day', for Osiris, 'Lord of Eternity', is the conqueror of death and has become for all of us the symbol of our own immortality. The evening Sun is also represented as Tum, who is depicted in the form of a king who has a crown (♙) on his head and bears in his hands the royal sceptre (♟) and the sacred *anch* or emblem of life (♀). After his invocation the adept praises the setting Sun whose glory is emblazoned across the darkening sky.

tā - k   χu em pet
Thou givest splendour in Heaven

em bennu   āq per
*as a phoenix   going in and
              coming forth*

The Lustration

Having made sure there is ample incense burning, the adept prepares to contact the Shining Ones of Egyptian tradition. These are identical in nature to the elemental rulers who figure in Western magical lore, and will serve the magician in exactly the same way. To begin with, the magician makes a lustration at each of the cardinal points, beginning with the east. This involves dipping the herbal posy into the bowl of water and asperging each point in turn. As he does so he visualizes the Shining Ones manifesting as shafts of light or as minor god-forms (*axemiu*). Returning to the altar he now dips the posy into the bowl of milk and again asperges the cardinal points. Back at the altar he sprinkles a final libation to the right, to the left, and lastly in front of the altar, reciting the appropriate words as he does so.

Au ári - nà   neter -
                heterpu
I have made offerings

en neteru perχeru en
*to the gods and
sacrificed to*

χu
the Shining Ones

The Sacrifice

If a blood sacrifice is to be performed, this is the time to do it. But first the adept must hold aloft the ritual dagger and proclaim himself king of creation. The vic-

Seχem - na   enti
*I show my mastery over
all living things*

tim's blood is then mixed with the milk and honey before the adept proceeds to make a further libation, repeating the words already spoken (*Au àri-nà*, etc.).

The adept is now ready to take upon himself the identity of the Sun god who, as the master of all life, has lordship over the Shining Ones and their divine guardians. The adept symbolically assumes his new role by placing a gold ring upon his finger and tracing the astrological symbol of the Sun above his heart.

The climax to the ritual is now at hand and the advice already given in the description of the kabbalistic ritual should be followed here. The mantra provided opposite may be recited while the adept works himself up to the required state of frenzy. A different mantra is necessary if the ritual is to have a sexual climax.*

The ritual climax demands the merging of the self with the Sun. This means that the adept will become filled with solar energy which he then projects towards his chosen ritual intention. As he feels himself possessed by the forces evoked he should *silently* recite the words of consecration. On no account must these be spoken aloud. They have not been translated into English.

em   tes
with this knife

Nuk   neb   sesep
*I become one with the
Lord of Light*

Maat Heru   tà - na
*O Eye of Horus,
grant unto me*

                  *the secret
                  longings of*
setatu   àb   *my heart*

Ba - à   pu   neter

Ba - à   pu   heh

χaχ   er   suit
Swifter than light

χu

hem - k
*O Shining Ones,
return now*

---

* In that case the following is spoken by:

(i) the male adept

Henen - à   em   Àmsu

(*My phallus is that of Amsu*)

Such was the sexuality of Amsu that he was said to be the father of his own mother.

(ii) the female partner

Àuf - à   Net

(*My flesh is of Net*)

The orgasm should be visualized as an outpouring of the particular intention under the appearance of molten gold.

Postcommunion

The adept's first task when he has recovered is to dismiss the Shining Ones as he would their kabbalistic equivalents.

âr ḥeru   pet
to the heights of Heaven

Seb - nâ   uru

quāḥ
I have walked beside the Great Ones

The adept now strikes his gong or gavel ten times (eleven if the rite was dedicated to Seth) and reviews his ritual experience before returning to the everyday world.

His immediate task on conclusion of the rite will be to enter a careful record of his experiences in the magical diary. The flowers he has used to mark the four elemental points must then be burned.

am quāḥ mâ

seb - sen
just as they pass close to

neter   pui   â'a   χu
God who, mighty and resplendent,

aper   nebu
is the sum total of all things.

Although the text may take some time to read, the Egyptian ritual takes only a short time to perform. This makes it eminently suitable for those of us who have busy lives to lead. Another virtue is that once you are thoroughly familiar with it you can perform it entirely in your imagination, visualizing the ceremonial as you go along. Only the words, spoken in a 'just voice' (*Ma-Khru*), need be uttered aloud. It is true that you may not at first be able to achieve in this way the complete self-abandonment which marks the climax of the rite, but even so your mind may, by a process known as *Per-Khru*, generate sufficient intensity of feeling to accomplish your magical intention. And, of course, whenever your mind dwells on the rite, it at once makes contact with those Egyptians who thousands of years ago performed the same actions and spoke the same words as you are now doing.

8

CEREMONIAL magic such as that described in the last chapter is something anyone can do, but it does help considerably if you happen to believe in what you are doing. It is all very well warning the aspiring occultist that he should not expect his ritual work to be accompanied by signs and wonders, but unless something out of the ordinary happens once in a while he is bound sooner or later to ask himself whether it is all worth the effort. It is true, of course, that the effectiveness of a magical operation can always be verified, but results may be slow in coming. In the meantime the novice magician is often left with the uncomfortable feeling that the pentacles, invocations and numerous names of power are just a load of meaningless mumbo-jumbo. Such a reaction is perfectly understandable, especially as all good occultists are gifted with a healthy streak of scepticism. But scepticism is sometimes liable to run riot. This can happen at any time; for example, you may be, as you think, engrossed in your ritual when all of a sudden the assembled esoterica will strike you as being ridiculously out of place in the familiar surroundings of your own room. Or the sound of a neighbour's television set or the noise of a car in the street outside will bring you back to earth with a jolt, and at once you begin to feel rather embarrassed by the whole affair.

Feelings of this sort are difficult to avoid. The danger is that they may persuade you to abandon your occult studies before you have properly embarked on them. Fortunately, there is less chance of this happening if you learn to prepare yourself for the inevitable doubts and uncertainties that will at some time or other assail you. Try to remember that everyone, no matter what he is doing, has occasional moments of crisis when he wonders whether his time might not be more profitably employed elsewhere. Perhaps these occur all the more frequently when one is engaged on something that lacks the utilitarian goal of most ordinary activity.

As far as magic is concerned the cause of all these difficulties is that we are dealing with a dimension of which few of us have any direct experience. For years we go through life blissfully unaware of the astral world, and then one day our interest in occultism forces us to accept a whole new concept of existence. The mental readjustment required for this is far from easy. The whole thing is also made more difficult because at the start of our magical training we are all expected to take the astral world on trust. It might, of course, be argued that those who have never visited Africa must similarly take the existence of that continent on trust, but the comparison is too facile. The reports of people who have been to Africa are sufficiently numerous and uncontradictory to warrant acceptance, and in any case the existence of Africa is something capable of empirical verification. Not so the astral world. All we have here are the recorded and, alas, often contradictory impressions of a few magicians, none of which can be confirmed by empirical experience. Even so, the case for the astral world is not quite as hopeless as it seems, since the process known as astral projection offers all of us a chance to discover its existence for ourselves.

Astral projection, you will recollect, is the means by which we are able to transfer our consciousness to the etheric double and make it responsive to our will. As was said earlier, the moment when you find yourself outside your physical body will be one of the most thrilling in your life and will convince you more than anything else that there are far more things in heaven and earth than are conceded by conventional materialism. Unfortunately, although some people can manage astral projection at their very first attempt, there are many more who find they must wait months or sometimes years before they can step out of themselves into the body of light. The trouble is that the final piece of mental gymnastics needed to shift the seat of consciousness is a knack that cannot be taught. Yet it is a knack that anyone can acquire with practice, and there is no need to feel despondent if you are unsuccessful at first.

We have discussed the nature of the astral body at some length in Chapter 1, where we described it as a thought-form moulded from or impressed upon the etheric fabric around us. In the East many names have been given to this thought-engendered body, and their prevalence suggests that its existence is something known from universal experience.* Nor is there any shortage of good books on astral projection, and you should endeavour to read as many of these as possible.[1] It goes without saying that the more you understand about what you are trying to do, the greater your chances of success, so it is as well to familiarize yourself with the subject. Some things need to be clarified beforehand, however.

In your reading you will find that most authors treat the astral body as a sort of natural adjunct to the physical body, thereby implying that men are born with their astral counterparts intact. My own view, set out in Chapter 1, is that the astral body, being a thought-created form, is the product of man's conceptual thinking. The difficulty about the other view, which argues that the astral body is an entity in its own right, is that, given the fact of evolution, there is no reason why every bird, cow, stickleback or dinosaur should not also have its etheric double, not to mention the astral counterparts of all the bugs, beetles and bacteria in existence. This, of course, might indeed be so, and the propagators of the doctrine would assert that man is different because he has within him a divine spark that elevates him above the rest of physical creation. But, as we have seen, science lends no support at all to the view that man is spiritually privileged in this way.

Another theory canvassed by some writers on astral projection, especially those who are interested in magic, is that the astral body is only one of the supra-physical bodies with which men are equipped. They then go on to speak of one bodily sheath after the next, until the poor reader must suspect that he has more layers of body than an onion has skins. Again no attempt is made to justify the theory except by an ingenuous reference to arcane tradition.† The esoteric fundamentalists who follow this particular tradition believe also in original sin on a cosmic scale, which they pompously

---

* The 'travelling soul', as it was called, appears as a mannikin or, just as often, an insect in Indian art, while in ancient Greece it was usually depicted as a butterfly. Elsewhere in Europe it has been represented as a dove, although in Egypt hawks, owls and ravens were favourite images for it.

† In fact this particular tradition springs from Buddhist and Vedantic teachings where the astral body (*linga sharira*) is the vehicle for prana (*pranamayakosha*). As such it is one of the several *koshas* or sheaths enclosing the principles that make up man.

call the primary deviation, and in such other oddities as life on Venus, the Holy Grail* and – of which more later – the lost continents of Mu, Lemuria and Atlantis. All of which goes to show that salt has more uses in magic than just warding off demons.

Nowadays few of us are ever aware of our one 'thought body', let alone the countless variants wished upon us by some occultists. However, if we are to practise astral projection we must give the astral body the benefit of the doubt and acknowledge its existence. Unless we do so we shall never persuade our consciousness to vacate our physical bodies. It will, after all, be understandably reluctant to take a leap into the void. Astral projection is difficult enough as it is.

Luckily we can make things slightly easier for ourselves by practising one of the visualization exercises mentioned earlier. This is the one which involved 'looking' at a room from a different position from that occupied by the physical body. This is only an *imagined* projection of consciousness, but proficiency at it will go a long way towards helping you accomplish the real thing. It is important therefore that you work at this psychological trick until it becomes almost second nature.

There are many ways of attempting projection, but leaving aside differences of detail there are three main methods.

The first method achieves very swift results if the experimenter is at all sensitive or impressionable. Primarily it entails the visualization of the astral body and then by an effort of will the projection of consciousness into the visualized form. If you are at all clairvoyant, then this is the method to adopt, since it is quite possible that the form you visualize will be the actual etheric double perceived clairvoyantly. On the other hand, if, like most of us, you have to use your imagination to visualize the form, the latter will integrate with the astral body as soon as projection occurs.

The form you have to visualize will, of course, be yourself, but it helps considerably if the figure has its back to you, for this then saves you the surprisingly difficult task of visualizing your own features. When the form has been built up, it must be charged with energy by imagining a shaft of light flowing into it, or, if you prefer, the light can be channelled into your physical body and thence

---

* Rid of its embarrassingly Christian associations, the Grail becomes a precious chalice brimful of astral concentrates. Substances similar to these are alleged also to have been stored in the Ark of the Covenant, although when the Temple was sacked in A.D. 70, the Ark, it is said, contained only stones and some badger skins dyed purple.

directed into the visualized form beside you. This latter method has the advantage of increasing your identification with the form you have created so as to make it easier for you to transfer your consciousness into it. Begin by making the form move at your command, raising its arm, turning to left or right, etc. At last when your rapport with it is complete, draw on the last reserves of your imagination and step straight into your body of light.

The second method involves no visualized forms, but a certain amount of imagination is again required. You should lie on your back, relax your body completely and imagine that you are gently floating upwards. Some people suggest you begin with your feet, imagining these rising slowly in the air followed by the rest of your body, others that the imagined levitation should begin from the base of the skull. Whichever happens, you will suddenly find that the sensation of floating on air becomes so real that you at once know you have vacated the physical body. The astral form will then right itself from its horizontal position, thus enabling you to look down at your replica apparently fast asleep on the bed. Another way of achieving the same result is to will yourself to a different part of the room, as you have done so often in your meditation exercises. If your will-power is not all that abundant, it is a good idea to eat something salty before going to bed so that you are left with a terrific thirst. Place a glass of water conspicuously on the other side of the room and while lying on the bed fix your mind upon it. With luck, the urge to quench your thirst will give your consciousness the shove needed to transfer it to your astral double.

There is also a third, but I think more unreliable, method of projection which becomes possible once you realize in the middle of a dream that you are in fact dreaming. Occultists claim that the dreamer's consciousness is then 'projected' into the dream, and that if he could but wake up he would find himself occupying his astral body. The trouble lies, you will find, in waking yourself up at the right moment.

Additional details on how to effect astral projection are provided in the time-table suggested at the end of this chapter. Meanwhile a few words must be said about what to expect when you are outside the physical body.

The first thing you will notice is that your surroundings are bathed in a violet monochrome, although occasionally the scene appears to be sepia-coloured, like an old photograph. A curious phenomenon is that the objects in your room may appear to emit a radiance of their own, but you will soon grow accustomed to this. It is essential that you at once dissociate yourself from your physical body, since your consciousness will seek to return to it at the slightest opportunity. There is certainly no need to fear that you will remain for ever locked out in your astral body. On the contrary, your main job will be to stay inside it. You will find that much of the 'pull' that draws you back to the physical body will come from the silver cord or thread that unites it with its astral double.[2] This cord may be semi-solid in appearance, or it may be no more than a trail of vapour. Forget the old story that death occurs instantly the cord is severed; you may be assured that no amount of tugging on your part is going to break the vital link.

When for the first time you do manage to stay out of your body you may find that you are in danger of being carried off by the magnetic tides which flow through the ether. To stop this happening you must immediately assert your control over the astral vehicle. Even so, you will not want to remain stationary for long since the whole object of astral projection is to go places. The astral body, it has been said, can journey anywhere in the physical world, but it is not clear to what extent such travelling is limited by conditions of time and space. Because of your magical interests it is more likely that your astral body will seek to voyage in the astral world which is, after all, its natural habitat. The mere wish is enough to superimpose the astral landscape on the physical surroundings about you. The blue haze will then give way to a world as real and full of colour as the everyday world with which you are familiar.

Once out of the body you can travel in the physical world or else restrict your itinerary to the etheric planes. Where you choose to go in the physical world is your own business and need not worry us here. As far as the etheric planes are concerned, two forms of astral travel are possible. The first is a journey through the astral world as represented on the Tree of Life; this is astral travel proper. The second, while it still takes place on the etheric planes, involves travelling through time to see places in the physical world as they were centuries or even millennia ago. For convenience occultists refer to this as time-travel, although it is a great deal more complicated than merely flitting back through time.

Let us first of all turn our attention to the astral world. When you see the astral landscape you will at once be reassured to find that it looks so familiar. Astrographically you are situated in the region of Yesod and, more precisely, in that area which Egyptophile occultists call the Antechamber of Osiris. This is where the dead pass their time between incarnations, gratifying their whims and uncon- sciously shedding in the process the aggregate personality of their previous incarnation. Here you may glimpse the faces of people you have known and loved, but you are unlikely to linger among them. Instead your astral body will be swept along towards the next sefira. Gradually, as you journey along, the astral scenery will bear less and less resemblance to the physical world you have left behind. Instead you will find yourself in an exciting place where light and colour rather than form predominate. Certain forms will nevertheless appear from time to time and, thanks to your acquaintance with the hermetic correspondences, these will inform you of your exact whereabouts on the Tree of Life.

The things you see and hear from then on are incapable of description, since our language cannot cope with the ineffable experiences that await you. To recount them would necessitate translating them into the words we use for sensory experience, which is just what they are not. The problem is an old one; it plagued the mystics who, try as they might, could never convey the sublimity of their vision in language comprehensible to their fellow men.[3] Suffice to say that you will see many wonderful things when you tread the psychedelic rainbows of the astral world.

The splendours of the astral world notwithstanding, there will be many readers who are more attracted by the possibilities of time- travel. This is a pity, for although time-travel is always interesting, it can do little more than satisfy the curiosity of those who indulge in it. However, an occasional time-journey will certainly do no harm provided (if you value your reputation for sanity) you are careful not to boast about it to your sceptical friends. Let us see why and how the astral body can apparently voyage through what we call time.

Briefly, time-travel is possible because the traveller's astral con- sciousness has left the physical plane where chronology is dependent on an assumed relationship between time and space. Here on earth our whole notion of time is subjective, being relative always to the person who measures it. In the astral world, however, the limitations of a three-dimensional reality no longer apply. Instead the conscious- ness dwells in what we may call absolute time, an eternal present which embraces both past and future. The best proof of the existence of absolute time comes from precognition, and we shall examine the concept further when dealing with that subject. For the present we need state only that the individual consciousness freed of its physical trammels is freed also of the temporal restrictions normally imposed upon it.

The sad thing is that our minds are so conditioned by these restrictions that the astral self will often remain voluntarily subject to them. The whole idea of a coexistent past, present and future is so alien to us that we are wont to carry our old ideas about relative time into the astral world. Indeed, many astral voyagers who desperately want to travel through time find they never succeed in doing so because of a deep-rooted conviction that the whole thing is a lot of baloney. The only cure is to reflect on time for yourself, to read some of the admittedly difficult books on the subject and, most important, to familiarize yourself with astral conditions so that they cease to be related by your mind to the physical world. Given then that you can accept the theoretical possibility of astral time-travel, your only remaining task is to take flight.

So little is known about the subject that there are few general rules to impart. It may be useful, however, to look at a typical time-journey, in this case one recently undertaken by a friend who has allowed me to quote her own account, written, as all magical records should be, immediately after the event. Apart from writing out some of her abbreviations in full, I have not altered her spontaneous report in any way. I must emphasize, however, that it is offered here by way of example only and not as evidence of time-travel. I should explain too that my friend – let us call her Ann – used to live in Croydon and one day in 1960 decided that she would like to see her home town as it was some fifty years ago. She knew, of course, that 'some fifty years' was far too imprecise and so went back exactly fifty years and selected a date, September 24th, which happened to be her mother's birthday. As for the time, four in the afternoon seemed to her a good hour to pick for her voyage of discovery. Here in her own words is what happened:

7.15. Formed Q.B.L. and Lux Mir.* Lay down. Very drowsy –

* The kabbalistic cross and Lux Mirabilis. The latter is an exercise beloved of many Western occultists. It involves visualizing the body slowly enveloped in coils of ketheric light – rather like a mummy in its wrappings.

probably too much supper. Afraid I might drop off to sleep, but projected after about ten minutes. Rid myself of spare astro-plasm* and passed into A.W. [astral world]. Before entering too far into Y [Yesod] willed myself at Croydon, 4.0 p.m., 24 September 1910. Everything went dark but a small light started flashing in the distance. As I got near, saw a shape with a curlew's head (Thoth?).† Lights began sparking all over the place – all colours like a kaleidoscope. Experienced an unpleasant bursting feeling and then darkness again. Gradually the dark-ness changed into a blackboard with the date 24 September scrawled in chalk across it. Before it appeared a young woman, hair piled up and a cameo brooch at her throat. She was laugh-ing, but no noise came out. After a while she picked up a blue gingham duster and wiped the board. Clouds of dust rose up – blinding, choking. I shut my eyes.

When I opened them I knew I'd made it.

My first surprise came with the sight of so many horse-drawn vehicles. And the ripe smell of horses! (You'd never suspect that from old photos.) I was standing outside an ironmongers – there were some strange-looking teapots (samovars?) and coffee percolators on display in the window. The people passing on the pavement seemed to walk straight through me which was a bit unnerving to begin with. Most of the men had moustaches or beards, with fancy watch chains much in evidence on their waistcoats. The women had long skirts and long-sleeved blouses. Thought I might be dreaming so as I knew I might not be staying long I tried to find my bearings. The ironmongers was called Hammond and Hussey which rang a bell. Across the road I caught sight of some posters plastered on a wall. No sooner had I noticed them than I was over there. A little black and white dog skidadled as if he'd sensed my arrival. He almost

* This is a word some occultists use to describe the 'stuff' of which their visible astral bodies are apparently composed. What Ann means here is that she willed her astral body to disengage itself from the physical shell so as to resist the 'pull' we men-tioned earlier. When she did this her astral body would have shed some of its etheric 'substance' which was then channelled into the silver cord. It is this process to which Ann is referring when she speaks of 'getting rid' of superfluous astroplasm.

† Thoth was known as the Measurer of Time. He had an ibis head, not a curlew's. Both the ibis and the curlew have long beaks, but unlike the dull-brown curlew the ibis has a fine white plumage and a jet-black neck.

tripped up a clergyman as he went. (Thought: Did the dog run away at that exact moment in 1910? I suppose he must have done. If so, was I there then to frighten him? Again the answer must be 'Yes'. Presumably one cannot change the past, but the past when it was present could, I suppose, be affected by the future. All v.v. metaphysical.) Back to the posters. One of them was advertising 'the greatest show on earth', Lord John (George, surely) Sanger's circus. It was due to visit the town on Friday, 30 September (which makes the 24th a Saturday – hence the busy street). There were some other posters – one for the Electric Theatre and its 'choice animated pictures', another for a cinema in Thornton Heath. I can't remember the second cinema's name (Essoldo?), but I remember it promised to pay its patrons' tram fares from Croydon and serve free teas between five and six. Anything for business. There were some other posters there. (I spent too much time looking at posters.) One was for American roller skates, another for a variety show, its star billed as the queen of the fairies. (I thought I'd remember the lady's name, but I can't for the life of me think of it.)

Next I turned to the street again. Saw a van advertising Jay's Furniture Stores. There appeared to be advertisements everywhere – on all the walls, shop windows and carts. Rather an awful mess. Everything looked less orderly than it is now. But much more character. Found I was in the old High Road and realized what a lot of changes there had been. That did it. The instant I thought of modern Croydon I blacked out straightaway and began to spin like a top. In the darkness I glimpsed a rag doll in a dark pink dress also spinning madly. I think the black and white dog was barking somewhere as well. A terrible pain deep inside my ears – the sort you'd get in an unpressurized aircraft. All of a sudden – in a flash of vivid blue light – I saw my room again. With a painful click* I was back in the body. Woke up straightaway still with headache and heart thumping thirteen to the dozen. The time was 7.45. I can't have been 'out' more than five minutes. Began this record at ten to eight and it's now eight-o-clock. Everything still very clear except for those few names that have gone clean out of my head.

* This click is something many people claim to hear when their consciousness rejoins the physical body. I know of no explanation for it, although the proximity of the brain, the physical seat of consciousness, to the inner ear may well provide a clue.

3 June. 8.30 a.m. This morning woke up convinced that the first
name of the fairy queen was an Elsie something. She was queen-
ing it at the New Hippodrome. Forgot to mention last night
that the price of admission to the cinema was 3*d*., children 2*d*.

Some people may feel that Ann was somewhat unambitious when
she decided to visit the Croydon of fifty years ago. It is not hard to
think of more interesting excursions she might have embarked upon
while she was about it. No doubt too readers can think of many
famous scenes from history at which, given the opportunity, they
would like to be present. But travel to historical events demands
a great deal of expertise. The greatest difficulty about it is that the
astral traveller will already have his own idea of what things were
like at, say, the crucifixion, the storming of the Bastille or on the
deck of Nelson's flagship at Trafalgar. This means that his consciousness will tend to hover uncertainly between the actual
happening and its own preconceived notion of what took place.
When this happens the astral journey usually transforms itself into
a self-induced dream. It is far better therefore to know where you
are going but to have no very clear idea of what to expect when you
get there. In Ann's case it is true that having lived in Croydon she
may have seen what it looked like years ago from old photographs,
but as photographs merely reproduce the real thing, this knowledge would have done her no harm. On the contrary, it may even
have helped. Where things do go wrong is when our idea of the
destination we have chosen is based on a subjective reconstruction –
our own or other people's – which can never be completely accurate.
It is this that often deflects the astral self from its goal.

It might be argued, of course, that Ann's astral journey was really
no more than an exceptionally vivid dream. You will recall that she
herself recognized this possibility in the middle of it. Ann's reaction
was a sensible one, however, for she began at once to make a careful
note of her surroundings, paying particular attention to small details
of the sort that might be verifiable later. She did not waste time
looking at the ladies' dresses or the gentlemen's moustaches; these
would have provided her with good 'period' recollections but would
have convinced no one, not even herself, of the reality of her
experience. Instead she carefully examined the posters plastered on
a wall, she peered at shop windows and noted names and dates.
Then she was able to check up on what she had seen. She discovered,

for example, that the Thornton Heath cinema the Electric Palace (not the Essoldo) had in fact paid its patrons' tram fares. She learned too that 'Lord' George Sanger had had a brother called John who toured England with his own circus, although Ann found no one who could remember whether the show had ever visited Croydon. In the end, enough details had been corroborated to convince her that she had on this occasion travelled back through time. She has now promised herself a return trip in order to see what was the name of the young lady who had been billed as the queen of the fairies.

Among the lessons to emerge from this example is the need to be completely objective about your time-journeys. If you accept them without question you will become unable to distinguish dreams from reality. And time-travel, you should never forget, is concerned only with reality. For that reason any experiment which is not capable of some verification must, I fear, be rejected as unproven. The imagination is always ready to create its own form of reality, and occultists by the very nature of their vocation seem especially vulnerable in this respect. You should bear in mind therefore that an undemanding acceptance of every astral experience may turn you into a certifiable lunatic, but never, never, into a competent magician.

There are some further points which should perhaps be mentioned about the astral body. When you enter it for the first time you will probably see your astral self fully clothed, although to talk about clothing in this context suggests – as does the word body – that the astral double is closer to its physical partner than is actually the case. It is true that it is an etheric replica of our flesh-and-blood selves, but being essentially immaterial it is of an entirely different nature. This becomes a little easier to understand if we think of it in terms of light. Let us imagine that you are about to take a photograph of someone who is standing about ten feet in front of the camera. As you press the button the variation in light-waves caused by the physical presence of whoever you are photographing will immediately register on a piece of sensitized film. This then carries the likeness of the person photographed. The astral body may be compared with the light-waves which travel between a photographic subject and the film inside the camera. Like these it is essentially formless, and to that extent imperceptible to our senses. When our consciousness 'sees' the astral body, it registers the effect of its existence in much the same way as a film registers a disturbance in light-waves. In other words, our thinking processes formalize the physically formless. At the same time they impose on it – out of habit perhaps – a few additional details of their own so that, for example, when our clairvoyant vision 'sees' the astral body, it generally appears fully clothed.

Some readers may by now be wondering how the astral body can ever indulge in the luxury of thinking, since its consciousness is divorced from the physical brain where all thoughts are said to originate. It is not easy to provide a satisfactory answer to this, just as it is no simple matter to explain telepathy, although telepathy undoubtedly exists. The real answer may lie in the fundamental differences between the astral and material planes of existence. On the material plane, where sensory impulses predominate, it is only natural that thought should be a physiological process located in the cerebellum; the brain is thus indispensable to it. But the same does not hold true in the astral world, where in the absence of physical stimuli the brain becomes unnecessary. In its place the individual consciousness receives and reacts to direct impressions. In other words, it thinks conceptually, as it did to a lesser extent in the material world where conceptual thought was already capable of a causal independence from sensory experience.

The essential formlessness of the etheric body at once removes the need for speculation about astral sexuality. Because sexual attraction is a *physical* response, and its gratification likewise physical, it stands to reason that there is little scope for adventure in the astral world. No doubt in some cases people do retain a few of their old urges when they die, especially if they die in their prime. However, bereft of their senses, it is doubtful whether even the most lecherous will find much to get worked up about in the Elysian Fields. There the entire mode of existence is completely different from our own, although in order to understand it we are compelled to relate it to what we know from our own experience here on earth.

Some newcomers to occultism often wonder whether physical deformity is automatically reproduced in the astral body. But such thinking is again due to an over-emphasis on the bodily aspect of the astral self. Here the use of such words as 'double' and 'replica' scarcely helps and these have perhaps been bandied about too freely in earlier pages. Strictly speaking, the astral body is the double not of our physical bodies, but of our *identity*. The trouble is that because our mind is used to thinking of our identity in corporeal terms (and what could be more natural in a material world?), it is a physical likeness that becomes impressed on the etheric strata. With the demise of the physical body, however, this astral impression ceases to be appropriate. The astral consciousness becomes aware of its discarnate identity and has no further need for a formal representation. It is true that for a time it may cling out of habit to a faithful replica of its physical body, and spiritualistic revenants will often speak of themselves as if still clothed in flesh. However, this is a short-lived habit, especially in the case of those who, because of illness or deformity, have no cause for wishing to retain a post-mortem likeness of their former physical selves.

As to the actual passage of consciousness into the astral body at the moment of death, this is something we shall look at later. For the present our interest lies in the temporary transition which takes place during astral projection. The time-tables given below are what might be called a five-day course in projection. It is not essential that you follow it, but your chances of early success will be enhanced if you stick to a routine such as this rather than make one or two desultory attempts now and again. For the purpose of the time-table we have taken 11 p.m. as the hour at which projection will be essayed. The exact time, however, will be a matter of individual choice, although care must be taken to keep to the same hour on each successive day. It is also important to maintain a record of your experiences, so have a notebook handy.

Once you have acquired the knack of projection your need for a special time-table will cease and you can then project as and when you please. The purpose of the time-table is simply to help you find the required knack. You will observe that the preliminaries tend to become progressively more complicated, but if you meet with success at the first or second attempt there is certainly no need to stay the course. Nor, on the other hand, should you give up in despair if you have got nowhere after the fifth attempt. There is always the second method to be tried and if that too fails you can return to the first with fresh vigour. It might be a good idea to have a rest for a week or more between each five-day marathon, although experienced occultists have argued with some justification that projection is more likely to be achieved when the physical body is debilitated. That presumably is why chronically sick people often recount 'out of the body' experiences to their incredulous doctors and relatives. But unless you are on a month's magical retreat it would be foolish to exhaust yourself unnecessarily – especially if, like most of us, you must get up to go to work the following morning. Bon Voyage!

METHOD I

Day 1

10.30 p.m. Light incense and candles

10.35   Perform kabbalistic cross

10.40   Practise projection of consciousness to various parts of the room

10.45   Relaxation

10.50   Commence visualization of astral form

10.55   Bombard form with visualized ketheric light

11.00   Transfer consciousness to form

Day 2

10.30 p.m. Light incense and candles

10.35   Perform kabbalistic cross

10.40   Relaxation

10.45   By way of practice, 'transfer' consciousness to matchbox

10.50   Visualization of form. Increase attunement with it until–

11.00   Transfer consciousness to form

Day 3

7.00 p.m. Period of fasting begins, interrupted only by one small glass of saline solution drunk every hour on the hour until –

10.00	Reflect on the Tree of Life as a guide to the astral world
10.30	Light candles and incense
10.35	Perform kabbalistic cross and Banishing Ritual of the Lesser Pentagram
10.50	Visualization, etc., of the astral form
11.00	Projection

Day 4

7.00 p.m.	Period of silence and fast begins. A little wine in which some mistletoe leaves have been steeped may be taken every half hour until–
10.00	Light candles and incense Smear *oleum magicale* on forehead, wrists and throat Perform kabbalistic cross and Banishing Ritual of the Lesser Pentagram
10.30	Relaxation and meditation on the astral world
10.55	Visualization of the astral form
11.00	Projection

Day 5

7.00 p.m.	Period of silence and fasting
10.00	Light candles and incense Apply *oleum magicale*
10.15	Lunar ritual. This may be performed with the intention of achieving successful projection after the ritual is over or, alternatively, the attempted projection may be made to coincide with the (non-sexual) climax to the rite.

METHOD 2

Day 1

10.30 p.m. Relaxation. The room should be dark but one candle may be burned. A joss stick may also be lit if the adept feels it helps him

10.40   Mantra. The continuous repetition of certain words will gently lull the conscious mind and activate its subconscious. The mantra may be something of the adept's own invention or one of the many mantric utterances alleged to induce euphoria. These include the Hindu invocation *Hari Krishna*, the Buddhist *Om Mani Padme Hum* ('Oh Jewel in the flower of the Lotus'),* or the Lotanic mantra of the kabbalists.† A mantra especially suitable for the task in hand would be the Latin *Progredior ad lucem siderum*

10.55   Imagined levitation

11.00   Actual projection occurs

Day 2

10.00 p.m. Relaxation and meditation on the astral body. Yoga enthusiasts should meditate on the chakra Svadhisthana, located in the spleen

10.30   Kabbalistic cross and donning of the crown of Abramelin‡

---

* In Buddhism this Sanskrit prayer is addressed to Avalokita. The *Om* is pronounced as two syllables (A – um).

† Gen. xxxvi 22. All the mantra means is, 'And Lotan's sister was Timna.' A Midrashic tradition claimed, however, that constant repetition of the original Hebrew brought transcendental bliss. The argument is that the inner linguistic elements of the verse emit subtle vibrations according with the character of each moment.

‡ This consists of a piece of parchment bearing the words MILON IRAGO LAMAL OGARI NOLIM. It should be fixed to the forehead by means of a band when, in addition to being a help in astral projection, it is supposed to endow the wearer with a knowledge of all things past, present and future.

10.35   Mantra

10.50   Imagined levitation

11.00   Actual projection

Day 3

As for Day 2
A magical oil should be worn
Fast and silence to be observed from 9.00 p.m.

Days 4 *and* 5

As for Day 3
The adept should perform an Egyptian ritual at sunset,
or a lunar ritual, provided the Moon is not waning, at
the time the Moon rises. The intention will be successful astral projection.

9

OCCULT WRITERS have never been too fussy about mentioning their sources, probably because many are none too respectable. Instead, they have preferred to refer vaguely to 'tradition' – arcane, esoteric or venerable – whenever a statement seems in need of support. There is no hardship in doing this, since the words 'arcane tradition' suggest something conceived long ago at Eleusis and thereafter cherished by only a few initiates. Such a tradition is ten times more satisfying than an unromantic footnote or a reluctant reference to a rival's textbook. However, I am glad to be able to describe exactly how I came across the information contained in this chapter.

About seven years ago, when I was living in Strasbourg, I managed to obtain a letter of introduction to a local wise man who was reputed to be something of an alchemist. His workshop, which I located only after much difficulty, was situated in a little back street beside an almost stagnant stretch of canal. Some of the houses in this neighbourhood actually backed on to the murky green water and all possessed a certain melancholic charm; hunched together and barely able to support their steep roofs, they seemed to decay before one's eyes, providing just the sort of locality where an alchemist might choose to live.

I had expected my alchemist to be an ascetic-looking person, probably white-bearded and certainly grave in speech and manner. On my arrival, however, I was greeted by a cheerful old gentleman whose portly figure and pince-nez made him look like a 'Phiz' etching of Mr Pickwick. His merry features certainly betrayed no indication of the long years he had spent at his spagyric labours. On the contrary, they seemed quite cherubic, a trifle worldly wise perhaps, but still cherubic.* Around us was a confusion of jars, retorts, alambics and cylinders, with precious liquids bubbling away contentedly. Despite the heat, the air, I noticed, was filled with a bracing scent which somehow reminded me of ozone or the smell of light rain on a warm summer's day. I have since learned that this atmosphere is characteristic of alchemical laboratories when the Great Work is nearing completion. I do not know if my alchemist knew he was on the verge of success, but if he did he gave no indication of it. Having found that I was interested in a small talisman lying on a table, he began to talk freely about its manufacture. And that is how, as I watched the old man pottering about testing pressures and taking temperatures, I learned all I wanted to know about talismanic magic. Since then I have read a great deal on the subject, but my reading has added nothing of substance to what I learned that day. What follows is a little of what I still gratefully remember of that educative afternoon.

Most of us at some time or other in our lives have put our faith in an object which we think may bring us luck. For years I turned up at examinations wearing the pair of socks I had worn when I obtained my school certificate. Darned and shrunken, they saw me all the way through school and university, until they eventually disintegrated during an unsuccessful driving test. It is doubtful whether the socks themselves possessed any special talismanic virtue but I do know that my own confidence in them soothed my nerves and, with the exception of the driving test, improved my examination performance. All over the world talismans and amulets inspire a

---

* Part of his work, I discovered later, was concerned with the creation of a homunculus or, as modern biologists would call it, a test-tube baby. These little creatures appear to have been fairly common in the 15th and 16th centuries, when they were a source of consternation to theologians, who were never sure whether a mannikin could possess an immortal soul. Jewish kabbalists, who believed they knew the secret of creation, also experimented in this field. Their usual method was to mould a human-sized figure out of river clay and place on it pieces of paper bearing certain holy names. The assembled kabbalists would then stand around the figure solemnly intoning passages from the book of Genesis, interspersed with more names of power and miscellaneous signs and symbols. At last, after the senior kabbalist had breathed into the figure's nostrils, it would glow eerily, shudder and then slowly open its eyes. It had become a golem or artificial man. The most celebrated haunt of golems was 16th-century Prague, where many kabbalistic scholars worked. One sorrowful-looking golem is said to have lived in a room above the Altneu synagogue, where it used to perform menial household tasks. It was examined and interrogated by King Rudolf II whose interest in the cognate sciences is well attested. The last recorded golem was in 19th-century Russia.

similar confidence in people from all walks of life, most of whom feel they need a little extra help to cope with the stresses and strains of living.

But the efficacy of a talisman does not depend entirely on the faith its owner places in it. Talismans exist which, unlike my late-lamented socks, contain a magical power which is their very own. They may work by influencing their owner's mind, it is true, but they succeed not merely because of the confidence they inspire, but because of their intrinsic magic. These are the talismans we shall be looking at in this chapter, since the rest are psychological boosters and nothing more.

The real magical talisman can be said to resemble a self-recharging battery. At the time of its preparation a propitious combination of angelic and planetary influences endows it with a specific type of magical energy. The exact nature of this energy will depend on the magician's reasons for wanting the talisman, but once the energy has been acquired, or, to put it another way, once the talisman has been 'charged', it will proceed on the principle of universal sympathy to attract a flow of similar energy from the universe. This means that while a talisman is using up energy in furthering the cause to which it was dedicated, it is also drawing into itself sufficient new energy to continue that function.

Thus a talisman works in a positive way, attracting the causal forces necessary to create whatever effect its owner desires. An amulet, on the other hand, has the more negative function of neutralizing certain causes before they can promote an undesired effect. To some extent both achieve the same result: an amulet which wards off bad health is, after all, doing much the same thing as a talisman which sets out to procure good health. For this reason, although this chapter is called Talismanic Magic, we will deal with amuletic magic as well. Indeed, we may occasionally offend purists by using both words without any distinction of meaning.*

We shall also look briefly at cursing which, like talismanic magic, is intended to attract causes that are desired by the magician but whose effect in this case is always unpleasant. That such magic is anti-social need hardly be stressed, but to ignore it would be to

---

* The word 'talisman' is derived (via the Arabic *tilsam*) from the late Greek word τελεσμα, which means a mystery. 'Amulet' is of Latin origin (*amuletum*), but its earlier etymology is unknown.

overlook the vindictiveness common to most human beings. Even so, I recommend no one to indulge in the practice; if the adept's good nature is not enough to restrain him, then he would do well to reflect that the malign force generated by cursing will recoil on him if for any reason deflected from its target. Even when a curse has successfully attacked its victim, the feelings of hate and malice needed to propel it to its destination will remain with the adept for a long time afterwards, souring his character and, far more dangerous, leaving him vulnerable to similar feelings from without.

As in the case of all magical work, the manufacture of talismans rests on the hypothesis that currents of etheric energy may be diverted to the world of dense matter where they can effect changes willed by the magician. In effect, therefore, the talisman is an object capable both of earthing the required force and of rendering it effective on the physical plane. Clearly, the magician's first task is to endow whatever piece of stone, metal or parchment he has chosen for his purpose with the talismanic qualities needed to make it function. First he must decide precisely what he wants his talisman to accomplish; a glance at the Table of Intentions will then reveal to him which group of planetary correspondences are appropriate. Let us once more assume that love is the thing the magician desires most, so Venus is the planet most likely to procure it. He sees from the Table of Correspondences that copper is the metal on which to engrave his talisman, since that is sacred to Venus, and that green is the corresponding colour, so that should copper be unobtainable he can always resort to green-coloured paper.* The other correspondences may then be fitted in as necessary. It is important that the construction of the talisman should take place when Venus is at her most benign. The adept will take care therefore to calculate the most auspicious time for its manufacture, just as he would set about timing a Venusian ritual. In that case, you will remember, he would be likely to choose a Friday, at the hour of Venus, when that planet was astrologically favoured or when the Sun graced either Libra or Taurus.

As to the actual design of the talisman, this can be left to the adept, provided he takes care to remain loyal to general esoteric tradition. He may, if he likes, copy one of the talismans illustrated in this and other magical textbooks. If he is following the kabbalistic

---

* Where paper or parchment is used it is often advisable to enclose it in a locket of the appropriate planetary metal. Gold and sometimes silver will do as alternatives.

system he will begin his talismanic work by forming the kabbalistic cross and then, with hands folded, recite the Blessing of Kamea:

'Blessed art Thou, O Lord, who hast sanctified Thy great Name and hast revealed it to Thy pious ones to show its power and might in the language, in the working of it, and in the utterance of the mouth: Yod-Hē-Vau-Hē.'

Next he turns his attention to his talisman on which he inscribes or engraves the three Hebrew characters כשם or, if space is precious, the abbreviation כ". This means 'in the name of' and is followed by the Tetragrammaton (יהוה) or by one of the divine synonyms or *shemoth.** Although this name may – and should – be written in Hebrew, Western occultists usually write its Roman equivalent. There then follows a mnemonic which represents a *shem* of the five archangels (Michael, Gabriel, Raphael, Uriel and Nuriel) and may be written in Roman letters (Argaman) or Hebrew (ארגמן). After this comes the talismanic intention which should if possible be reduced to one word; in the case of our example it would be 'Love'. If this cannot be done, the intention will have to be written out on a scrap of paper and reduced to its numerical root using the Hebrew numerological system. According to this the letters of the alphabet are endowed with the following numerical values:

1	2	3	4	5	6	7	8
A	B	C	D	E	U	O	F
I	K	G	M	H	V	Z	P
Q	R	L	T	N	W		
J		S			X		
Y							

---

* For ease of reference these are:

Yah	a contracted form of Yahweh (Jehovah)
Elohim	the ordinary appellative name of God
El	a similar name of God
Shaddai	the 'Almighty' or 'All Powerful One'
Adonai	'Lord', a substitute for Yahweh
Tzabaoth	'Of Hosts'
Yod	
Hē	
Vau	abridged forms of the Tetragrammaton.
Hē	

Let us assume in order to show how this works that the adept hopes to win the affection of someone called Mary Smith, so that at its simplest the intention he writes down will be 'Love: Mary Smith'. Converted into numbers, the message becomes 3765: 4121 34145. These numbers have now to be added together, and if the total has two digits or more these must again be added until a single digit, the 'numerical root', is at last reached. In our example the sum of all the numbers comes to 46 which in turn adds up first to 10 (4+6) and then to 1 (1+0). It would thus be the number 1 that appeared on the talisman, followed, if there were room to spare, by the words *Amen* and *Selah*. Up to this point therefore our imaginary talisman looks something like this:

Figure 6

So much for the obverse of the talisman, which may be regarded as the magician's contribution to the operation because it serves to give direction to the astral force.* On the other side the talisman will bear the symbols of that force and they, by the law of micro/macrocosmic sympathy, will shortly conduct the force itself down on to the physical plane. Planetary symbols are perhaps the most commonly used, but they are not always explicit enough to capture the aspect of the force most likely to satisfy the particular talismanic intention. That is why a special symbolism has been carefully worked out over the centuries by magicians. Not only is this her-

---

* All magicians are agreed that to be effective talismans demand a reciprocal effort from the user. The medieval visionary Arnold of Villanova (1235–1311) was so convinced of this that he recommended they be recharged daily by their owner's thoughts. He also taught that while talismans were godsends to those struggling on the path of life, they could only benefit people who were pure in heart and mind.

metically correct, but time and usage have conferred upon it an astral potency of its own. The talismans illustrated below are based on this symbolism and may therefore be used with confidence.*

We have already seen how the effectiveness of ritual magic depends on the sacramental quality of the rite performed, culminating as it does in the consecration of the celebrant. In the same way a talisman must first receive an infusion of supernatural life if it is to bridge the astral and physical worlds. This becomes possible when it is made the object of a ritual intention so that it can become suitably consecrated as the rite attains its climax. If he prefers, however, the hard-pressed magician can skip the ritual preliminaries and simply *will* the power into the talisman, helped – if will-power is scarce – by concentration, mantric recitation, masturbation or anything else he can think of. Given the adept's dedication, the right time and the correct symbolism, nothing in heaven or earth will stop the appropriate force from linking up with the talisman. It will then have been 'charged'.

Some occultists, especially those who, following Paracelsus, like to explain magic in psychological terms, claim that if anything is charged at all, it is the mind of the magician. The talisman, they declare, remains unaffected except that it now becomes a visible reminder of what has happened. As such it stimulates the magician's mind to produce thoughts which, by attracting 'sympathetic' aspects of the cosmic mind, will gradually create the conditions needed to achieve the ambition for which the talisman was created. This leaves the talisman with scarcely more power than my examination socks, in which case there hardly seems any point in going to the trouble of making one. However, I think this theory is disproved by experience; talismans work even when their owner is sceptical, and amulets preserve the wearer from dangers quite unknown to him, not to mention the fact that curses will work on unsuspecting victims. But if the psychological explanation seems the more convincing,

* The adept may construct a talisman for others besides himself, although ideally they should be present when the work is done. If this is impossible they must be told the exact time of the operation in advance so that they can meditate on the talismanic intention and associate themselves with the magician's efforts on their behalf. After consecration the talisman should be wrapped in soft leather or in silk of any colour save black or brown until such time as it can be worn by the future owner. An occult tradition insists that the adept should accept no payment for his services, although common sense, always more reliable than occult traditions, suggests that this is a case where if the labourer is worth his hire, he is also worth his keep.

then you may accept it. You will certainly require some explanation to satisfy your mind, since talismanic magic really works, as you will discover for yourself when you try your hand at imitating some of the following designs.

KABBALISTIC CHARMS

Figure 7

This is probably the best-known of all charms, although it is not widely used by modern kabbalists. From its original purpose as a prevention against plague, tooth-ache and assorted ills it has grown into a general good luck charm. Scholars claim that it is composed of the initials of the Hebrew words *Ab* (Father), *Ben* (Son) and *Ruach ACadsch* (Holy Spirit), while others regard it as a derivative of the Hebrew injunction *abreq ad habra*. Its earliest appearance among non-Semitic people suggests, however, that it is really no more than a corruption of the Basilidian form *Abraxas*. The word was usually written on parchment and hung from the neck (often in a small pouch of soft leather) by a linen thread.

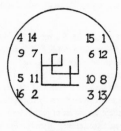

Figure 8

Any talisman engraved on silver when the Moon is well aspected is said to ensure general good fortune for its owner. A suitable inscription in such a case would be the numerical one given above, which is associated with Jupiter. This association means, of course, that the talisman would also be effective when engraved on tin. The symbol at the centre of the talisman is that of Bethor, planetary spirit of Jupiter.

Figure 9

Made of gold and bearing the astrological symbols of both the Sun and its spiritual patron (Och), this is an excellent talisman for attracting wealth and friendship. When inscribed on paper and kept in a gold locket worn around the neck it has the reputation of being lucky for gamblers and those in search of hidden treasure.

Figure 10

This talisman is traditionally associated with Sandalphon, the

name given to the guardian angel of Earth.* The intelligence
responsible for the physical evolution of our planet, Sandalphon is
subordinate only to God and the Archons. That such an angel
exists is not too difficult to accept, although it would probably be
wrong to personalize 'him' too greatly. Unfortunately, Jewish
tradition in the Midrash has done just that by maintaining that
when the prophet Elijah ascended to heaven in his fiery chariot he
was promptly turned into an angel called Sandalphon who became
the custodian of Earth.† Most people nowadays will find it hard
enough to take the fiery chariot seriously, let alone the angelic meta-
morphosis. The symbolism of this talisman may be interpreted as
the angelic stewardship (♕) of Earth (⊕) being entrusted to
Sandalphon who is represented by fire (Δ). On the other hand,
the same symbols can also be read as Elijah's departure from Earth
(⊕) in a fiery chariot (Δ) and his subsequent promotion in
Heaven (♕). Whatever its real meaning, this interesting talisman
is held to be of great value to all Earth's children especially those
engaged in occult or philosophic studies.

Figure 11

This healing amulet incorporates the divine monogrammaton

---

* I.e. to the sphere of Earth (Malkuth). The reader will recall that Uriel is the
Regent of the element of Earth. In Jewish lore Sandalphon's job in the heavenly court
was to weave garlands for the Almighty, but he also had a more down-to-earth function
since it was he who differentiated the sex of every embryo.

† A similar fate awaited the Prophet Enoch, who after his death became the Angel
Metatron, 'Prince of the Presence'. Jewish tradition has it that Metatron is the Master
of Heavenly Song when, presumably, he works closely with Michael who is believed to
be the leader of the holy choir.

with the solar imagery of Raphael, archangel of healing. It is startlingly effective in both preventing and curing all manner of sickness. It may be struck on gold or inscribed on parchment.

Figure 12

In this second healing talisman the concentric circles represent the Inner Earth, or primary manifestation of the four elements. These elements are here regarded as the physical components of man and their common well-being is entrusted to the Archangels Uriel and Raphael, both of which are agencies of the one God. Sometimes the centre of the circle contains the astrological symbol of the Moon. This is because of an esoteric tradition linking Uriel with the 'old' Moon which – according to the same tradition – preceded our present Moon in Atlantean days. Its displacement in the heavens is said to be the cause of the seismic disturbances on Earth which finally resulted in the destruction of Atlantis.

The talisman may be engraved on gold or silver or inscribed on parchment.

Figure 13

This talismanic inscription is part of the 'Magic of Light' of

Abramelin the Wise. It should be written on parchment, and if placed on the forehead before sleeping it will assure the wearer prophetic dreams.

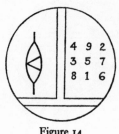

Figure 14

Figure 15

Figure 16

The use of these richly symbolic talismans has in the past been confined to practising magicians who have found them of tremendous value not only in their work but in their private lives as well. All three are equally powerful, but the first is particularly effective when one is dealing with the astral world. The figures represented on it express the divine name numerically and opposite them is found a symbolic 'third eye'. The second talisman brings enlightenment to questing minds (the initial A on the Chalice of Wisdom, a symbol of Binah, suggests Pallas Athene), while the third, known as the 'Crown of the Magi', guarantees the adept's mastery of all the forces he encounters. Here, the symbols surrounding the hexagram represent the *Chaioth ha Kadesh* or Holy Creatures, these being a man, a lion, a bull and an eagle (*Rev.* iv 7). Each of these symbolizes one of the four elements, the four letters of the Tetragrammaton and the four sublime injunctions of the Sphinx ('To know, to dare, to will, to keep silent'). In Christian symbolism the four Evangelists are also represented by the same creatures.

All these talismans may be struck on metal or drawn on parchment. Because of their connection with Saturn, figures 15 and 16 are best engraved on lead.

Figure 17

This love talisman should be made of copper, the metal of Venus, and bear the glyph of both that planet and its guardian spirit Hagith. Alternatively, it may be drawn on parchment in green ink, when it should be kept in a locket of silver or – if you can get it – copper.

Figure 18

Another love charm, a version of which is given in the famous *Key of Solomon*. Sometimes the Vulgate translation of Gen. ii 23, 24 is written around the periphery of the circle, although this is not really necessary.

Figure 19

The final kabbalistic talisman is the celebrated seal of Agrippa, which is a cryptogrammatic summary of several sacred phrases. It can be used to attract those benefic influences conducive to material and magical success.

EGYPTIAN CHARMS

There is no shortage of Egyptian charms. Those illustrated here are some of the several amuletic inscriptions known to esoteric students for centuries and more recently to Egyptologists. They may be consecrated at the climax of an Egyptian ritual and may bear the original hieroglyphics or their equivalents in Roman lettering. For that reason examples of both are given below.

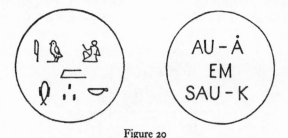

Figure 20

This is an all-purpose protective amulet which seems to have been popular once among the inhabitants of Abydos. Sometimes known as the Seal of Shabako, it is not clear what connection it has with the famous Shabako Stone on which is told the story of how the physical world was created by Ptah, or universal reason. The inscription, which merely declares that the wearer has obtained sovereignty over all things, may be struck on metal or drawn on parchment. An alternative version found at On (Heliopolis) incorporates some solar imagery which, if adopted, will have to be engraved on gold.

Figure 21

The most common Egyptian amulets are those bearing the god-form Khopri, traditionally depicted as a beetle. This insect, which as we have seen was believed to be self-generating, symbolized the emergence of new life from inert matter. Although natural history now informs us that there is nothing extraordinary about the beetle's nativity, the idea represented by Khopri remains a subject worthy of meditation. The beetle is depicted as being in the centre of a circle formed by a snake devouring its own tail. This again symbolizes the perpetual self-renewal of nature. In modern occultism the talisman has become associated with the post-mortem survival of the astral self. Some authorities teach therefore that the wearing of a scarab will ease the transition of consciousness from the physical to the astral body at the moment of death. The Egyptians used a different symbol for this, however, when they designed amulets to protect the discarnate soul. The example given below shows the serpent (*uraeus*) defending the soul from every evil onslaught by spitting out a protective shield of venom.

Figure 22

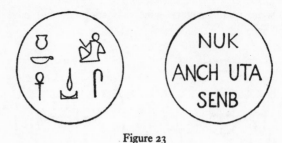

Figure 23

Originally intended to obtain or conserve health, this talisman is suitable whenever the intention is to ensure the physical or spiritual protection of the wearer. It should be struck in gold or silver or, if inscribed on parchment, kept in a locket of either metal.

Other Egyptian talismans concerned with the preservation of health and dedicated to Im-Hotep, patron of medicine, are of simpler design and consist of only one symbol which may be the *Anch* (♀) or the hieroglyph *Dad* (☥), which means health. The anch or ansate cross as it is sometimes called was the universal symbol of life. Some Egyptologists have stated that it represents a dam holding back the waters of the Nile, but there are others who see in it a sexual symbolism.

CURSES

It is a sad fact that magicians are more famous for their curses than for their blessings, although less cursing goes on than popular fiction supposes. One way of harming one's enemies is to send an artificial elemental after them. These elementals are forms created by the magician's imagination out of the elemental power generated by ritual. The nasty-minded adept can let his imagination run riot here and fashion the most grotesque monster which is then dispatched like a hound of hell to effect its master's business. Occult fiction is full of stories that tell of the havoc wrought by such elementals and it was a favourite theme of Algernon Blackwood who, as a former associate of the Hermetic Order of the Golden Dawn, knew full well what mental damage could be caused by psychic attacks of this nature. It is said that in the 'twenties a magical lodge in Hampstead created an artificial elemental which they hoped

would disrupt a rival fraternity newly established in the neighbourhood. But someone tipped off the intended victims who promptly
held a meeting at which the aggressor was sent back where it came
from. Meanwhile the original Hampstead group, fully confident of
their success, were sipping tea in their sanctuary when in burst the
turncoat elemental. Pandemonium broke out at once; teacups were
hurled in the air by invisible hands, sandwiches flung across the
room and an ivory Buddha sent crashing through a gilt-framed
portrait of Mme Blavatsky. From that day forth no member of the
group could escape the attentions of the elemental that each had
played a part in creating. It was described as looking like a giant
sea anemone equipped with spindly legs, and for the next few weeks
it was to haunt members at their work, in their homes and even in
their beds where it once tried to envelop a lady adept in its gelati-
nous embrace. This may sound very far-fetched and, indeed, the
whole thing may be attributable to collective delusion, but I do
know that only after due and lengthy ceremony was the creature
finally got rid of. Fortunately its visitation did some good, since
it for ever deterred that particular group from dabbling in that sort
of thing again.

As far as talismanic magic is concerned, the curse may be regarded
as an object designed to attract malefic forces to whomever the
magician has in mind during the course of its manufacture. Its
function is thus similar to that of a talisman, except that the latter
creates benefic conditions. Not that the job ends here, for tradition
has it that a curse must be 'willingly' (i.e. unwittingly) accepted by
its intended victim. That is why magicians in the past have spent
hours working out how they might pass on their curses without
arousing suspicion. However, as I said earlier, cursing is something
you would do well to leave alone.

ANTIDOTES

There is always the risk that some morning you may yourself get
up to find one of these nasty curses lying on your doormat. The
thing to do then is to neutralize it as quickly as possible. Place the
curse in the centre of the following diagram which should be drawn
on a large sheet of paper. This will give you some temporary protection while you work out what to do next. It may be some comfort
to see that the copious symbolism in this diagram looks sufficiently

effective to hold back a whole phalanx of demonic agents, and by now you should be able to recognize in it various divine grammatons, the Tau and other sacred symbols including two 'marvellous candles' which are taken no doubt from the famous *grimoire* of 'Little Albert'.

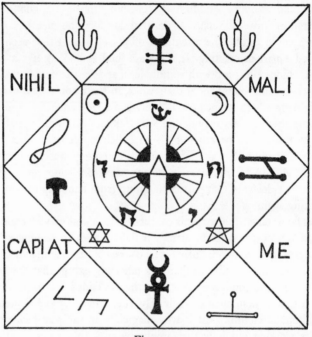

NIHIL MALI

CAPIAT ME

Figure 24

What you do next will depend on the nature of the curse, so you must try at once to identify which sefirothic force it represents. For example, if the curse were engraved on a piece of iron, you would find on working through the Table of Correspondences that iron is the metal of Mars and that Mars is the planetary associate of the fifth sefira. The chances are therefore that the kliphothic force evoked in making the curse which, by now, will be bearing down on you, is that of Geburah. So far so good. Now all you need do is perform a rite of Mars during which the force is evoked in only its positive aspect and not, as would be usual, in its balanced duality. The reason for this is that the negative aspect represented by the curse will immediately conjoin with the positive aspect in order to form a neutral unity which will harm no one. After this, all that remains to be done is to wrap the curse in the paper on which it rests and either burn both, if this effects a chemical change, or, if more convenient, throw the lot into the sea or any pool or river. (The ultra-cautious may first consecrate the water by adding a pinch of salt and uttering the appropriate words.)

Figure 25

We shall conclude this chapter with a talisman specially designed to allay the effects of other people's cursing; its symbolism will be apparent to every reader. This amulet will at least afford you some protection from the harm others wish upon you. To be on the safe side, however, any curse you come across should be ritually neutralized.

THE ART OF PROPHECY

MANY PEOPLE suppose that being a magician turns you into something of a soothsayer as well. This can be embarrassing, especially when friends who know of your occult interests start passing you their dirty teacups in the hope that you can discern their destiny among the slops. People, often perfect strangers, will come up to you at parties, and, having announced that they are Aquarians, Virgoans or what have you, will calmly await your analysis of their character and matrimonial prospects.

That precognition is possible must, I think, be admitted by anyone who bothers to study the evidence.[1] Some readers may even have had personal experience of precognitive dreams, or have had hunches which turned out to be correct. It would be wrong to attribute all such experiences to precognition, especially when coincidence plays so large a part in our lives, but there are cases where predictions have come true in so detailed a way that coincidence has to be ruled out. A much-quoted example is found in the annals of the Society for Psychical Research, and involves the investigator Dr S. G. Soal and a 'direct voice' medium, Mrs Blanche Cooper.[2] During a seance held early in 1922, Dr Soal received a message from a spirit purporting to be that of an old school friend called Gordon Davis. This 'spirit' had already offered Soal some evidential proof of its identity at an earlier seance. Now the voice began to speak of a terraced house with a 'funny dark tunnel' beside it. This house was situated in what the voice described as 'half a street' with the letter E predominant and five or six steps 'and a half' leading up to the front door. Opposite the house stood 'something' which none of its neighbours shared, 'not a veranda' but something like one.

The voice then described the interior of the house, referring to an upstairs room with a very large mirror and several pictures depicting 'glorious mountains' and seascapes. Reference was also made to some very large vases and 'funny saucers'. Turning its attention to a downstairs room the voice described 'two funny brass candlesticks' on a shelf and 'a black dickie-bird on the piano'. Mention was also made of a wife and small son.

At the time of the seance Dr Soal believed that Gordon Davis had been killed in action during the First World War. However, three years later, in February 1925, he learned with some astonishment that his friend was still alive and living in Southend. His address was 54 Eastern Esplanade and when Soal went there on April 18th he found it to be a terrace house on the sea-front ('half a street') with a promenade shelter directly opposite ('something ... not a veranda'). Six steps led up to the front door, the topmost step being little more than a thin slab ('five or six steps and a half'). Soal noticed too that between each pair of front doors in the terrace was a covered passage ('a funny dark tunnel') leading to the back. Inside the house more surprises were in store for Soal. In an upstairs drawing-room he found a very large mirror suspended over the fireplace and, on the wall, seven pictures, six of them scenic views in which sea and mountains figured prominently. There were also five very large vases in the room, together with two saucer-shaped plaques ('funny saucers'). Downstairs – just as the voice had promised – were two brass candlesticks, the only ones in the house, and on the piano a porcelain kingfisher perched on a black pedestal ('a black dickie-bird on the piano'). Even sceptics must concede therefore that Mrs Cooper had provided what turned out to be an amazingly accurate description of the house and its interior during her seance with Dr Soal some three years previously. But the real cause for amazement comes when we read that although the seance with Mrs Cooper took place in January 1922, *Gordon Davis, his wife and small son did not move into the house in question until nearly twelve months after that date.*

There can be no disputing the facts. Dr Soal, experienced investigator that he was, had made careful notes of his seance with Mrs Cooper, and these had been signed, dated and witnessed. The subsequent discovery of Gordon Davis, his move to 54 Eastern Esplanade, the details of his home there – all these were fully corroborated. We cannot therefore avoid the conclusion that the voice, whoever it belonged to, which spoke through Mrs Cooper in 1922, had described in minute detail things that had not yet taken place. It is a clear case of precognition.

The real difficulty about accepting such cases of precognition is that they upset all our orderly notions about time, and the mind does not like this at all. So accustomed are we to conceiving of the passage of time in three-dimensional terms that our mind spontaneously rebels against the possibility of a future which already exists, fearing perhaps that our precious freedom of will may turn out to be an illusion if every event in our lives has already been mapped out for us.

Thus the idea of precognition becomes one that our tidy-minded consciousness is not prepared to tolerate. As a result, most of us are persuaded to ignore the possibility altogether. Fortunately some people, among them Bergson, Ouspensky and Dunne, have tried to tackle the whole problem of time, a problem that has also preoccupied imaginative writers like Proust, H. G. Wells and J. B. Priestley. Much of the latter's book *Man and Time*[3] is taken up with considering the various theories about time in order to see how well precognition fits into them. Priestley puts forward the interesting idea that precognitive dreams may be more frequent than is generally imagined, but that the waking consciousness is so hostile to them that they get shoved into oblivion within seconds of their emergence from the subconscious. He goes on to suggest, following Dunne,[4] that we might try sleeping with a pad and pencil under our pillow, so that immediately on waking we can record whatever dream memories are still with us. These can then be compared with later events to see if there is any correlation between them.

For the purposes of this chapter we shall avoid being drawn again into the free-will versus determinism controversy and confine ourselves to working out a theoretical justification for precognition. Plausibility rather than philosophical proof must be our aim, and those readers who want really to get to grips with this difficult but fascinating subject are advised to read some of the books which deal with it in greater depth.

Most of us see time as the back-cloth to a sequence of events taking place during our progress from birth to death or, as we shall call it, A to B. If we pause to think about our journey at any point, let us call it X, between A and B, we become aware of three things: a past made up of A to X, a present, X, and a future, X to B.

Of these three, however, only the present, X, possesses any real meaning; it is the infinitesimal moment which forms our 'now'. Beyond X lies a future as yet devoid of reality, and behind it a past that is in a sense only subjectively real, being filled with remembered experiences. As we continue our journey towards B, the widening distance between A and X accumulates memories of what has happened at various points along the way, each point representing a present now past. The future (X to B), on the other hand, is filled only with an unknown potential which cannot be realized until acted upon by the steadily advancing present (X). In other words, we face an amorphous future whose eventual form depends on a series of forthcoming presents. For that reason the future, being formless, should not be foreseeable.

And there the case would rest were it not for the evidence which clearly suggests that the future can on occasion be foreseen. Faced with this evidence we can do one of two things: we can attribute all recorded cases of precognition to fraud, coincidence and unconscious inference, or we can reconsider our views about time. The first course is the easier, but to adopt it would be to ignore the cases like that of Gordon Davis which cannot be conveniently explained away by fraud, etc. Far more honest would be to square up to the fact that the future has at times been predicted and so must in some way or other already exist – otherwise the future would not be there to predict. And if, as we have posited, the future already exists, then our journey from A to B must lead not, as we thought, towards an amorphous future but to a destination where we are expected. This is what Eddington had in mind when he declared that events do not happen, but that we happen upon events.

Things may become a little clearer if we exchange the As, Bs and Xs of our earlier example for the more homely picture of a passenger on a train. The time is 10 a.m., and as he looks out of the window beside him our passenger sees some cows grazing in a field. Soon they are lost to view and in their place he sees some lambs frisking on a hillside. The time is 10.02 a.m. The cows he saw at 10 a.m. belong to the traveller's past, while the gambolling lambs are a part of his present (10.02 a.m.). Yet those same lambs were already frisking merrily at 10 a.m. and only the physical limitations of the railway carriage prevented him from seeing them.* Indeed, had he put his

* This example, though useful, is not completely satisfactory since the action of the lambs at 10 a.m. would not necessarily have been the same as that observed at 10.02 a.m.

head out of the window at 10 a.m. he might well have seen them sooner.

Like the traveller, our idea of time is limited by our presence in the physical world where we occupy both space and time. Our notion of time is related to our notion of space; as our senses are simultaneously aware of only three dimensions, height, length and breadth, so our consciousness adopts a spatial notion of time characterized by similar limitations. When we took the example of the man in a train we became aware of the limitations imposed on him because we ourselves were not confined inside the carriage. From our vantage-point outside we could observe that the cows and lambs he saw were not, as they seemed to him, successive phenomena, but were coexisting in a common present. As we have pointed out, had our traveller put his head out of the window he too would have been able to appreciate this, for he would then have overcome the ordinary limitations of his environment.* This is exactly the sort of thing our subconscious can do – for example in dreams – when it is no longer subject to conscious control. At such times it dwells in what we have elsewhere called 'absolute time', an all-embracing present akin to the state of timelessness many mystics claim to have experienced. Here it is able to see past, present and future not as separate portions relative to the body's occupation of space, but as an eternal 'now'.

Precognition therefore is nothing less than the conscious mind's awareness of the timeless vision presented to the subconscious when the latter has been liberated – in dreams, trance or under hypnosis – from its normal constraints. In general these glimpses of the future are quite involuntary, so that the primary aim of divination is to

* Here we must leave our example of the man in the train or else we shall be led into a process of infinite regression. This is because although we as observers are in absolute time compared with him, that time is still only relative as far as we are concerned. This is like the example which I think Priestley quotes, of a man who wished to paint a certain landscape. To make the picture complete he decided to paint himself into it. But no sooner had he done so than he realized that to make the picture really complete he would have to paint in himself painting himself painting the scene in front of him. And so on ad infinitum. I prefer an example that used to fascinate me as a child. On the label of the brand of coffee essence called Camp coffee is depicted a kilted army officer being served a cup of coffee by an Indian servant. On the tray which the servant held was a bottle of Camp coffee complete with label, so that the regression of servants and coffee-drinking officers was unending. Fortunately, however, the absolute time attainable by the subconscious is removed from the three-dimensional world of matter. For that reason it is safe in its poly-dimensional world from the threat of infinite regression.

encourage the voluntary departure of the subconscious into absolute time. The conscious mind has then to be kept in a state of receptive passivity so that it will accept whatever images are conveyed to it by the temporarily dislocated subconscious.

This dislocation of the subconscious is the *modus operandi* of crystal-gazing, where the scryer tries to suspend all conscious mental activity by fixing his attention to the exclusion of all else on the crystal ball. The subconscious is then given free rein to travel in absolute time and the images observed there are duly 'seen' inside the crystal. For those who are interested, the best results are achieved when the crystal is placed on a piece of black paper on which the following Egyptian figure has been drawn in white chalk.

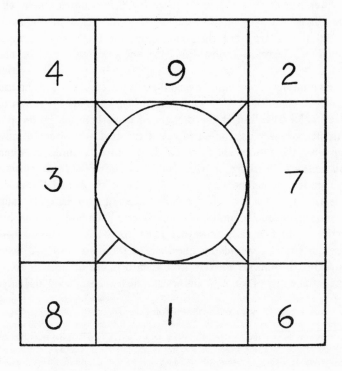

Figure 26

The prolonged study of tea-leaves, Tarot cards and possibly the exposed entrails of animals can release the diviner's subconscious in just the same way. The magician with prophetic ambitions should cultivate an ability to move at will into the four-dimensional realm of absolute time. Already his magical training and knowledge of astral conditions will have fitted him for the task, while concentration and meditation will help bring it to fruition.

Another way of achieving success is through the use of ritual magic. As the Table of Intentions has shown, the appropriate rite is a Mercurial one and Hod will be the sefira to which the adept directs his attention. Some magicians prefer, before the start of their rite, to frame a particular question about whatever aspect of the future concerns them. The answer will then be apprehended either at the climax to the rite or later in the form of a dream. At no time, however, should there be any deliberate straining for an answer, since given half the chance the fickle consciousness will be all too ready to supply its own. It is far better to forget all about the matter until the time comes for the answer to rise, often in allegorical terms, from the subconscious levels of the mind.

As a means of obtaining precognitive experience ritual magic has much to commend it. We know that when he tired of testing the *I Ching** or baulked at the thought of constructing a horoscope, Aleister Crowley usèd often to resort to ritual as a means of discovering the future. He followed the practice favoured by some magicians of working in pairs and then addressing questions to whichever partner became god-possessed at the sexual climax of the rite. Crowley has left a detailed account of a series of such workings conducted in Paris when Victor Neuburg became his active partner in a homosexual rite.[5] As Neuburg approached orgasm Crowley would fire questions at the deity they had been invoking. Neuburg's answers were then believed to emanate from the astral entity to which, in his ecstasy, he had abandoned his body.

* According to Chinese tradition the emperor Fu-Hui once saw a mysterious dragon climb out of the murky waters of the Yellow River. On its back were the curious shapes that were to become the *I Ching*. This event took place in 3000 B.C., but regardless of whether the story is true or not, the *I Ching* is certainly the oldest known method of divination. It consists of pieces of bone which may be cast to form eight trigrams and these in turn combine to make up sixty-four hexagrams each containing six tendencies. The interpretation of these shapes enables the diviner to deal with every possible human situation.

Whether the god himself supplied these answers or whether they proceeded from Neuburg's own subconscious is irrelevant: the information received was satisfactory and that was all that mattered.

It is not, of course, necessary to emulate the methods used by Crowley and Neuburg to obtain details of the future. Sex is only one way of surrendering yourself to the powerful forces evoked by ritual. Provided that surrender is achieved, no matter how, there is every chance that the questions you ask will receive the right answer.

Sometimes the answer the magician seeks comes not in a convenient flash of inspiration but later in a dream. The dangers here are that it may become distorted in the process, and that the waking consciousness, being rationally biased, will be reluctant to preserve a dream experience where reality and fantasy intermingle. The usual pad and pencil at the bedside are the only precaution you can take, but frequently the dream will have fled from memory even before you have a chance to reach for them. Fortunately, the conscious mind becomes more amenable once it has learned to accept the theoretical validity of precognition. Dreams are then more easily remembered and the ability to look into the future is slowly acquired. Once again, patience and understanding are all that are called for.

What we have been discussing so far may be described as intuitive precognition, since all the conscious mind does is be still while the subconscious imprints its message on it. However, there are other methods of divination which involve the conscious mind in a far more active role, since they work on the assumption that observable things can themselves be pointers to the future. This is as it should be, for the whole of nature is a dynamic process dedicated to the realization of its evolutionary goal. Thus by observing what is, we are able to infer what will be. This is exactly what scientists do when they tell us that a stump-tailed macaque monkey will lose its stump in a few hundred years, or that our own small toes are doomed to extinction. These and other pieces of scientific induction like every statistical projection are no more than an exercise in precognition based on existing data.

The magical adept does much the same thing when he endeavours to deduce the future from his observation of natural phenomena, be they the stars in the sky or the lines on someone's palm. Sceptics will quickly protest that it is one thing to look at a monkey's backside and prophesy the eventual disappearance of its tail, but quite another to deduce the future from the flight of birds or the position of the major planets. The difference between them is that the first method begins with the particular and sticks to it, while the second proceeds from the particular to the general. On their own terms, however, both methods are equally valid: the first confines itself to the external aspect of nature, while the second searches for an inner meaning – which, after all, is the whole basis of magic.

The inner meaning of things arises from their common existence on the plane of matter. We must leave the physicists to explain, label and quantify the essential properties of matter, although it is becoming increasingly clear that these properties bear out the hermetic thesis. This, you will recall, supposes the interdependence of all things within a universal scheme, so that the part reflects the whole and vice versa. It is what Blake so picturesquely described in some famous lines in 'Auguries of Innocence':

> To see a World in a grain of sand,
> And a Heaven in a flower,
> Hold Infinity in the palm of your hand
> And Eternity in an hour.

It is also what on a practical level has been unfolded in the theory of correspondences where we have presented to us the exoteric aspect of the fundamental unity of all physical things.

The most renowned system of divination from observable phenomena is probably astrology. Its supporters maintain that events here on Earth run parallel to events in the sky, because both depend ultimately on the same vital force.* Palmistry, the arrangement of cards, the drawing of lots and myriad other divinatory practices rest on this same basis, which supposes that as the universe is one great design, any event occurring in one part will have important repercussions elsewhere. For this reason the study of particular events,

---

* This is not the only explanation. Dr Jung defended astrology by arguing that what a horoscope did was crystallize a particular moment of time and so reveal the microcosm's relationship with the macrocosm which contains it. He also suggested that the hitherto unsuspected influence of inanimate objects might one day furnish a causal basis for astrology. Those who are interested in learning more about his views are recommended to read the essay he wrote in collaboration with W. Pauli, *On the Nature of the Psyche* (see C. J. Jung, *The Collected Works*, vol. 8, *The Structure and Dynamics of the Psyche* (Routledge and Kegan Paul, London, 1960)).

however insignificant, is held to inform the enlightened observer what future events are thereby presaged.*

The pity is that methods of divination, the so-called 'occult sciences', have for so long been over-simplified and commercially exploited that by now they are largely discredited. Some of them, it is true, seem highly suspect at the best of times – including such polysyllabic wonders as alectryomancy, where a cock pecks pieces of grain spread over letters of the alphabet; aleuromancy, where messages are enclosed in small balls of dough; alomancy, which is a form of divination with salt; anthropomancy, the scrutiny of the entrails of sacrificial victims; and so on right through the alphabet via empyromancy, lampadomancy, molybdomancy, until we reach xenomancy or divination from the appearance of foreign visitors.

If he wishes, the adept can at once start observing things around him in order to detect their relationship to future events. For those who distrust their own observation there is a vast literature available on astrology, palmistry, the Tarot† and other methods of fortune-telling. These books will teach you to predict the future, often in considerable detail, from the evidence presented to you.

To sum up, therefore, there are two methods of looking into the future: the first is intuitive, and proceeds from the subconscious to

---

* These lines from Francis Thompson are particularly appropriate:

> When to the new eyes of thee
> All things by immortal power,
> Near or far,
> Hiddenly
> To each other linked are,
> That thou canst not stir a flower
> Without troubling of a star ...   ('The Mistress of Vision')

Sir Isaac Newton also taught that every particle in the universe affected every other particle.

† The Tarot cards are probably the ancestors of our present playing-cards, although their exact origin is obscure. One tradition maintains that they were first designed by the ancient Egyptians and brought from Europe by the gypsies. Another attributes their invention to a group of 13th-century kabbalists living near Fez. Many sets of Tarot cards exist, including the Tarot of Vergnano, the Tarot of Marseilles, the German Tarot and the Tarot of Etteila. Among the modern versions are those designed by A. E. Waite, Papus and Knight-Littel. Each set consists of 78 cards. Of these, 56 belong to the Minor Arcana and are divided into four suites (cups, wands, pentacles and swords). The remainder form the Major Arcana or Tarot trumps, and on each is pictured an allegorical figure. Behind these quaint little figures in their medieval settings are said to lie the most profound secrets of hermetic philosophy.

the conscious mind; the second depends on the activity of the conscious mind, and is a process of induction from given data. In most cases of precognition, however, there is a little of each. Astrologers describe how they often get hunches while staring at someone's natal chart so that they are able to supply details which cannot be inferred from the information they have before them. The same thing happens to palmists as they peer at the lines criss-crossing someone's hand. Such 'clairvoyance' supplements the inductive process and arises from the release of the diviner's subconscious into absolute time. There it sees realized what the conscious mind in its study of cards, palms or planets sees only in unfulfilled potential.

The adept with prophetic ambitions must decide, therefore, by which of the many methods available he is going to realize them. He should strive to understand both what he is doing and why he does it, so that all levels of his mind co-operate fully to discover what nature chooses to conceal. Who knows, he may end up as the success of every party he goes to!

11

ONCE AT A party where I had drunk rather more than was good for me, I started arguing the case for the supernormal with the author of a book on psychical research. A large bejewelled lady who, it later turned out, was a Christian Scientist, listened attentively to our discussion and when it was over drew me aside. 'A word in your ear', she whispered, 'about demons.' As the demon drink had by then reduced my resistance to nothing, I had little choice but to listen to her as she warned about the evil spirits waiting to pounce on anyone who went within ten feet of a ouija board. I am afraid I took none of it very seriously. But at this point I intend having a word in your ear about the same subject. I cannot help wondering if my remarks will be treated as lightly as I treated those of Mrs Eddy's disciple. I hope not. Like her I honestly think they warrant attention.

If this were an encyclopedia of demonology – and there are such things[1] – we would now be faced with the horrible task of cataloguing all known demons – and there are thousands of them of every shape, size and hue. The problem is compounded too by the fact that one demon may have myriad different shapes and often just as many names to go by. Fortunately, this work can safely be left to the encyclopedist although, unlike the magician, he is never likely to find himself conversing with the real thing. Let us look at the subject of demons within the context of practical magic.

Up to now we have tended to treat all astral forces as impersonal, which is quite in order since the power used in magic is impersonal. And yet everyone who reads occult literature or has any experience of magic will soon be brought up against forms which seem every bit as personal as the adept himself. And if on occasion the beings that turn up during ritual work are not exactly personal, then they are certainly not formless, abstract forces. The novice magician must not be astonished therefore if he finds himself confronted by human shapes, or by shapes whose likeness may or may not exist in the natural world.

In an earlier chapter we discussed in some detail the objective reality of such forms. By now the reader who has already tried his hand at magic may even have discovered their reality for himself. If so, he will know that the great forms encountered in the master rituals, be they elemental or angelic, are on the whole quite well disposed towards him. This is because the ceremonial preliminaries and the form of each rite are designed to ensure that all undesirable influences are kept firmly at bay. But a time will come when the magician's experiments may introduce him to the delinquents of the astral dark, those devils and demons so beloved of story-tellers the whole world over. These forms again, you will remember, are essentially forces, although a number of them do seem to have acquired a formal identity of their own. To call them 'evil' would be an over-simplification, but in this case life becomes much easier if we allow ourselves to be over simple. We shall call them evil for the good reason that given the chance they would do us immeasurable harm.

The shapes generally assumed by demons are far from horrendous – at least to begin with, when their owners may still be trying to give a good impression: little children, gentle old folk and beautiful young people of either sex are some of their favourite human disguises. Though not themselves human, they will frequently display as much resourcefulness as the most cunning human being. They will flatter, charm, threaten and cajole the adept with consummate skill in an attempt to gain the upper hand, and the unwary magician can all too easily succumb to their clever ploys. What do they hope to achieve by all this? Being the forces of disorder and imbalance, they seek first of all to upset the ritual and so thwart the adept's intention. However, this is subordinate to their chief aim which is to destroy anyone, in this case the magician, who dares approach their domain.* Their hostility arises from the fact that ritual success

* As Lactantius says in his *Divinae Institutiones*: 'These spirits, defiled and abandoned, roam across the face of the earth seeking comfort in their perdition by destroying men. Thus they fell everything with their tricks and stratagems, their deceits and wiles.'

depends on joint action by the two constituent aspects, positive and negative, of a perfectly balanced force. Now such action is something quite abhorrent to an unbalanced force irrevocably separated, as it often is, from its complementary aspect. It feels menaced by the magician and so does all it can to remove him in order to restore the chaos which is compatible with its inherent nihilism.

Physical assaults by demonic agents are comparatively rare, though by no means unknown, and there is scant risk of the careless adept's being battered by some scaly science-fiction monster. However, a physical battering would be preferable to the psychological assault to which he is more likely to fall victim: the science-fiction monster will still be there, but the adept alone will see it; the pain will still be acute but his body will bear no scars. In other words, his hell will be a secret one, a private madness that no one else can share or begin to comprehend.

From this there arises the ever-present need for caution before you scale the heights of magic. Even in the foothills there lurk dire perils, which is why the rites so far described should not be undertaken lightly. When someone sets out deliberately to contact the astral world, be that world inside or outside his mind, he at once faces many dangers which only knowledge can help to overcome. But even the cleverest and most knowledgeable magician realizes that the demons of the pit are waiting for the one false step that will deliver him to them.

These dangers should not be exaggerated, and need not, of course, deter you from practising magic, unless you happen to be a very nervous person in which case you should keep clear of all forms of occultism. Magic is probably a great deal safer than driving a car, although, as in motoring, care and skill are all that are needed to ensure safety. If, therefore, you come across a *grimoire* containing a demonic invocation which you are tempted to try, you may do so without too much risk provided the correct ritual observances are made.

Many people, it seems, are attracted to the idea of seeing demons. It is as if they seek reassurance that the bogies which haunted their childish nightmares* are genuine after all. Little good, however, can come from consorting with the shadier inhabitants of the astral world unless, of course, your ritual intention is a negative one. In

---

* The word is in fact derived from the Anglo-Saxon *maer*, meaning sprite, or elf.

that case these creatures will, without too much persuasion, do their utmost to help you realize it since their appetite for destruction and discord appears to be insatiable.

One of the ways of contacting the demon kingdom is to use a revised form of the master rituals, generally the kabbalistic version, since in the west more is known about the demons of that tradition than any other. (Better the demons you know than those you don't.) For this experiment the adept, clad in black, draws his magic circle and Triangle of Art in the prescribed manner. Inside the circle he formulates the kabbalistic cross before proceeding to perform the usual banishing ritual. On this occasion, however, only the eastern, southern and western stations are 'purified'. That of the north is left as it is, unattended by its archangelic guardian.* Turning now to this station, the adept places a candle there or else sacrifices some small living thing, whispering as he does so the name of the demon he hopes later to summon. The self-anointing and other preliminaries follow in the usual way, except that incense is conveyed to the northern station and allowed to burn there. Henceforth, whenever he approaches that station the adept will kneel and whisper to the Earth the demon's name.†

As soon as the customary transition from Malkuth to Yesod has taken place, the adept summons the fiend by calling the name eleven times. A period of waiting follows during which the magician focuses his attention on the Triangle of Art and recites certain words.‡

---

* It should be noted that some demonophiles substitute the following names for those of the four archangels: Magoa (east), Paymon (west), Egym (north), Amaymon (south). In his *Magia naturalis et innaturalis* the great Dr Faustus changes the order slightly and replaces Magoa with Oriens. From him we also learn that the demonic equivalents of the elemental angels are Samael (fire), Azazel (air), Azael (water) and Mahazael (Earth).

† There is no shortage of demons to choose from – according to Talmudic tradition there are no less than 7,405,926 of them. The following is a very short alphabetical selection: Abac, Aldai, Aliseon, Asmodeus, Ayperos, Bathim, Casmiel, Chameron, Densor, Destatur, Dumosson, Eparinesout, Esmony, Estiot, Glasyabolas, Gomeh, Guthac, Iat, Lilith, Mandousin, Marbas, Naydrus, Pruslas, Pursan, Valefar.

‡ These might be nothing more than the mantric repetition of such ancient evocatory formulae as, 'Palas aron azinomas', 'Xilka, Xilka, Besa, Besa' or 'Bagahi laca Bachabé'. The *Key of Solomon* recommends the recitation of nine divine appellatives: Eheieh, Yod, Tetragrammaton Elohim, El, Elohim Gibor, Eloah Va-Daath, El Adonai Tzabaoth, Eloi Tzabaoth, Shaddai. More appropriate would be the names of the six Authors of Wickedness: Acteus, Magelsius, Ormenus, Lycas, Nicon and Mimon.

Some time later the demon, if so disposed, will respond to the summons, although at first the adept will merely sense its presence as it stalks like some curious beast along the perimeter of the circle. Eventually, however, it will assume a visible form within the triangle. Should it appear anywhere else it must be commanded to depart forthwith: only an experienced magician can cope with an errant demon, and even then there can be problems. Assuming that the form has turned up in the right place, it will soon begin to act and talk in a very friendly manner; do not forget, however, that its winning ways conceal a sinister intention – namely, to get the adept out of the circle and into its clutches. Nor should the circle be abandoned if the demon tries a little intimidation by suddenly producing a hellish host of friends and neighbours. This is what happened to Benvenuto Cellini in sixteenth-century Rome after he had made the acquaintance of a Sicilian priest with occult leanings. One night the two of them, accompanied by a couple of friends, repaired to the Coliseum where they planned to evoke demons. Here is Cellini's account, from his autobiography,[2] of what happened:

The priest, clad in the impressive manner of all conjurors, began to draw strange and wondrous circles on the ground. He had made us bring along a stock of rare perfumes and some incense which gave off a foul and noisome odour. When all was ready he opened up the main circle and taking each of us by the hand led us inside. He gave the pentacle to another necromancer, his partner, who was commanded to burn incense at the due and proper times while the rest of us were bidden to look after the fire. Finally the incantation began.

The ceremony had been going on for over an hour and a half when all of a sudden the Coliseum became filled with legions of devils. I was busy with the perfumes, but the priest guessing that a sufficient number of infernal spirits had assembled, turned to me and said 'Benvenuto, ask them something.' Whereupon I replied, 'Let them bring me into the company of my Sicilian mistress, Angelica.' That night, alas, we obtained no satisfactory answer from them, but I was at least glad to have indulged my curiosity.

The magician now told me that a second visit would be necessary and he promised that I should then be satisfied in whatever I might ask. He warned me, however, to bring with me a small boy who had never had knowledge of woman.* And so I took along my young apprentice who was then about twelve years of age. With us also were Vincenzio Romoli, my companion on the previous occasion, and a certain Agnolino Gaddi, who was a close friend of ours. When we reached the appointed place the priest began the same preparations as before, but this time they were far more elaborate. He then placed us inside the circle which again was more artistically and solemnly drawn than last time. Having entrusted the care of the perfumes and fire to my friend Vincenzio who was assisted by Gaddi, the magician handed me a pentacle, ordering me to turn it towards whatever direction he indicated. I instructed my apprentice to sit beneath the pentacle. Now began more marvellous incantations during which the magician summoned by name a vast multitude of demons, leaders of several legions, whom he interrogated in the name of that eternal and uncreated God who reigns for ever, using the Hebrew language as well as Greek and Latin. Almost at once the amphitheatre became filled with demons a hundred times more numerous than at the earlier conjuration. In the meantime Vincenzio, helped by Gaddi, was busily tending the fire and burning on it a large quantity of precious incense. Prompted by the magician I once more expressed my wish to be reunited with my Angelica, after which the sage turned to me and said, 'Listen, they have just disclosed that in the space of a month you shall be with her.'

He then asked me to be brave and stand beside him since the legions about us were a thousand more than had been summoned. Worse than that, they were of an exceedingly dangerous kind. Thus as soon as my question had been answered we felt obliged to dismiss them as civilly and as gently as possible.†

---

* In some countries small children are still used for clairvoyance, it being thought that their young minds are more receptive to the supernormal.

† As was emphasized in the chapter containing the master rituals, astral forms must be dismissed at the conclusion of every rite. In demonic evocation this is especially important. The courteous form of words in which Cellini's priest addressed the demons in the Coliseum may have been on the lines of the following dismissal, which is typical of many found in medieval *grimoires*: 'O demon, seeing that thou hast duly answered all my questions, I hereby license thee to depart without injury to man or beast. Depart, I say, and be thou willing and ready to come to me whenever conjured to do so by the sacred rites of magic. I now beseech thee to withdraw quietly, and may peace remain for ever between me and thee.'

By this time the young lad beneath the pentacle was in a state of extreme terror and swore that there had gathered in the place a million fierce men all bent on our destruction. In addition there were four armed giants of tremendous size, each doing his best to force a way into our circle. The necromancer who by now was himself quivering with fear, tried again to dismiss politely the assembled hosts, while Vincenzio trembling like an aspen leaf took care of the incense. Although I felt as scared as any of them I strove hard to conceal my fright in the hope that my example would put fresh courage into the rest. The truth is, of course, that I had already given myself up for dead, especially when I beheld the abject terror of the magician.

The boy with us had put his head between his knees and kept moaning, 'I shall die in this position for we are all most certainly doomed.' I told him to look up, assuring him that all he would see were smoke and shadows, but when he raised his eyes he cried out, 'The whole place is on fire and the flames are about to fall on us.' Then, his face covered, he sobbed that our end was inevitable. Again the magician bade me remain calm and burn the correct incenses. I therefore turned to Vincenzio Romoli and told him to do this at once. As I did so I caught sight of Gaddi who was so frightened that he scarcely knew where he was and looked as good as dead. Seeing the gravity of his condition I shouted, 'Gaddi, at times like this a man should make himself useful instead of yielding to fear, so move yourself and help me with this incense.' ...

Fortunately, Cellini's steadfastness saved the situation; at last the demons departed, enabling the exhausted party to make for home. For the historian of magic this has always been a favourite anecdote, but for magicians it is much more. For them the semblance of courage which the narrator maintained, thanks to his self-control, has become one of the first lessons they must all learn. Though often quaking, countless adepts have remembered Cellini's advice to Gaddi and have made themselves useful rather than succumb, as weaker men would, to the pandemonium around them.

Perhaps the picture of Cellini and his friends surrounded by devils is a good one to leave with you at the end of this cautionary chapter. As promised, we have had a word in your ear about consorting with demons. The best word, of course, is, don't.

12

B Y NOW it may seem to the reader that, given the Table of Intentions and the master rituals, everyone has all he needs to realize his fondest wishes. Because the potential efficacy of each rite is guaranteed *ex opere operato*, nothing apparently stands in the way of success. Unfortunately, this is not quite the case. It is true that every rite is capable of effecting whatever intention lies behind its performance, but capability does not automatically ensure success. The trouble is that things can and often do go wrong – an astrological calculation may be inaccurate, the correspondences inappropriate or the adept may at the last minute fail to assimilate the power always evoked by ritual. These, however, are mistakes which in retrospect can usually be identified and so corrected on future occasions. A more serious cause of failure is the karmic handicap that most magicians start off with.

Recently the word karma has tended to become all things to all men, so we had better state exactly what it means in the present context. Each of us goes through life with the characteristics of whatever moment marked our arrival on the physical plane. The cosmic tendencies of that moment, in occult language its 'vibrations', then accompany us through life and determine its general trend. One of the purposes of astrology is to reveal this trend to us through an interpretation of the planetary configuration that coincided with our birth.

Because these natal 'vibrations' determine the trend our life will take they are particularly important to the idea of reincarnation. Earlier we explained how a quintessential consciousness or, to follow Kant, a *noumenon*, is able to survive the death of our astral personality just as it has survived the death of countless earlier personalities. This is the vital spark which, when due to begin a new incarnation, joins up with the nascent personality of a new-born baby. How this union takes place is still a mystery, but we may suppose that the vibrations characterizing the moment of birth attract from the astral world a *noumenon* whose spiritual evolution can be advanced by the sort of life destined for the incipient personality. For that reason a personality is often said to inherit at birth a karmic debt which means that its subsequent failures and successes are to some extent what the *noumenon* has merited during previous incarnations. Life thus becomes a remedial process governed by the law we call karma.

Now the purpose of magic, you will recall, is to effect changes in conformity with the will. Sometimes, however, the changes desired by the magician will conflict with what is meant to flow from the law of karma: an adept may want instant riches, while karmic law demands that he endure penury for the good of his soul. In such cases karmic law generally, though not always, prevails.

When karmic law is overcome, the adept is usually first made to recognize the lesson he would have learned had things taken their normal course. In occult language he is said to confront the Dweller on the Threshold, which is a personalized form of his aggregate debt to date. This then removes from him his karmic obligation and so allows his magical intentions to be realized. Many occultists find that their early experience of magic is marred by a curious run of bad luck when things just will not go right. It is as if they must submit to a sort of purgatory during which they gradually loosen a long-accumulated karmic debt. Time and again novice magicians lament their misfortunes, complaining that far from improving their lot, magic has made it much worse. Fortunately these ill effects do wear off after a time and are soon forgotten once success starts to attend each magical operation. So if your ritual work does not immediately meet with the sure-fire success you expected, be patient and try to understand why.

These last few paragraphs are perhaps unduly pessimistic, since karmic restraints are not as many or as binding as is suggested. Indeed, an experienced magician can often overcome them quite easily, although unless at the same time he learns why they were necessary, he will be faced with an identical set of conditions in his next incarnation. As always, understanding is the key that frees the individual from the otherwise remorseless cycle of death and rebirth.*

With experience therefore the adept can be sure of overcoming whatever karmic handicap may afflict him; if one method of realizing his wishes should fail, he will know of at least a dozen others he can try. And if each of these is individually unsuccessful, their cumulative effect is often sufficient to bring ultimate success. Such knowledge is something that comes only with time but in the next few pages we shall examine three magical intentions, all important ones, in order to see to what extent the ritual recommendations in the Table of Intentions can be supplemented. The intentions chosen for this purpose are love, eternal youth and healing.

LOVE

There are probably more love charms in existence than stars in the sky. Some are quaint, some crude and a few quite beautiful, but all are potentially effective. Their merit lies not so much in the procedures they recommend as in the effect they have on the mind of whoever performs them. Firstly, they concentrate his attention on the person of his choice, in whose mind a reciprocal interest is telepathically aroused. Secondly, they link the adept's intention with the 'love aspect' of the universal mind. The charm he is engaged on then draws down the force needed to accomplish the intention behind it.

From this it will be clear that a talisman, suitably consecrated, is an indispensable weapon in the lover's armoury. In addition, however, he has a vast stock of other charms, spells and incantations to assist him. One is given below. It belongs to Celtic magic, which is eminently suitable for people of European descent as it is the

---

* The thought of past lives fascinates many people, and previous incarnations can sometimes be recollected once some external stimulus attunes the subconscious to the etheric wavelength that carries the appropriate memory record. The pineal gland is said to play a part in this process. When the necessary stimulus has been received the adept should allow his mind to wander freely as in the exercise known to psychiatrists as the 'free association test'. It is important to record all the impressions that rise up on the stream of consciousness, since among them will be the clues needed to piece the past together. Later, during meditation or ritual, these clues will afford direct access to the wavelength where further details are stored.

native druidic tradition of our continent.* Called Lover's Mandrake this charm was still used at the beginning of the present century by love-sick farm-hands in central Wales. The version given below retains the Welsh incantations, but a translation is provided for those who wish to use it.

The ritual, as its name suggests, involves that notorious vegetable the mandrake (figure 27). The true mandrake (*Mandragora officinalis*), a member of the potato family (*Solinaceae*), grows in Mediterranean countries where it is valued not only for its magical

Figure 27

---

* Julius Caesar tells us that the Druidic Order sprang up in Britain and spread to Gaul. It remained the custom, however, for candidates for the priesthood to travel to Britain to be instructed in the mysteries of druidism.

properties but also as an emetic, purgative and narcotic. In China the celebrated herb Ging Seng and in America the May Apple both go by the name of mandrake, as does the flag (*Iris pseudoacorus*) in some northern European countries. These plants have in common a root formation that bears some resemblance to a human shape. In Britain a plant called White Bryony (*Bryonia dioica*) is often used as a mandrake for the same reasons, and because of its wide distribution is recommended here. Found in moist hedgerows it is identifiable by its long trailing stems and vine-shaped leaves (figure 28). The adept's first task, then, is to find his mandrake.

Figure 28

The rite* is undertaken when the Moon is waxing, the best time

* It will be seen that these instructions for harvesting mandragore differ from those given in the *Herbarium of Apuleius*, where the adept is told to tie his dog to the plant and then persuade it to tug the root from the ground. In this way it is the dog, not its master, who goes mad and dies on hearing the shrieks mandrakes are supposed to give when being dragged from the earth. Modern occultists and the R.S.P.C.A. may rest assured that the dog is in fact unnecessary.

being when the Pleiades occupy the night sky.* The adept rises before dawn and silently makes his way to the site where his mandrake lies buried. He must equip himself with a torch and spade, since his first task is to dig up the plant without damaging its precious root. As he digs, the adept recites the following mantra which, apart from its magical purpose, will help him contain his temper: '*Gwyn eu fyd y pridd, y gwreiddyn a'r noson hon.*' 'Blessed be this Earth, this root, this night.' When at last the root has been exhumed, the adept may return home with his prize. The chances are that he will be disappointed to see how little his root resembles a human form. The most he can hope for are a few protuberances that might with some imagination be said to resemble arms and legs. This is where nature must be helped along, for the adept has now to carve the root very slightly in order to give it a more acceptable shape. Thanks to his surgery the mandrake should end up with two arms, two legs and some sort of face. Thus fashioned, the root represents the person with whom the adept is in love, and so it must be named. For this it is sufficient to hold it in the left hand and forming a pentagram over it with the right, say, 'I name you N. N.' Needless to say, any sexual characteristics the root may present should not blatantly contradict those of the person named. There is no need to be too fussy about this, but it would clearly be inappropriate to leave a lady mandrake with a phallus-like nodule between her 'legs'.

The next step is to return the mandrake to the earth. Ideally, its reburial should be in a churchyard or at a crossroads, since both places are sacred to Hecate, Queen of Magic. Fortunately, the adept's own garden will do as a second best. So too will a flower-pot or window-box. The top of the root should be covered with soil, but a few green shoots may be allowed to peep out above the ground. A cross should then be traced with a silver object across the topsoil where the mandrake lies interred.

All that then remains to be done is to mix together one part milk with three parts water to which are added a few drops of the magician's own blood. This libation is poured slowly over the soil while the appropriate words are spoken:

> *Wrth y bedd y gwaed a'r llaeth*
> *Wnaeth gadw N. i mi'n gaeth.*

* These stars, the seven daughters of Atlas, can be seen in the eastern sky before sunrise around June 15th. They set shortly before sunrise early in November.

> Blood and milk upon the grave
> Will make N. evermore my slave.

You will be glad to know that with this the adept's pre-dawn labours are over and he may return thankfully to bed.

For the next few weeks the only attention the mandrake will require is occasional watering, but the adept should make an effort to visit it every other day. When the next lunar cycle begins he may dig up the root again one hour before sunrise, reciting the following words as he does so:

> *Lloer lân dy wên a gwen dy fron*
> *Rho' dy fendith y noson hon*
> *Ar fy nghais er gwan fy nghri*
> *A boed i'm cariad garu fi.*

> Moon above so palely shining
> Bestow this night thy sacred blessing
> On my prayer and ritual plea
> To fill N.'s heart with love for me.

By now the mandrake will have acquired tremendous talismanic properties. It will form a common link between the adept, the person it is meant to represent and the cosmic mind. Its preparation, however, is not yet over, for it must now be dried. This can be done by hanging it up in a well-aired room. It should also be passed through some Venusian incense at least once a week. This process takes some time, but the hasty adept can cheat slightly by putting the root in a warm oven or on top of a radiator in order to accelerate the natural drying process. To preserve its Venusian association, however, the mandrake should be placed on a paper bearing the following Venusian inscription:

Figure 29

Whatever means of drying the mandrake are adopted, certain words must be spoken over it. These are:

> *Y gwres a lysg y ffrwyth bach hy'*
> *Yw'r fflam sy'n llosgi nghalon i.*

This fruit is scorched by that same heat
Which warms my heart with every beat.

At last the mandrake is ready for the final piece of magic, assuming that the desired effect has not already taken place. The adept obtains a silver pin or needle and plunges it straight through the little creature's heart, not with any intention of harming it, but merely to smite it with love for him. As he does so, he 'projects' his magical intention with all the force he can muster. The mandrake, still impaled, should then be left on a window-sill where it can see the Moon at night. There it will do its utmost to win for the magician the love he wants.

Those who quail at the effort involved in this charm may be interested in another which also has some horticultural connections. This one is called the Magic Rose, and in order to perform it you must rise between three and four on any morning in June and pick a full-blown red rose. Return to your room and hold the flower for a full five minutes over a chafing dish in which charcoal and sulphur of brimstone are burning.* The flower should then be folded in a piece of paper bearing your name and that of the person you love. Seal the paper with three seals and bury it under the tree where the rose was gathered. The letter A, representing the Latin tag *Amor vincit omnia*, is traced over the spot. There the rose is left until July 6th, when at midnight it must be dug up and the little parcel taken to your room. Sleep with it under your pillow for three consecutive nights and you will enjoy dreams of great portent.

Such dreams, incidentally, can also be induced by grating together a walnut, hazel-nut and nutmeg. This powder should be mixed with butter and brown sugar so as to make several pellets. Seven of these should be taken one hour before retiring in order to induce

---

* You may care to know that by burning sprigs of rosemary you can, it is said, induce feelings of warmth in the heart of your beloved. A more passionate warmth can be aroused by administering the herbal aphrodisiac given in Appendix 1.

revelatory dreams. An invocation to Brizzo, goddess of sleep, is supposed also to help.

Sweet dreams!

ETERNAL YOUTH

In the past, several famous magicians have looked remarkably youthful even in old age; among them were Cagliostro and Casanova, whose smooth skin was much admired by the pock-marked courtiers among whom they moved. Similarly, the youthfulness of the mysterious Comte de Saint-Germain remains a source of interest today even if he was not, as popular belief once supposed, over two thousand years of age.[1] But the pursuit of youth, unlike its attainment,* is far from being confined to magicians: millions dedicate their money, time and energy to the same goal.

Before we proceed on our own search for youth it is as well to be clear in our minds what we are after. The most important thing to remember is that the quality of youth consists of more than just a youthful appearance. The latter may, with a little effort, be acquired temporarily by people who are no longer young (some suitable recipes are given in an appendix). But what these people possess is really no more than a physical simulacrum of youth, a smooth young mask through which old eyes peer. The point is that youth is as much a state of mind as a bloom on the skin, and your first task is to recapture that state of mind. To do this, retire to a quiet place at a fixed time each day. There surround yourself with things associated with your youth or things whose taste or smell transports you back to younger days. It is impossible to tell you exactly what you need; clearly it is something you must work out for yourself. For the narrator in Marcel Proust's *A la recherche du temps perdu*, the taste of a cake dipped in tea, or the accident of stumbling over an uneven step, were just two of the things that

---

* There is a sad little story about the elixir of life that some magicians claim to have found. In its heyday the Order of the Golden Dawn had among its members a venerable gentleman who years previously had brewed this most precious of liquids. Unfortunately, he had been too afraid to drink it. When at last he found his courage it was only to discover that every drop of the vital elixir had evaporated!

The recipe for one such elixir was given – ironically enough on his deathbed – by Trithemius. Its ingredients are calomel, gentian, cinnamon, aniseed, nard and mace. The recommended dosage is 5 grammes of the mixture taken daily in wine.

could plunge him back through time. For you it may be the scent of pine-needles, the feel of sand or the taste of wild strawberries that will release a flood of memories more vivid than any induced by a voluntary exercise of the mind.

Above all, do not underestimate the power of thought in these matters. If constructive thinking can mould the etheric substances that lie outside yourself, how much more easily can it induce changes in that intimate fabric which is your body and which is but a tangible expression of yourself. The phenomenon known as stigmata, and the physical effects of certain hypnotic suggestions, are clear proof that the mind can bring about physical changes. Truly, to think young is to look young.

As for magical methods of rejuvenation, we shall look first of all at two celebrated, if somewhat drastic examples, which are of academic interest if nothing else, because each has found its way into literature. The methods employed are rather sinister and as one involves ritual murder and the other its astral equivalent, neither can be recommended.

In the first of these rejuvenating rituals the magician seeks to exchange his own decrepit body for that of a young and healthy person. This demands a great deal of thought since not only must the person chosen be fit and youthful, but he must have a vulnerable astral body. In addition, the victim's natal horoscope should offer the prospect of an agreeable life, so the adept has the added burden of finding a victim whose birth date is astrologically propitious. The preparatory work is far from easy, especially for someone who presumably is already close to senility.

Once the victim has been lured into the magician's sanctuary he is rendered unconscious and placed inside the magic circle, his head pointing westwards. A special lunar ritual is performed, projection of the astral body taking place at its climax. Immediately afterwards the magician leaves his own astral body and gate-crashes his way into that of his bewildered victim. In general little, if any, resistance is encountered and the dispossessed victim will automatically seek refuge in the astral shell newly vacated by the adept. At this stage two things are possible: the adept can either sever the silver cord linking his old astral and physical bodies, thus ensuring the convenient demise of his former identity; or he can direct his new astral body into its physical counterpart and then kill off the old self as it lies sleeping beside him. An understanding accomplice can perform this task for him, if he prefers, so that all there is left to be done is to dispose of the superfluous body. The magician, proudly flexing his youthful muscles, can then begin to contemplate the exciting new life ahead of him.

The second of these rejuvenating techniques is based on the same principle but demands a very close telepathic rapport between the adept and an accomplice. Again, the adept has first to set about finding his new body, which in this case will be that of a small child whose astrological prospects are attractive. The child need not be brought to the scene of the ritual, but his exact whereabouts must be known to the magician. Once more the rite adopted is a lunar one, at the end of which the adept projects from his physical body. Having assured himself that the astral body of his victim is both accessible and capable of possession, he mentally instructs his partner to 'kill' his now-useless physical body. The aim is to destroy this body completely so that the astral self has no compunction about leaving it for good. In this way it can more easily be persuaded to assume the personality of the young victim. Sometimes the importance placed on destroying the physical body and making it unattractive led to its being horribly mutilated, and this fired the imagination of writers and poets who overlooked the esoteric significance of the act.

Rumour has it that the Roman poet Virgil, who was not unacquainted with magical practice,[2] attempted rejuvenation by this method. The story, as we now have it in a rather fanciful version,[3] is that Virgil persuaded a servant to chop his body into small pieces which were then cast into a barrel of salt. There they were to remain for nine days while an oil lamp burned continuously nearby. Throughout this critical period strict secrecy was to be observed with only the magician and his accomplice aware of what was being essayed. However, after seven days had passed the emperor began to miss his favourite court poet and fearful lest some mishap had befallen him, seized the servant and made him confess what had happened. With his retinue in tow, the emperor rushed to the spot where the barrel was standing, and peering over the rim beheld Virgil's head. Such was his rage at what he took to be a clear case of murder that he promptly killed the luckless servant. No sooner had he done so than there appeared on the scene a naked child who ran three times round the cask and cursed all present for their inopportune meddling.

In his *Metamorphoses* Ovid describes similar attempts at rejuvenation conducted by Medea on Aeson and others. In these a grievous wound which in ordinary circumstances would prove fatal is inflicted on the patient. It is likely that the poet was here drawing on what he had heard about the ritual suicide involved in such ceremonies as we have just been discussing.*

Not all methods of rejuvenation are quite as gruesome as this, although the ones that are known to work make heavy demands on whoever decides to try them. For example, there is an ancient procedure described by Cagliostro in his *Egyptian Freemasonry*, and later reproduced by Eliphas Lévi in the *History of Magic*.[4] This involves a retreat of forty days and a regimen to daunt all but the most dedicated. The adept should retire to a deserted part of the country, taking with him only one friend or loyal companion. The retreat commences at the Full Moon in May when for the first seven days a strict fast has to be observed. During this time the adept should drink only May dew collected from sprouting corn with a cloth of pure white linen.† A few sweet, fresh herbs may be eaten during the day if the pangs of hunger are irresistible, and at night a meal of white meat, followed by a piece of wholemeal bread dipped in honey.‡ Before retiring to bed the adept bathes in warm water in which such aromatic herbs as sage, valerian, vervain and balm have been steeped. At dawn on the seventh day the adept performs an Egyptian solar ritual, and that night swallows seven

---

* 'As soon as she saw that all was ready, Medea pierced the old man's throat with her drawn sword allowing the stale blood to gush out ... The emaciated features at once vanished, together with all sign of pallor and decay, the hollow wrinkles filled out, the body was refreshed and its limbs grew strong again. Aeson stood astounded, remembering that this was how he had been over forty years ago.' *Metamorphoses* VII.

† Dew – and May dew in particular – has always been thought to have curative properties. In the 17th century it was widely used as an eye lotion and as a cure for skin disorders. A reputed cure for goitre was to gather May dew just before daybreak from a young man's grave. The patient then passed his hand three times over the grave before applying the dew to his neck.

Soil also was held to be beneficial to health. Sir Francis Bacon, having observed many robust-looking ploughmen, believed its smell alone to be a tonic. Gurdjieff believed that the smell of cattle was therapeutic, and the authoress Katherine Mansfield was made to inhale it in the Master's cow-sheds at Fontainebleau.

‡ The Comte de Saint-Germain once attributed his longevity to a diet of oats and white chicken-meat. In modern France the name Saint-Germain tea is given not to an elixir of life but to a laxative drink containing senna.

drops of the miraculous draught known as *aurum potabile*, or drinkable gold.

As the metal of the Sun, gold was held precious by most ancient civilizations. But the gold used in medicine is not the base metal with which most of us are familiar, but a special version of the *aurum raymundi*, or transmuted gold distilled by successful alchemists. It is the 'vital dew' of Ostanes the Mede; the tincture of Marianus; that blessed liquid which Khalid ben Yesid eulogized in the *Book of Crates*. For Chinese alchemists it was the *tau* whose essential properties are listed in the works of Ko Hung, the great fourth-century sage. Although Ko Hung recommended herbal medicines for prolonging life, he always insisted that immortality could be gained only by partaking of the divine elixir.

Few readers will be able to obtain a bottle of spagyric gold unless they know a co-operative alchemist. A substitute must therefore be concocted. In making it we are guided by those occult correspondences that form the basis of practical magic. The ingredients listed in Appendix 1 have been chosen because of their ability to combine secretly to produce the same effect as the rarest and finest *aurum potabile*.* After swallowing this the adept has completed the preparatory stage of his retreat.

There next follows a more inactive period, during which he retires to the privacy of his room and seeks in quiet reflection to recapture the feeling of his youth, its pleasures and its sadness. From now on his evening meal consists of a broth of lean beaf and rice seasoned with sage, followed by a glass of fresh orange juice. On the seventeenth day the adept takes, on waking, six drops of the Balm of Azoth, increasing the dosage by two drops until the thirty-second day. The Azoth which gives its name to this balm is, strictly speaking, that happy conjunction of circumstances which results in the transmutation of base metal. In chemical terms, therefore, the Azoth may be described as a universal catalyst since its function, like that of the philosophers' stone, is to encourage change. True to alchemical tradition the Balm of Azoth used here comes under the influence of Mercury. In rejuvenation its aim is twofold. In the first place, it acts as a mental stimulant, reinforcing – and thus helping to realize – the experimenter's desire to recapture his youth. Secondly,

---

* The ingredients given later both for this and other tonic medicines owe nothing to Lévi, whose writings on this topic smell of quackery. Apart from their use in this operation the prescribed draughts are of immense everyday value.

it helps to induce all the necessary physiological changes – you will see that many of its ingredients are famous for their tonic effect on the human organism.

Throughout this time the adept must perform a solar and a mercurial ritual on alternate days at the most suitable time. These rituals, conducted according to the kabbalistic tradition, will be dedicated to youth. On the thirty-second day the magician takes to his bed and from then on swallows a dessertspoonful of Universal Medicine at the hour of Mercury. This medicine is said by Lévi to be nothing less than astral mercury. However, other occultists associate it with the *prima materia* of spagyric theory where it forms the essence of all material things. The Chinese call it the *tao* which, according to them, assumes various different properties according to the presence of varying proportions of Yang and Yin. Being of the Earth it would seem to belong to the sphere of Malkuth, and so its manufacture traditionally takes place under the joint auspices of Uriel and Sandalphon, Regents of the Earth.

On the thirty-ninth day, *dies terribilis et sublimis*, the magician must drink the *rōs vitae*, the very dew of life, which Lévi describes as the Elixir of Acharat. Ten drops are taken in two tablespoonfuls of red wine at the climax of a solar ritual.* This rite is dedicated to the pagan god Maponus,† who on this occasion becomes both Sanat Kumara and the divine youth of Tifareth. Like him, the adept hopes to span eternity and yet remain untouched by time.

So there you are. When next you find yourself with forty days to spare, here is a good way to spend them. It is said that the Cardinal de Rohan submitted himself to this ordeal and emerged looking half his age. There is no doubt that the rest and the diet would do

---

* For the sake of completeness it should perhaps be mentioned that some adepts do without a specially prepared elixir. Instead, profiting from the active co-operation of a male companion, they adopt as their elixir what Verlaine once described as:

> *Lait suprème, divin phosphore,*
> *Sentant bon de la fleur d'amandier ...*

Cf. Eliphas Lévi, *Transcendental Magic*, p. 134.

† Maponus was venerated by the Celts of northern Britain, but his name survives (as Mabon) in Welsh mythology as well. There was something of Apollo, Mars and Mercury about him.

One school of occultism dedicates this ritual to Belatucadros, a Celtic deity whose name means 'Bright and Beautiful One'. In my opinion this is based on a misunderstanding. Despite his name, Belatucadros seems to be a Celtic version of Mars in his military role. Indeed he is frequently invoked (as at Netherby) as *Deo Marti Belatucadro*.

nothing but good to anyone, and when combined with a touch of magic who knows what miracles might be worked?

HEALING

Raphael is the archangel traditionally associated with good health. He is often described as standing in the Sun, and the solar rays typify his healing ministry.* Their warmth and brightness enable us better to imagine and so benefit from the remedial power available when we invoke his assistance.

Sunlight and healing were likewise associated by those great Sun-worshippers, the Egyptians, who attributed a therapeutic role to Ra when, as Lord of the Rays, he was depicted as the source of life, health and physical fitness ($\frac{\circ}{+}$ ⌿ ⎪). In the classical world the health-giving sun became linked, at least from the fifth-century B.C., with the fire-robed god Apollo, to whose shrine at Delphi people flocked to consult the oracle about their health. Certainly for the Romans Apollo was the supreme health-giver, and was in addition the father of Aesculapius, god of medicine.

Rituals intended for healing or the promotion of good health are usually performed on the seventh or twentieth day of the *lunar* month. The origin of the first of these dates may lie in the classical tradition that Apollo was born on the seventh day of the month. Because this supernal nativity occurred in the shade of a palm tree, palms have always been sacred to him. In kabbalistic tradition they are sacred to Mercury, which reminds us that in the Fourth Homeric Hymn it was Apollo himself who bestowed divine powers on Hermes (Mercury), so that here the correspondence is not accidental. Some magicians perform an annual ritual on July 13th, intended to provide a year's good health, but the only apparent significance of that date is that the Games (*Ludi Apollinares*) were held in Rome on the 13th.

Before you turn to magic to obtain good health, make sure that you have overlooked none of the material details conducive to the same result. Magic is but a part of the process and it would be wrong to think it can be used as a quick and easy panacea when a couple

---

* His name means 'God Heals', and in the Book of Tobit he appears in the guise of Azarias or 'Yahweh helps'.

of aspirins will do the job better. In some occult circles it is fashionable to denigrate the medical profession and resort instead to herbal nostrums, spirit-healers or other forms of fringe medicine. Any occultist so disposed would do well to try orthodox medicine as well, if only because it is wise to hedge one's bets.

There are many theories as to how astral therapy works; multi-coloured rays, angelic ministers, spirit doctors and magnetic currents are among the most common explanations offered. What probably happens is that the astral power evoked by the magician or healer acts upon the patient, probably via his astral body, in such a way that his subconscious wills recovery. There is no hocus-pocus about this: the *cure* as well as the cause of many diseases may be psychosomatic. Because this process involves the subconscious mind it can be applied to other people without their conscious co-operation. All that happens is that the force created by ritual is directed to the patient's subconscious where it can begin its recuperative work.

Sometimes the process may be a slow one, in which case you should sustain your efforts and consider how best to supplement them: a more auspicious time for your ritual work; the importation of additional correspondences; a specially constructed talisman – all these can help.* The co-operation of the patient might also be sought so that he can get on with a little useful Couéism of his own. This is particularly important in the case of a patient whose resolve to get well has been undermined both by disease and, as often happens, by the indifference of mystique-conscious doctors. Coué taught that ideas which cause or prolong disease may be eliminated by means of auto-suggestion, even if this involves no more than the daily repetition of his famous maxim, 'Every day and in every way I grow better and better.' In his view it was no good exhorting sick people to buck up or shake off their diseases if deep down they were already convinced that they were doomed. That was why the conscious will to live was often insufficient unless nourished by an inner certainty that recovery was possible. This certainty is what the Coué method still seeks to instil in a patient.

During his treatment the patient should, if possible, be encouraged to let his mind dwell on solar imagery. Let him imagine

---

* Attention might also be paid to the microcosmic correspondences of the ten sefiroth. These are: Kether, cranium; Hokmah, left side of face; Binah, right side of face; Hesed, left arm; Geburah, right arm; Tifareth, heart and chest; Netsah, loins and hips; Hod, legs; Yesod, reproductive organs; Malkuth, the whole body.

himself soaking up the Sun's rays while his illness evaporates from his body. In this way the appropriate astral forces will be attracted to him. Try, surreptitiously if need be, to surround the patient with as many as possible of the correspondences used in your ritual. An excellent link can be forged between him and your efforts on his behalf if you transfer to his bedside some of the things used in your rite; for example sprigs of heliotrope or laurel might be used. These objects will also attune his subconscious to the solar and tifarethic influences needed to ensure his return to health. Once again the details must be selected to suit the circumstances of the case and by this time you should know how to work these out for yourself. Needless to say, you should never worry a sick person with your magical preoccupations, especially if all he wants is peace and quiet. Relapse, not recovery, will be the result if you bully a chronic invalid into filling his mind with sunny thoughts while he lies reciting mantras in a bed bedecked with laurels.

It is an excellent idea to place a small vase of wood sorrel (*Oxalis acetosella*) beside the patient's bed, since this freshens the atmosphere considerably.* Another good idea is to keep a candle or votive light burning in the room, since the flame not only symbolizes the evocation of astral aid, but shines like a beacon in the astral world where it attracts all the desired influences. Ritual incense may also be burned, although you should always consult the patient before importing incense into the sick-room. Finally, talismans, often inscribed with the word *Ananīsapta* and dedicated to the spirit Buer, are also effective, as the protection and cure of disease were among their earliest functions. Do not forget, however, that all talismanic objects must be prepared according to the instructions given in an earlier chapter.

People who are new to occultism frequently ask what magic can and cannot achieve in matters of health and sickness. They know, for example, that no amount of incantation on their part is going to cause a new leg to grow after the first has been amputated. And yet

---

* Among the accomplishments of many magicians is a knowledge of herbs and their use in medicine. Within the system of correspondences each herb has been assigned to one of the twelve zodiacal signs or brought within the influence of a certain planet. Given an acquaintance with these correspondences and those (already listed) which relate various bodily parts to the Zodiac, the adept can prescribe appropriate herbal remedies. Readers who obtain an edition of Culpeper's *Herbal* will discover for themselves the astrological correspondence attributed to many of our native plants.

they know or have heard that organic changes do occur as the result of astral therapy. The latter can dissolve tumours, unlock joints, revive dead muscles and repair cell damage. Why then can it not cause new limbs to grow? The answer probably lies in the fact that what magic does, according to the definition given earlier, is effect changes so that organic changes are fully within its scope. The production of new limbs, however, would not involve a change in something already present but a creation *ex nihilo*, and that seems to be something not even magic can accomplish. Where change is concerned, however, you may apply magic with the confident assurance that it can and will work wonders.

There will be occasions when no amount of magic or medical attention will arrest the progress of a disease. Neither physician nor occultist can expect to challenge nature and not lose once in a while. We might end this chapter by reminding ourselves that in our lives we should always be ready to face the certainty of death; indeed, part of living is simply a preparation for it.

13   DEATH AND THE MEANING OF LIFE

ACCORDING to Schopenhauer, death is the inspiration of all philosophy since it prompts us to look for a meaning to the brief span of time we spend on Earth. In our search for this meaning our main concern is often to discover some reason for hoping that our personality will survive the grave. Hope of physical immortality, though not entirely lacking, has generally been much rarer than the fond belief in some nonphysical after-life. And yet the former is, if anything, more scientifically tenable. For death is not, as might be gathered from natural observation, the universal heritage of all living things. On the contrary, simple organisms like the unicellular protozoa continue to reproduce *ad infinitum* by splitting in two and, provided no calamity befalls them, leave no corpses in their wake. Research has shown too that when optimum conditions prevail, as for example when they are artificially created in a test-tube, pieces of animal tissue can be kept alive indefinitely. Muscle cells and nerve cells have both been successfully cultivated in this manner. From this biologists have inferred that living cells are potentially immortal, although their interdependence within a larger unit, such as the human body, means that any accidental flaw in the system can upset the general ecology. This brings in its train a variety of regressive and degenerative changes which lead eventually to the termination of the cell's vital capacity. It would seem, therefore, that longevity depends on a general functioning of the whole organism which, like the proverbial chain, is only as strong as its weakest link.

Whether physical immortality is desirable remains a debatable point, but it is unlikely to exercise men's minds in any immediate way for a long time. For it is clear that unless men succeed in reproducing for themselves the ideal environment that exists *in vitro* when tissue is cultivated artificially, they have no prospect of achieving the immortality of which their constituent cells are capable. Nevertheless these facts do indicate that rejuvenation and the fabled longevity of the Comte de Saint-Germain and Methuselah are at least theoretically possible.

In Chapter 1 we discussed the indissoluble link between our thinking processes and the physical structure of the brain. Here we are at one with science. Where occultists depart from the scientific view, however, is in their belief that there also exists a psychogonic extension to the human organism, which, for want of a better word, they call the astral body. This astral form is intimately associated with the physical body, being a natural product of its cerebral behaviour. Nevertheless, like any thought-form, the astral entity enjoys a quasi-independent existence not irredeemably bound up with that of the physical body. On the death of the body the human consciousness, which is no more than an accrued awareness of itself, is immediately taken over by the astral double. This is perfectly understandable, for once the sensory mechanism of the physical body has ceased to function, the self-awareness to which it formerly gave rise has more in common with its astral personification than with a physical corpse. In other words, the personality departs from the body and so survives its dissolution.

A similar process may well occur on every occasion in life when consciousness is temporarily suspended. We know from experience that concussion or anaesthetics cannot destroy the self-awareness of a lifetime. If they could, there would be no return to full consciousness once the physiological effects had worn off. What probably happens is that the displaced consciousness* is sympathetically attracted to the astral body where it takes up temporary residence, returning to the physical body once the physiological changes that expelled it are removed. When that happens the body is said to have 'regained' its former consciousness. The occultist would further argue that in cases of prolonged coma the consciousness is denied access to the physical body. This theory loses some of its superficial improbability if one remembers that the astral body, though conveniently described as an adjunct to its physical counterpart, is not

---

* The subconscious, not being subject to the same physical effects, may continue to function as it does under hypnosis or psychoanalysis.

a mysterious cocoon, or something we trail along behind us like a coloured balloon. Rather, inasmuch as it occupies space at all, it can be said to permeate our physical selves. Like the surgeon and psychologist, therefore, the occultist can happily confine his attention to the patient on the bed without worrying about some imaginary wisp of ether floating near the ceiling.

When the physical organism has deteriorated beyond a certain point, the consciousness becomes intuitively aware that death is inevitable. Its intuition is not always correct, of course, but having relied for so long on the physical vehicle for all its information it is well qualified to judge when that machine is finished. During this period the consciousness will hover uncertainly between the two bodies at its disposal until recovery or death at last decides which one it will occupy. Meanwhile it can observe the faces of people who have already passed into the astral world where they wait to welcome the new arrival. Here we have the explanation of the deathbed visions which are so frequently reported.[1] Naturally, in cases of violent death the transition to the astral body is so brusque that it can often be quite a while before the consciousness finds its bearings. Lord Dowding described in his books how during the war the distressed spirits of dead airmen used to appear in his home circle, many of whom had not realized that they had quit this world.

It is a nuisance to have to call the post-mortem personality 'the astral body', when the more usual word 'spirit' is not only shorter but is also free of the stellar connotations which beset the epithet astral. However, the astral body does apparently retain certain semiphysical characteristics which render the word 'spirit' an unsatisfactory alternative. Nor would 'spirit' be consistent with the anti-dualistic stand we have taken.

This confusion is not a new one; clearly it existed in the minds of the ancient Egyptians who accredited the *ka* with a semi-material existence after death. We are probably correct in linking the *ka* with the astral body, since it is usually depicted as a discarnate personality endowed with all the characteristics of its owner. It is what the Greeks later called his εἴδωλον or double.* Though subordinate to the physical body, the *ka* retained an independent life of its own and could move freely from place to place, separating itself from the physical body when it wished and reuniting itself to it at will.

* The Egyptian word *sekhem* means the same.

Only after death did the *ka* permanently leave its physical counterpart and really come into its own.* It is likely that the funeral offerings found in the pyramids were intended to sustain the *ka* in its postmortem life. The Egyptians believed that another component of man was his spiritual body, or *sādḥu*, which corresponds to the consciousness we have been discussing in this chapter; it was that part of man which had obtained the knowledge and power that rendered him incorruptible. In the *Book of the Dead* a deceased person is said to 'look upon his body and rest upon his *sādḥu*',[2] and souls are further said to 'enter into their *sādḥu*'.[3] However, a more likely candidate for the part we have ascribed to consciousness is the Egyptian *ba*, a word which means 'sublime' or 'noble'. The *ba* is incorporeal and dwells within either the physical body or its attendant *ka*. Like the latter, it is often depicted as a human-headed bird. This multiplicity of names is confusing, but clearly reflects the Egyptian attempt to identify both the semi-physical astral body and the consciousness that animates it. That all these various names were but synonyms of the one thing was recognized, since it became customary to regard them all as representing the one deceased person whom religious tradition identified with Osiris. For our own purpose in this chapter we need only emphasize yet again that the astral body is not a wraith, but an etheric thought-form living in a world whose scenery is similarly the product of thought. From now on, however, we shall refer to an astral body that is animated by post-mortem consciousness as the astral self. The term 'astral body' sounds too much like a cadaver lost in space.

Probably the first thing that strikes the astral self once it has passed into the astral world is the similarity between its new surroundings and the physical world it has just left. There are trees, gardens and houses, just as on Earth, although *revenants* are apt to describe them as 'different' or 'more beautiful'. The reason for this, as has been mentioned before, is that occupants of the astral world

---

* In this respect it resembles what the Egyptians called a man's *khaibet* or shadow. This again was supposed to have an independent existence and be able to separate itself from the body, being then free to travel wherever it pleased (cf. Greek σκιά and Latin *umbra*).

It should be noted that in the East the post-mortem astral body (*mayavi rupa*) is often distinguished from the one that accompanies us through life (*linga sharira*). This, however, does not seem to be the case in Tibetan lamaism where the astral form (*delog*) enjoys a continuous existence. Here we find also that thought-forms are known as *tulpas* or *tulkus* according to the degree of permanence acquired.

more or less create their own environment, and as each has a fairly definite idea of what he wants in paradise, few are disappointed. It is also understandable that many new arrivals find their earthly habits hard to shed in an environment so closely resembling that of the material world. The Egyptians, while aware that the deceased enjoyed a 'spiritual' existence after death, nevertheless thought of it in corporeal terms,* and spiritualist accounts of the 'summerland' show the same attitude. Indeed, most spiritualistic literature consists of banal and idiosyncratic descriptions of life beyond the veil where, it seems, musically minded people gather in vast halls to listen to spirit orchestras, doctors pursue their researches in well-equipped spirit laboratories (without recourse to vivisection), great writers write, and where, since someone must keep the lawns trim, spirit gardeners garden contentedly. We even have reports of animal-lovers running rehabilitation centres for cattle slaughtered in the Chicago stockyards and suddenly transported, much to their bewilderment, to lush spirit meadows! Everyone, in short, is assured of a heavenly time, all of his own making.

However, eventually these pleasures cloy, and the moment comes for the consciousness to withdraw from the astral form and continue its evolutionary progress, either by returning to Earth to occupy the incipient astral identity of a new-born baby, or by commencing its astral pilgrimage. The mechanics of all this are a complete mystery and at this stage the processes involved admit only of speculation. We can only suppose, reasoning from the observable effects, that the experiences which make up the astral self are somehow distilled to produce the individual behind the personality. This individual, which may already have survived many reincarnations, is the quint-essential self that gravitates back to Earth or, if it has nothing more to learn there, moves joyously on towards the fountainhead.

To all intents and purposes the earthly return of the individual, the kernel, as it were, of several personalities, is on all fours with the doctrine of reincarnation which envisages a long chain of incarnations stretching behind each one of us. Such former lives are for the most part unremembered, although occasionally, as we have explained, an apparently trivial incident may induce a fleeting

---

* Thus in the fifth dynasty King Unás is said to eat well and perform all his bodily functions after death. Like the Mohammedans later, he is able to gratify his passions in the next world (*Amenti*). The other world of the Tibetans (*Bardo*) also resembled the physical world, much to the confusion of the deceased.

recollection of something that happened in a previous incarnation.* The memory chain can sometimes be reforged by a hesedic rite in which all that was past becomes present. Even so, the difficulty about remembering past lives is that the subconscious, given a free rein, will set about inventing previous incarnations that accord with its own pretensions to grandeur. This is why so many people claim to have formerly been Egyptian princesses, Chinese courtiers or Roman legionaries, and why we never find among them an erstwhile street-sweeper, stevedore or lavatory attendant.†

Occultists have the advantage over their fellow human beings in that when they die they know what to expect. Many of them will have already travelled in the lower astral during their experiments in astral projection. It is true that spiritualists share this knowledge to some extent, but the occultist, because of his long experience with thought-forms, also understands something of the laws that govern his new environment. He will not take at their face value the spirit concert halls and the spirit cows he sees grazing in spirit meadows. This does not, of course, prevent him from enjoying good music or finding pleasure in the contemplation of a pastoral scene. However, because he has spent so much of his time on Earth seeking the reality behind the forms, he will not linger as long as some in the lovely lotus land that lies beyond the grave.

But this knowledge also assists the occultist while he is still on Earth, for his belief in reincarnation enables him to regard his trials and tribulations as part of an educative process by which the individual is constantly refined so as to become worthy of its destiny.

---

* Since the emergence of mankind the population of the Earth has been increasing, although the rate has accelerated significantly only in recent years. This might suggest that the dwindling supply of earthbound individuals in the astral world does not match the growth in birth-rate. However, conceptual thinking always engenders an astral form, and if there is no astral consciousness waiting to inhabit it the form merely develops an identity of its own. In this way a new individual enters the reincarnationary scheme. Another possible problem, almost the converse of the last, might arise if the population on Earth declined, for example as a result of widespread birth-control, so that there was no opportunity for astral individuals to incarnate. This is unlikely to happen, however, since some individuals do not, of course, require further earthly experience and so the number of Earth-orientated individuals in the astral world is also dwindling.

† Occultists, even the most eminent among them, are not free from the habit. Mme Blavatsky claimed to have been Paracelsus in a previous life. Dion Fortune identified herself with Vivien le Fay Morgan, and Aleister Crowley claimed to have been, among others, Apollonius of Tyana, Edward Kelley, Cagliostro and Eliphas Lévi.

Many newcomers to occultism question the value of reincarnation, nevertheless, arguing that our inability to remember past lives robs it of any purpose. Their view is that unless we know why we have merited our present afflictions, no benefit can be gained from them. It is, they say, no good attributing adverse conditions to karma when we have no idea how the karmic debt was incurred. There is something to be said for this view, and our counter arguments can be no more than personal opinions. However, the idea that retribution for past transgressions will be meted out in subsequent lives is not essential to reincarnation; it is merely a Hindu and Buddhist interpretation of what is elsewhere regarded as a normal after-death occurrence. The ethical implications came later and an inability to appreciate them need not compel anyone to reject the phenomenon itself.

The attitude of primitive people to reincarnation is best understood if we recall that to them the 'soul' enjoyed an existence which could in certain circumstances be completely free of the body. It was this view which lent support to the theory of travelling souls. Given that these souls could travel while the body slept, it was thought that they would also escape when the body breathed its last. Their immediate ambition would then be to gain access to another body which offered them the opportunity of beginning a new incarnation. Any body, it seems, would serve the purpose, and animals or insects were frequently thought to harbour human souls. A Celtic tradition* even maintained that transmigrating souls found refuge in trees and plants, somewhat in the manner of Philemon and Baucis to whom Greek mythology attributed a similar fate. In general, however, the Greeks believed that human souls were reinstated in a human body.

There is evidence to suggest that Pythagoras believed in reincarnation, and the doctrine was certainly taught by Plato. It was later adopted by the Neo-Platonists from whom it spilled over into the Gnosticism of the first century. Metempsychosis, another name for reincarnation, was one of the heretical tenets of the Manichean movement, and the same notion cropped up again in the Middle Ages in the writings of the kabbalists. The idea was suppressed whenever possible by the Church, which envisaged then, as it still

* Julius Caesar draws special attention in his *De bello gallico* to the Celtic belief in reincarnation.

does, only one earthly incarnation followed by eternal bliss or torment according to one's deserts. In modern times the same theories
have percolated from the East where, as we have just seen, they are
closely allied to the idea of rewards and punishments. Whether you
agree with the ethical implications is a matter of choice, although in
my opinion the relentless process of death and rebirth would seem
devoid of value without some sort of moral purpose behind it. If,
however, you find the whole notion of karma and past sins alien
to you, the best course is to forget them. Instead try with Plato to
accept your present life and possible past lives as an opportunity
for continuing self-improvement, a mysterious but necessary part
of our human evolution.

To sum up, therefore, death entails the removal of consciousness
to the astral body. There it starts an existence, by all accounts idyllic,
in a thought-susceptible region of the lower astral. Gradually the
individual behind the personality withdraws of its own accord in
order to link up with a new astral body here on Earth or else proceed
on the next stage of a journey which leads, according to some, to the
beatific union of God in His glorious transcendence.

All this has little bearing on the actual practice of magic. And yet
the pursuit of practical occult knowledge should always be accompanied by speculation about the meaning of life and the part death
plays in the scheme of things. The word speculation is used deliberately; all must be speculative while so many important questions remain unanswered. It is for this reason that the views given
here must be treated as only the expression of a personal opinion.
Others – occultists, atheists or even Jehovah's Witnesses – may be
much closer to the truth. The sad thing is that some occult books
present the reader with categorical and all-too-often conflicting
statements about the nature of things. Judge these as you would
judge everything else, in the light of your own knowledge and
experience. While you practise magic, therefore, strive after a better
understanding of the laws you manipulate, the forces you unleash
and the sublime mysteries you encounter. And if by chance you are
fortunate enough to find the meaning of life, then keep it to yourself. Each man must find his own answer; if there is an answer to be
found. The light, you will remember, is within yourself.

14

THROUGHOUT this book we have been discussing what some occultists call 'low' magic. Although the epithet is intended only to distinguish one form of magic from another labelled 'high', it has managed to acquire a derogatory meaning which it scarcely deserves. Low magic, generally speaking, is magic whose rituals are dedicated to the attainment of specific ends such as making money or curing warts. There is nothing reprehensible about this; but because high magic is dedicated to more worthwhile-sounding ends like self-fulfilment or mystical illumination, it has, over the years, made other forms of magic seem vain and rather trivial.

It is silly to despise low magic, as some people do, on the grounds that it can lend itself to, selfish abuse; so, of course, can many other good things in life. Low magic is, in any case, important because it provides those who aspire to high magic with a useful apprenticeship. Eventually you will come to realize that it is only the tip of the magical iceberg and then, if it makes you feel better, you can tell yourself that you have at last caught sight of the path towards high magic. In anticipation, let us now look briefly at this path since it is here and not among simple spells and incantations that lie those 'mysteries' which are a part and parcel of the great occult tradition.

Part of this tradition maintains that human beings did not originally belong to the physical world. Instead, like the angels whose incorporeal nature they once shared, they formerly dwelt in the astral light where they could rejoice in the intuitive comprehension of God's mystery. However, unlike the angels, whose passive adoration makes them seem like docile sheep, mankind was endowed with a will of its own, a privilege God had otherwise reserved only for Himself. And it was this will, the divine spark within them, which persuaded men to rebel against the benevolent authority of God. Here we have the old story of spiritual pride, as a result of which, according to the occultists, human beings were demoted to the world of matter and, supreme indignity, clothed in flesh. Since then each one of us has inherited the blot of original sin which can be expurgated only after repeated incarnations in this valley of tears.

That at least is how the story, derived partly from Gnosticism, goes. However, evolution – if not common sense – makes nonsense of the whole theory, although if we take care to remember that it is just theory, we shall not be too put out when we encounter this and other theories in occult literature.

Nearly all esoteric schools, including, strangely enough, those that show most distaste for the world of matter, look back nostalgically to a golden age when the Earth was a young and happy place. This, in their view, was a time when great teachers, emissaries from the upper astral, went about instructing mankind in the arts and sciences. So successful were they that civilization soon reached standards of technological achievement far surpassing those of our own age. Interplanetary travel was just one feature of life in those halcyon days, enabling more teachers to travel here, this time from Mars and Venus where life had apparently advanced still further than on Earth. The Moon was quickly colonized by our ancestors, but being a cold, inhospitable place it proved unpopular compared with our own milk-and-honey world.

But this phase came to an end with an almighty bang. Some occultists say it was the fault of a few black magicians (magic being at that time both respectable and widely practised); others blame a clique of ambitious scientists who abused the knowledge they had gained. Whoever's fault it was, the bang occurred, propelling the Moon, by then decolonized, far off into space and plunging a whole continent called Atlantis into the sea. It is sometimes claimed too that one part of the Earth detached itself to form our present Moon, but there is no one view among occultists about this. All agree, however, that the Moon we now have is a late replacement.*

Not all the Earth's inhabitants perished in the great catastrophe,

---

* Alas, one of the things noticed by scientists examining recent rock samples from the Moon is that they are far older than the minerals on our Earth.

but apart from a few saintly beings, Masters of the Great White Lodge, the superhuman teachers packed their bags and went. Gradually the beautiful buildings crumbled, the works of art were destroyed and, worst of all, the books containing great wisdom were allowed to turn to dust. There then followed a regression to a primitive culture, our so-called Stone Age, and it is to history we must turn in order to see how civilization has since striven to regain its former pristine glory.

What truth is there in all this? As evidence of a prehistoric civilization, occultists point to certain Mayan relics, the terraces at Baalbek, Aztec symbolism and, unfailingly, to the mysterious stone figures on Easter Island.* It is said that the explorer Colonel Fawcett stumbled across some survivors of this civilization after his disappearance in the Brazilian jungle. Forced to live among them until his death, he is alleged to have recounted his experiences through several mediums, telling how his hosts made practical use of thought-energy a thousand times more powerful than anything known to modern science.[1]

Before we dismiss the so-called evidence adduced in support of the occultist argument, we should remember that many archaeological discoveries do pose grave problems. Those Easter Island figures, for example, weigh up to fifty tons each and no one has yet explained how they were transported to their present location from the volcanic crater of Rano-Roraku.† Then, again, there has been the discovery of objects made of various aluminium-based alloys in an ancient burial mound at Kouang-Sou in eastern China. Some of the objects found here in a tomb belonging to a general of the Tsin dynasty (313–250 B.C.) were formed of an alloy of copper and aluminium which modern metallurgy has taken two thousand years to reproduce.[2] In the same part of the world archaeologists have

---

* Most recently of all they have shown an interest in reports of man-made structures lying submerged off the coast off the Bahamas. These were photographed by the explorer Dimitri Rebikoff and have been compared with the megalithic monuments found on the continent of Europe. For further details see *The Times*, January 29th, 1971.

---

† The ideogrammatic inscriptions on the back of some of the statues have been compared with Egyptian hieroglyphics and taken to show that the island was colonized by refugees from the Old World, possibly from Atlantis. Tradition has it that these people arrived there with their leader, an Atlantean chieftain called Hotu-matua. The Polynesian-sounding name and the island's situation off the *Pacific* coast of South America render such theories very suspect indeed.

unearthed carvings fashioned from realgar, a mineral substance composed of arsenic monosulfide: realgar is both dangerous to handle and well-nigh impossible to carve. Numerous examples of the same kind can be cited. They may not make a clear case for an antediluvian golden age, but they do suggest that the case is as yet unproven.

Much the same can be said of Atlantis. We noted earlier that lost kingdoms are a subject of enduring interest to occultists, who speculate endlessly about the social *mores* in such places as Mu, Lemuria and Shamballa. But nowhere intrigues them more than Atlantis, which they regard as the former centre of all that was marvellous in the ancient world. While reconciled to the idea that Atlantis is for ever lost beneath the waves, many still claim to be in telepathic communion with some of its erstwhile inhabitants. In London there is a group which devotes itself to the teachings of a certain Helio-Arcanophus who, according to his disciples, was a leading figure in Atlantean society. Other occultists, denied access to such dignitaries, content themselves with the 'memory' of previous incarnations spent in Atlantis (whose popularity in this respect rivals that of ancient Egypt). It often happens, too, that any esoteric teaching which cannot be fitted with a credible pedigree is attributed to Atlantis. After all, apart from Helio-Arcanophus and a fellow spokesman said to live in China, there is really no one around to challenge such statements. A newcomer to occultism must ask himself therefore just what there is to the legend outside the over-heated imagination of some occult writers.

The name Atlantis is given by Plato in his *Timaeus* to an island in the Atlantic Ocean. According to him the size and position of the place were revealed to Solon by some Egyptian priests, who described it as a mighty kingdom, larger than Libya and Asia Minor combined, which, some nine thousand years previously, had been situated beyond the Pillars of Hercules. Though a martial nation whose armies, it was said, had once conquered most of the countries of the Mediterranean seaboard, the Atlanteans were apparently a happy people; in another work, *Critias*, Plato describes the ideal society they had evolved. The notion of a kingdom submerged in the Western sea crops up again later, and Arabian cartographers were particularly fond of marking the imagined location of Atlantis on their maps. From then on the myth survived intact up to the time of the Renaissance, when attempts were made to rationalize it by identifying the lost country with, among other places, the Americas, Scandinavia and the Balearic Islands. French humanists, among them Montaigne, were also inclined to accept the truth of the story, and the factual existence of Plato's island was vouched for in the eighteenth century by no less a person than Voltaire. Having survived that long, the credibility of Atlantis is, not surprisingly, still a subject of debate among contemporary scholars.

There are plenty of books on the missing continent and they make fascinating, if not over-convincing reading. Recently, two rather more objective reviews of the same subject have appeared almost simultaneously in the bookshops.[3] They identify Atlantis, not for the first time, with the early Minoan civilization which once flourished on the island of Crete. Both books argue that the volcanic eruption of Santorin, which seismologists say must have generated three times the thermal energy of Krakatoa, destroyed the Minoan civilization. Some remarkable evidence, both archaeological and geophysical, has been adduced in support of this theory, although none of it satisfactorily explains why Plato located Atlantis far to the west of Crete beyond the Straits of Gibraltar.

For myself, I tend to the view that centuries before our era began there may well have been a country which became the Atlantis of folk memory. There may even have been several such places, since many old stories tell of the disappearance of islands, promontories and coastal cities. The original Atlantis had probably reached a comparatively high level of cultural and technological development, perhaps because it enjoyed certain natural advantages. Its people, freed from the struggle to survive, may have devoted themselves to art and philosophy, so earning the esteem of their less fortunate neighbours. The exact fate of the country may never now be known, but whatever happened the memory of its achievements could easily have survived.

But formidable arguments can be marshalled against even this view. For one thing there is the curious absence of any detailed records of Atlantis until the time of Plato. Even then the Egyptian priests who recounted the story to the visiting Solon failed to specify the cause of the calamity that befell the island. It seems odd, if not suspect, that this catastrophe should fade into oblivion while the memory of Atlantis persisted. Perhaps the most damning argument of all is the fact that history affords neither the time nor the cultural gap to accommodate a lost civilization. In the end the real explanation of Atlantis may lie in human psychology: people want to believe in it. Thus, whatever its historical validity, the place has by now been assured of an archetypical existence – and there's no knocking that!

Let us leave Atlantis and move on to consider the occultist view of the post-Atlantean world and its inhabitants. Although most occultists would object to being called racialists, it remains true that much of their writing is concerned with race. Some of it, especially the unblushing exaltation of Aryan virtues* found in books produced in the 1930s, might well have gladdened the heart of Adolf Hitler. Nowadays the emphasis has changed slightly. Faced with the encroaching tide of miscegenation, occultists confine their racial theorizing to the seven divisions of the Atlantean race and their history. It seems that with the unhappy end of the golden age these seven sub-races diffused to become the root-races of all the ethnic groups now overcrowding our planet. The term 'root-race' is a confusing one, however (racial prototype might be a better expression), since it is also the name given in esoteric literature to the main colour divisions of mankind.

Whatever root-races really are, each of them had at one time its own Manu or Instructor whose task it was to guide the race entrusted to his care along a preordained path. Occultists believe that the memory of these and other Manus, such as Merlin, Odin and Osiris, lingers on in folklore where the original instructors have become heroes and demigods. In her book *Applied Magic* the occultist Dion Fortune lists a few of the better-known Manus:

Rama was the Manu of the Aryan Race.

Melchizedek was the Manu of the Chaldean and early Semitic Races in addition to his Atlantean connection.

Narada was the Manu of the First Atlantean Race.

---

* E.g. Dion Fortune, *Applied Magic* (Aquarian Press, London, 1962), p. 85: 'The White Race contains not only the most evolved – the Aryan – but also the Semites ... Owing to certain Atlantean errors, the Jewish section of this Race have brought the Archetype to the West without themselves being fitted to use it. This is the "Curse of the Jews" and dates from long before the birth of Jesus.' These post-diluvian races are not to be confused with the four earlier races which are said to have preceded our present species. Of these some were semi-physical, some giants and some hermaphroditic.

Asuramaya was a Manu of an earlier Lemurian Race which had mingled with the early Atlanteans, and he 'lived' in Atlantis in these earliest days. He was the 'teacher of the starry wisdom' to the ante-diluvian world even as was Melchizedek to the post-diluvian, and was the first astronomer. In Atlantis he worked with and under Narada. Euclid – who is a Lord of one of the Wisdom aspects of the Western Tradition ... was not only a great human teacher but also had on the Inner Planes an aspect manifesting a direct 'beam' from Asuramaya (somewhat analogous, but less in degree and origin, to the manifesting of the Christ by the Lord Jesus), which was more than an 'overshadowing'.[4]

In addition to its Manu, each race also possesses a guardian angel whose job it is to watch over the archetypical idea which the particular race represents. This archetype is the original divinely conceived racial pattern, and its angelic custodians are sometimes referred to as the 'personalized principles of Archetypical Fire'. These personalized principles see to it that their ethnic protégés settle in the territory assigned to them, there to establish themselves as one nation or more. An angel of this sort is believed to have watched over the Jewish people while they journeyed under Abraham's leadership from Ur to Canaan and again when they were led out of Egypt by Moses.[5] It is further claimed that while each nation remains strong or true to form, its archetypical consciousness will always be attuned to the mind of its guardian angel. However, once decay sets in, the racial angel promptly absconds, transferring its stewardship to another nation whose character better reflects the angelic driving force or inner principle.

The difficulty about examining the occult view of race is that as a general term the word 'race' is not one of which ethnologists are over-fond. For example, they would shudder at the way some occultists speak of a Celtic race, since according to them the Celts were a mixed bunch of people who just happened to share a common language. But let us for a moment forget the niceties of ethnology and consider the evidence derived from our own experience. This surely indicates that just as there are physical and mental differences among individuals, so there are similar differences among groups of people. And these groups we may, for want of a better word, call races. To admit such differences is not, of course, to assert that one race is inherently superior to another. We are merely saying that geographical and environmental factors can – and do – determine group as well as individual characteristics, thanks to which certain races may develop particular aptitudes. It is for this reason that occultists will often speak of the 'green ray' of the Celtic race, as a result of which the Celts possess a strong romantic streak manifesting itself in their music and poetry. To this extent generalizations about race, though no less fallible than other generalizations, can be said to be borne out in reality.

From here it is not too difficult to go on to accept that if an intelligent motivation underlies every evolutionary process in the universe, then the development of racial groups is no exception. You will recall that in magic an angelic agency is generally held responsible for the evolution of each species. Racial angels can be regarded therefore as agencies of this sort, since it is they who guide the members of a race towards their collective destiny. As guardians of the racial archetype, they also personify that ethnic over-soul which has so fascinated C. G. Jung and his school.

This is not to deny that external factors are responsible for racial characteristics; the existence of racial angels suggests only that these factors may occur more by design than by accident. In other words, although they may well be the tools by which races are fashioned, they really tell us nothing of the hand that wields them or the pattern it copies. Unlike the ethnologist, who studies effects and their immediate causes, the occultist contemplates the whole ethnic scheme and finds it to be consistent with what he already knows of the universe.

But by stating that racial characteristics are angelically imposed we introduce determinism with all its attendant difficulties. And this time instead of individuals it is whole races who are bound up in a remorseless karmic system. However, even this appears quite reasonable once we relate it to the theory of reincarnation: racial differences have always been necessary to ensure that reincarnating 'souls', with all their divergent educative needs, are satisfactorily catered for on Earth. For some, a life in the New Guinea bush may be just what they require, while for others the most suitable classroom may be the floor of the London Stock Exchange. In this light the history of each race can be seen as a therapeutic process designed for the good of its members, which lends some meaning to the apparently undeserved suffering endured by some races and the relative comfort of others.

Like all determinist theories, however, this one has its pitfalls. The admission that races get what they deserve may do much to reassure the better-off among them, but will hardly appeal to the less fortunate. More serious still is the risk that such thinking will lead among the former to an easy acceptance of the status quo. This, after all, is what has been happening in the world until quite recently although, hopefully, men are now becoming less concerned with what divides them and more aware of their common humanity.

At first sight this new trend may seem to invalidate the emphasis which occultists have in the past placed on races and their angelic guardians. In fact, it is a logical development of the esoteric view, as we can see when we reflect on the fact that individuals are constantly reincarnated in order to improve themselves. Although there may be lapses from time to time, the general reincarnating trend must be a progressive one. As the years go by an increasing number of those who come back to Earth have less and less to learn, thanks to the experience they gained in previous lives. Thus the demand for such basic self-tuition as might be gained from a Stone Age existence in Papua is fast declining. For that reason the time has now come when the Papuans and other formerly backward races can begin to prosper. There is still, of course, a gulf between the rich and poor races, but with the passing of time this gulf will grow smaller as the need for it declines. In short, the spiritual evolution of mankind is detectable in the progress currently being made towards racial harmony and universal understanding.

These then are some of the theories that form the background to high magic. Again it must be stressed that they are only theories, and nobody is obliged to accept them. One final theory has still to be mentioned, however, and that is the esoteric belief that history can be divided into aeons of time, each coinciding with a phase of mankind's evolution. This idea is thought to originate in Hinduism, where the racio-cultural development of mankind is fitted into a Great Cycle of 25,900 years. This cycle is split up into twelve ages, each lasting about 2,000 years and named after one of the signs of the zodiac.* Because of the retrograde motion of the

* There is, of course, a respectable astronomical basis to all this, for we know that the spring equinox moves across the ecliptic at the rate of one zodiacal sign in every 2,000 years. The Greek astronomer Hipparchus (190–120 B.C.) was the first man in the West to discover this precession.

zodiacal equinoxes we are moving backwards through the twelve signs and have now come upon the threshold of the Aquarian Age, having just left the Piscean Age whose archetypical teacher was Jesus Christ. Rather than dismiss all this as a fanciful notion, we would do well to remember that the Hindu scriptures have been proved right on this sort of thing in the past. One thousand years before Copernicus the Brahmans taught that our earth was not the centre of the universe: from here they went on to calculate the age both of the Earth and of the universe in terms of light years which correspond with the latest estimates put forward by modern astronomers. It would be unwise therefore to regard the notion of zodiacal ages as the product of a superstitious geocentric mentality.

Even so, much nonsense has been written about the Aquarian Age, most of it by people who, like the late Mrs Besant and others, had a vested interest in its arrival. The truth is that we can do no more than surmise what the new age will be like. Often it is described as the golden age of man, presumably because utopian conditions will then prevail over the whole planet. For the present, however, we are said to be witnessing the demise of the sorrowing, sin-obsessed aeon of Pisces and its gradual replacement by the joyful humanism of the new era referred to sometimes as the era of Horus. This, of course, fits in perfectly with contemporary liberal trends, although many Renaissance men and women must have thought that they too were in at the start of a new age: the old order keeps changing.

The details of the Aquarian Age can be left for its self-appointed prophets to work out. As far as occultists are concerned, a sure sign of its coming will be a resurgence of interest in their subject. This, as we saw in our Introduction, is already happening. To some extent an interest in occultism is quite understandable in a century which, more than any other, is dedicated to scientific materialism; for it represents a reaction against the stifling omnipresence of technology, a refusal to accept science as the final arbiter on such matters as life, death, love and beauty. At one time men might have turned to organized religion for comfort, but formal theology is now tottering on its shaky foundations. People turn to occultism not, as some argue, because it is anti-rational, which it is not; rather because it alone promises to show that there may be more to man than science yet allows.

Magic nowadays is ceasing to be covertly esoteric and is emerging into the clear light of day, whence it should never have been banished. It still remains esoteric in the sense that only a few are aware of its mysteries, but they are no longer the secretive minority they once were. Who are they? A few years ago it would have been correct to say that they were the spiritualists, Theosophists and several other '-ists' both ancient and modern. But this may no longer be the case. Magic may in the end owe its revival not to the traditional stalwarts of occultism but to those young people all over the world who are now seeking to understand life through the exploration of the communal unconscious. By their use of drugs, music, meditation techniques and visual experiments they hope to induce states of consciousness which will open their minds to the transcendental reality behind the world of form.

These young people have not banded themselves into groups and as yet have no common philosophy. All they have done is sense that there may be more to life than the utilitarian existence towards which our materialistic society is orientated. Many have chosen to 'drop out' of our society altogether, while others, wiser perhaps, have tried to see if they can work out a more satisfactory alternative for themselves. Knowing that they and all around them are fundamentally one harmonious universe they strive to impart this message by their own, not always successful, example of peace and love and service.

But although they are more than just social reformers, it would be an exaggeration to dub such young people occultists. Certainly most of them have never thought of themselves in this way. And yet they are travellers on the path of magic. The trouble is that so few of them know it. As a result their search for life's meaning lacks the discipline which would direct their steps to the reality of the astral plane. In its absence they content themselves with the euphoria that comes from discovering a hitherto unknown dimension to life. They can thus rejoice at the existence of the astral world but, being ignorant of the passwords, cannot yet gain access to its full wonder. Here magic can help, for it is the means by which these Beautiful People, sons and daughters of Aquarius, can find that realm of being for which they, more than the rest of us, yearn like homesick children.

*

And here we come to the end of our introduction to
Or, as magicians would say at the end of their rituals, *Te*
it is over. In these pages I have tried to show that magical be
perfectly reasonable and not merely a curious aberration affe
certain people. Nor is it a form of escapism, as Freud thought.*
the contrary it seeks not to avoid the real world but to get to know
it better. If I were to sum up the aim of magic, I would describe
it as a search for that ultimate reality of which form is but the
external appearance. This, of course, is also the aim of mysticism.
But the mystic differs from the magician in that for him the visible
world conceals the reality he is seeking and for that reason must
be shunned. The magician, however, knows that matter merely
reflects reality so that by studying its manifested form he will
eventually discover its unmanifested essence.

Not all those who practise magic are aware of these things to
begin with. Often their ambitions are immediate and severely practical. Given time, however, the significance of the results that can
be obtained by ritual will strike all but the most myopic practitioner.
Without expecting it even he will suddenly find that he has been
brought face to face with the one tremendous secret that will trans-
form his life. At once he will start to wonder why he never saw it
before, forgetting that the nearness of a miracle can often blind
us to its presence.

For the successful occultist, therefore, magic becomes a way of
life and not a substitute for it. To him belongs the deep satisfaction
derived from identifying himself with the macrocosm of which he
is a tiny part. By attuning his mind to the universal forces around
him, he is able to expand his consciousness until everything is contained within himself. This he does by inducing supernormal states
of consciousness which enable him to contact forms of existence
that are not usually a part of our human experience. Hence his use
of symbolism, since it is the means by which concepts normally
impossible to define or comprehend can be rendered accessible
to the conscious mind. At the same time this same symbolism
awakens in the magician's subconscious all the intuitive knowledge
already stored there as part of his human inheritance. One with the

* In his *Psychoanalysis and Telepathy* (1921) Freud contends that an interest in
occultism is due to a need to compensate for feelings of personal inadequacy arising
from certain childhood experiences.

universe, he gathers up into his present all that was and will be, discovering a magical self-fulfilment by which he can both lose and find himself. His end, therefore, is but a beginning. May it be the same with this book.

τετέλεσται ἀλλά μόνον ἄρχει

APPENDIXES

APPENDIX 1 MAGICAL RECIPES

HERBS HAVE always interested the occultist, who recognizes in them Nature's way of promoting health and curing disease. In addition to their natural properties, however, they also possess certain occult virtues. That is why some of those named in this Appendix have no known medicinal value but have been included because of their hermetic significance within the universal system of correspondences.

Ideally, the herbs you use should be freshly gathered, although dried herbs are almost as good. When no specific astrological advice is given, the magician should gather his herbs while the Moon is waning in the spring or early summer months. The best time of day is just after the Sun has evaporated the early-morning dew. Care should be taken to see that the herbs are quite dry when picked, since wet herbs have a habit of turning mouldy.

Herbs can be dried by hanging them in bunches in a well-ventilated room, or spreading them out on shelves where they can be turned at regular intervals. In a cold climate the drying process may be accelerated by placing the herbs in a warm oven. When ready, the herbs can be used in any of the following ways:

i. *Brews*

These are prepared by putting fresh or dried herbs in a pan of water (usually one large handful of herbs to two cups of water) and heating it slowly almost to boiling-point. The mixture is then allowed to simmer gently for a further five minutes before being removed from the heat and left to stand overnight. If stored in a cool place this brew will keep for up to four days and even longer if intended only for external use.

ii. *Tinctures*

The preparation of tinctures is equally simple. In general, the combination is two ounces of powdered herb to one quart of liquid (alcohol, surgical spirit or pure vinegar). The mixture is stored in an airtight bottle for two weeks and the bottle shaken vigorously several times a day. The tincture is then ready for use.

iii. *Oils*

Here a handful of herbs is crushed to a powder and then placed in a half-pint bottle which is three-quarters filled with fine oil and a teaspoonful of pure vinegar. The tightly corked bottle should be placed in hot sunlight and shaken daily. Alternatively, the mixture may be warmed gently for an hour or so each day by placing the bottle in a bowl of water which is then heated slowly. The whole process takes roughly three weeks. A fortified oil can be prepared by straining off the oil every fourth day and adding it to a fresh supply of herbs.

iv. *Salves*

In this case the newly ground herbs are pounded into a fatty base, such as that provided by an ordinary, bland cold-cream. The combination is usually one tablespoonful of herbs to three ounces of cream. Another method is to add the herbs to some liquefied lard which is then heated for a further fifteen minutes before being strained off into a suitable container.

In magic, herbal oils and creams are widely used and were often mentioned during the witch trials. It was alleged that they made the wearer invisible, rendered him immune to pain and enabled him to fly through the air. These nocturnal flights were customary whenever witches and warlocks set forth to attend a sabbat. What they probably entailed was a successful projection of the astral body, although most people, including the participants, were convinced that their physical bodies became capable of flight. Imagination may also have played a part in this, since the most widely used salves contained belladonna or opium, both of which were calculated to produce hallucinations. These concoctions are described in detail by Wierus in his book *De praestigiis daemonum et incantationibus ac veneficiis*, liber iv (Basel, 1563). The Witches' Ointment given here is based on his writings.

1. OILS AND SALVES

(i) *Oleum magicale no.* 1

This is a general-purpose unguent of proven efficacy. An almost indispensable accessory to magical work, it may be prepared in a liquid (oily) or solid (cold-cream) base.

> *Lycopodium clavatum* (devil's claw)
> *Euphorbium* (wolf's milk)
> *Clematis vitalba* (traveller's joy)
> *Convolvulus arvensis* (cornbind)
> *Sambucus nigra* (elder)
> *Artemisia absinthium* (wormwood)
> *Umbellifera* (poison hemlock)
> *Atropa belladonna* (deadly nightshade)

The plants called ramping fumitory and red spur-valerian may be used as alternatives to any of the first six ingredients, with henbane an alternative to either of the last two.

Clematis vitalba and *Convolvulus arvensis* are advised for open-air work. Among other things they will, if combined with laurel leaf, assure you of good weather!

(ii) *Oleum magicale no.* 2

The second of the general-purpose oils is widely used in modern magic since it is particularly useful when dealing with the elemental kingdoms. It can have a liquid or solid base. Unfortunately, its narcotic ingredients mean that this *oleum* is sometimes difficult to prepare. The quantities should be carefully noted.

> Betel 30 gr.
> *Potentilla* (cinquefoil) 6 gr.
> *Hyoscyamus niger* (henbane) 15 gr.
> Opium extract 50 gr.
> *Atropa belladonna* (deadly nightshade) 15 gr.
> Cantharides 5 gr.
> Indian hemp 250 gr.

According to some authorities these ingredients should be added to a base composed of powdered sugar and gum tragacanth.

(iii) *Oleum Angelorum (Oleum magicale no.* 3)

This salve induces a pleasing numbness of the body and a sweet languor of spirit which are conducive to both meditation and the perception of astral forms. Often the adept will drift off after a time into a gentle sleep during which his subconscious will learn many things about the inner planes and their inhabitants.

Base: almond oil

Apium palustre (wild celery)

Aconitum lycotonum (wolf's-bane)

Populus balsamifera (poplar)

or

Betula lenta (sweet birch)

Atropa belladonna (deadly nightshade)

or

Hyoscyamus niger (henbane)

(iv) *Witches' Ointment*

This recipe, given by Wierus, was greatly favoured by medieval witches. It must be prepared on the day of Mercury and in his hour. It is important, too, that at the hour of its preparation the Moon should be in one of the air or earth signs and waxing. The appropriate signs are Taurus, Gemini, Virgo, Libra, Capricorn, Aquarius.

Umbellifera (poison hemlock)

Frondes populeae balsamiferae (poplar leaves)

Aqua aconiti lycotoni (juice of wolf's-bane)

Fuligo (soot)

2. TONICS

(i) *Aurum Potabile*

*Melissa officinalis** (balm)
Ocium basilicum (sweet basil)
Lonicera periclymenum (honeysuckle)
Calendula officinalis† (marigold)
Heather honey to sweeten‡

(ii) *Universal Medicine*

Mentha viridis (mint)
Convallaria majalis (lily-of-the-valley)
Lonicera periclymenum (honeysuckle)
Senecio vulgaris (groundsel)
Erica (heather)

A standard brew is prepared using wine as a base.

(iii) *Balm of Azoth*

Tanacetum vulgare (tansy)
Scabiosa arvensis (scabious/gipsy rose)
Ruta graveolens (rue)

Helianthenum canadense (rock rose)

or

Adiantum capillus veneris (maidenhair fern)

or

anthriscus sylvestris (chervil)

---

* Paracelsus was especially fond of this herb – as are the bees who have given it its name.

† The marigold is known as 'Aurum Solis' or Solar Gold.

‡ Some modern occultists use royal jelly as well as honey. This is the fluid which bees feed to their queen. It is obtainable from apiculturists and health-food shops, but its nutritional value is debatable.

(iv) *Rōs Vitae*

Orchis maculata (orchis)
Rosmarinus officinalis (rosemary)
Medicago sativa (alfalfa)

These ingredients are used to produce a small quantity of essential oil based on an oil of roses which can be prepared from fine oils and rose petals. Before use, the orchis tubers are finely ground and mixed with a little honey.

(v) *Potio Priapi (Herbal Aphrodisiac)*

Much nonsense has been written about aphrodisiacs – from rhinoceros horn to oysters and champagne. This little recipe depends on the amoritic virtues of vervain or *Herba Veneris* when used in conjunction with fennel. Both herbs may be combined in an infusion; or fennel water, obtainable from herbalists, may be used to prepare an infusion of vervain. These herbs are native to Britain, and should be gathered on a Friday, preferably during the passage of the Moon through the first ten degrees of Taurus or Virgo. The Moon should also be well aspected with Saturn and Venus.

Verbena officinalis (vervain)
Foeniculum vulgare (fennel)

3. COSMETICS

(i) *Witches' Eye-bright*

Boil one dessertspoonful of celandine (*Chelidonium majus*) and one of elderflowers (*Sambucus nigra*) in a pint of water. When required for use mix the herbal brew with one part milk and apply as an eye lotion.

(ii) *Skin Lotion*

Gently warm half a pint of buttermilk to which has been added a handful of elderflowers (*Sambucus nigra*), marigolds (*Calendula officinalis*), some geranium leaves and one or two garlic cloves. The mixture should simmer for forty minutes before being removed from the heat and left for five hours. It must then be reheated and have an ounce of honey added to it. When cold it may be used as a first-class restorative for jaded complexions.

(iii) *Anti-wrinkle Lotion*

Follow the previous instructions using half quantities and substituting the following herbal ingredients:

> *Arthemis nobilis* (chamomile)
> *Nymphaea alba* (white pond-lily leaves)
> { *Fragaris vesca* (strawberry leaves)
>
> or
>
> *Sambucus nigra* (elderflowers)
> *Dispacus fullorum* (teasel)

(iv) *Wart Cure*

Among the many wart removers recommended by folklore are the following applications:

> Juice of greater celandine (*Chelodinium majus*)
> Juice of poppy seed (*Papaver rhoeas*)
> Pulped houseleek (*Sempervivum tectorum*)

Supplement your efforts with a caustic pencil (*causticum medicamentum!*) obtainable from any chemist's shop.

WHEN YOU begin to study magical textbooks for yourself, you will find that not only have you to reject what is patently silly in them, but you must also spend time trying to work out the precise meaning of much that is left. This is because magicians have always had a liking for making things as complicated as possible. After pages of allegorical language they will frequently abandon the vernacular and launch into Sanskrit, Hebrew, Greek or Latin. Provided you have some knowledge of these languages or can at least lay your hands on a dictionary, you should be able to surmount even this obstacle. But worse is to come, for many magical texts are littered with enough cyphers and hieroglyphics to keep more than a dozen Champollions busy.

The alphabets illustrated below are designed to help you interpret some of the strange scripts you are bound to come across sooner or later.* Fortunately, many of the authors of magical books are on closer acquaintance not really as erudite as they wish to appear: what may look at first like Greek or Hebrew often consists only of English words transcribed into Greek or Hebrew characters. For that reason alphabets of both these languages are included in this Appendix.†

* Most of these alphabets are given in a famous compendium of occult lore called *The Magus or Celestial Intelligencer; being a complete system of occult Philosophy* by one Francis Barrett, published in London in 1801. Despite the 'great variety of curious engravings' which are promised on the title-page, and which include ten portraits of fiends, the opus is inexpressibly tedious.

† Not all magical languages are as simple, however. The Enochian tongue disclosed to Dr Dee (q.v.) by the angels and the Senzar language spoken by the Masters have a vocabulary and syntax of their own.

HEBREW ALPHABET

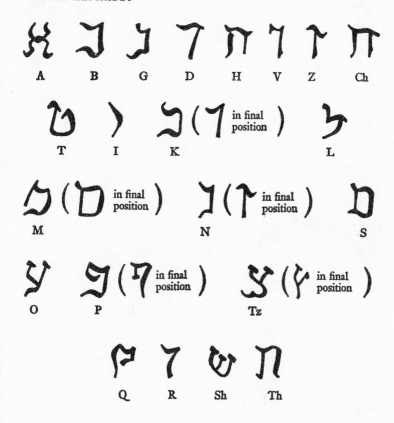

A	B	G	D	H	V	Z	Ch

T	I	K	(in final position)	L

M (in final position)	N (in final position)		S

O	P (in final position)	Tz (in final position)

Q	R	Sh	Th

THEBAN ALPHABET*

A	B	C	D	E	F	G	H	I	K	L	M

N	O	P	Q	R	S	T	V	W	X	Z	

* Theban is often used for talismanic inscriptions. So too is the 'Writing of the Magi'.

CELESTIAL SCRIPT

RUNIC OR FUTHORC ALPHABET

MALACHIM ALPHABET

The script known as 'PASSING THE RIVER'

WRITING OF THE MAGI

A MASONIC/ROSICRUCIAN ALPHABET

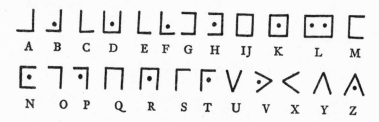

HIEROGLYPHIC ALPHABET

Based on the scholarship of Sir E. A. Wallis Budge (*The Egyptian Language*, Routledge and Kegan Paul, London, 8th ed., 1966), this script is used by some enthusiasts to prepare talismans.

GREEK ALPHABET

Aα	Bβ	Γγ	Δδ	Eε	Zζ	Hη	Θθ	Iι	Kκ
A	B	G	D	E	Z	Ee	Th	I	K

Λλ	Mμ	Nν	Ξξ	Oo	Ππ	Pρ	Σσ	Tτ	Υυ
L	M	N	X	O	P	R	S	T	U

Φφ	Χχ	Ψψ	Ωω
Ph	Ch	Ps	ō

OGHAM* ALPHABET

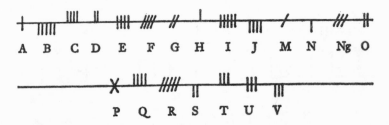

* Named after Ogamus, the Gaulish god of speech. Some occultists believe this to have been the written language of Atlantis.

THE PERSON who decides to study magic will often find himself in company as strange as anything he may encounter in the lower astral. In this Appendix he is introduced to some of his companions, past and present, in the art. The next few pages can offer no more than a short selection, but even so they introduce a motley crowd of people. Among them are saints, sinners, cranks and sages, most of whom showed a not ignoble ambition to penetrate the mysteries of nature. Some pursued knowledge for its own sake, or for the good of humanity. They, alas, are the minority. But whatever the faults of the others, who sought knowledge in order to profit from it, they are rarely dull. That, in the end, may be their saving grace.

Abano, Pietro de (*c.* 1250–1310). An Italian philosopher who studied medicine in Paris, then returned to Padua to practise as a physician. There he wrote some highly respected medical books as well as a treatise on magic called the *Heptameron* or *Magical Elements*. Accused of practising sorcery by the Inquisition, he was acquitted, but was later rearrested. He died in prison while awaiting trial.

Abaris (*fl.* 400 B.C.). This Scythian magician, famous for his long fasts and extraordinary feats of levitation, deserves a mention because he is reputed to have been the tutor of Pythagoras (q.v.).

Abramelin (*c.* 1400). Little is known of him except what can be gleaned from the introduction to the *Book of Sacred Magic, as delivered by Abraham the Jew unto his son Lamech* (1458). In this introduction, Abraham tells how he learned the secrets of the kabbalah from his father Simon before travelling to Egypt and thence to Constantinople, where he came across the secret books of Abramelin. In occultism there persists a tradition that those who follow Abramelin will sooner or later come to a sticky end. It may be a little unfair always to blame Abramelin, but at least you have been warned!

Agrippa (*Cornelius Agrippa von Nettesheim*) (1486–1535). This is the famous Agrippa whose work *De occulta philosophia* is a comprehensive defence of magic. In it the author argues that magic offers us the means of understanding God and His manifestation in nature. This book, and others in which Agrippa attacks *inter alia* the Church's distortion of the original Christian message, brought him not unexpectedly into conflict with the Inquisition. Agrippa travelled widely in Europe, and was both a soldier and a physician. In 1510 he was sent on a diplomatic mission to England. A sequel to the *De occulta philosophia* was later published by an imposter who styled himself 'Agrippa'. In it we are given detailed instructions on exorcism and the conjuration of spirits.

Albertus Magnus (*c.* 1200–80). The Great Albert, Bishop of Ratisbon, was a *doctor universalis*, or man of wide learning, who earned distinction as a scholastic philosopher, scientist and theologian. He was also an accomplished alchemist, and discovered the Philosophers' Stone, which enabled him to effect the transmutation of metals. Among his other recorded achievements is the construction of a statue so life-like that it became endowed with the gift of speech. He could also control the weather and perform a wide variety of marvellous feats. His posthumous reward was canonization by the Church in 1931.

Apollonius of Tyana (*fl. c.* 4 B.C.). A Greek philosopher who travelled widely in the East and is said to have visited India, where he was initiated into the Mysteries. The narrative of his travels, given by his disciple Damis and reproduced by Philostratus, is so full of wondrous events that by the Middle Ages Apollonius had come to be regarded as an entirely mythical character. Among his recorded exploits is the story of how he reanimated the corpse of a Roman matron who had died a short time previously. Besides working this and similar miracles, Apollonius went about preaching love and the forgiveness of one's enemies. In many ways his life resembled that of Jesus and, like him, Apollonius was believed to have ended his earthly mission by ascending bodily to heaven. Many Western occultists now regard him as their *Magister*, or spiritual patron, and commemorate his life by an act of dedication performed around sunset on May 1st. In 1854 the magician Eliphas Lévi (q.v.) performed a ceremony designed to summon the shade of Apollonius, but the experiment had somewhat mixed results.

Bacon, Roger (1214–92). A philosopher and lecturer at the University of Paris, he became a Franciscan in 1247, and later he lectured at Oxford; there his profound interest in mathematics, astronomy and chemistry developed. His great ambition was to provide a scientific foundation for the magical ideas prevalent in his time, and he conducted careful experiments to test his ideas on magic, alchemy and divination. He was imprisoned for four years after being accused of demonism by the superiors of his Order, and died a year after his release. His definition of philosophy is nowadays accepted by many magicians as appropriate to their art: 'The end of all true philosophy is to arrive at a knowledge of the Creator through knowledge of the created world.'

Barret, Francis. Author of a learned treatise called the *Magus or Celestial Intelligencer* (1801), which is described on the title-page as a complete system of occult philosophy. The book is likely to daunt anyone save the most dedicated student of magic, but is useful because it recapitulates almost everything contained in the old *grimoires*: Agrippa, Abano, the pseudo-Solomons, these and others are conscientiously plundered by the industrious Barrett. In addition, he offers his readers 'private instructions and lectures upon . . . the RITES, MYSTERIES, CEREMONIES and PRINCIPLES of the ancient Philosophers, Magi, Cabalists, Adepts, &c'. Those who would bring their minds to a contemplation of the 'ETERNAL WISDOM' were invited to present themselves at an address in Marylebone between the hours of eleven and two. It is not known who or how many visited the Magus in his private chambers, but it is possible that Bulwer Lytton (q.v.) was among them. Barrett is also believed to have gone to Cambridge to help run an occult fraternity at the university.

Benedict IX (d. 1045). One of the many popes who, by reputation at least, were gifted exponents of magic. Others include Gregory VIII, John XX, Alexander VI and Silvester II. The last-named is better known as Gerbert, a specialist in nigromancy and inventor of a bronze head capable of prophetic utterances.

Berossus (d. 280 B.C.). While a priest of Bel at Babylon, he translated the standard textbook on astrology into Greek. In later life he settled on the small island of Cos where many came to hear his prophecies. He has the dubious honour of being the accredited author of several *grimoires*.

Beuther, David. An alchemist who flourished in the seventeenth century, and was imprisoned for refusing to reveal his secrets. He committed suicide rather than part with them.

Blavatsky, Helena Petrovna (1831–91). Shortly after her eighteenth birthday, Mme Blavatsky deserted her home in Russia and her husband of two months in order to travel. Such travels are the classic beginning to many occult careers, but in her case they ranged farther and wider than most. She is believed to have visited Canada, North America and Mexico before setting out for India. Next she tried, unsuccessfully at first, to enter Tibet, eventually gaining access to that mysterious country in 1856. Afterwards she returned to Russia whence she emerged to fight for Garibaldi at the Battle of Mentana. The year 1873 saw her in New York, where she investigated the spiritualistic phenomena then in vogue. Although she accepted the genuineness of the raps and knocks heard in the seance room, she poured scorn on what she called their 'spooky' origin, and demonstrated that she could obtain the same and better results without recourse to ghostly assistance. By 1873 she had already attracted some devoted admirers, among them a Colonel H. S. Olcott (1830–1907) who was to be her lifelong 'chum', and William Q. Judge, future recipient of many of the Mahatma letters.

On November 17th, 1875, she and her friends founded the Theosophical Society. It aroused little interest at first, but in 1877 Mme Blavatsky produced her controversial masterpiece *Isis Unveiled*, which purported to be an esoteric history of mankind and religion. Two years later, Mme Blavatsky set sail again for India where the Theosophical Society was reconstituted in the Madras suburb of Adyar. Soon the phenomena were coming thick and fast, to the growing horror of Christian missionaries and the embarrassment of local Buddhists. In spite of scandals and a devastating report produced by an investigator from the Society for Psychical Research, the Theosophists continued to grow in numbers. When Mme Blavatsky, who had long been a sick woman, died in 1891 she had, it was estimated, some 100,000 disciples in countries all over the world. Mme Blavatsky's death is commemorated by the Society on May 8th ('White Lotus Day').

The years following her death were turbulent ones for the Society, with many defections from its ranks. It has, however, managed to survive the 'Christianization' inflicted on it by Mrs Besant (1847–1934), the bogus visions of 'Bishop' Leadbeater and the desertion of Krishnamurti. Unfortunately these batterings have left it somewhat hypersensitive to criticism, but there are hopeful signs that it is now becoming more robust and outward-looking.

At some time or other every occultist must tackle Mme Blavatsky's formidable opus *The Secret Doctrine*, although until one finds the courage to do so her *Key to Theosophy* is a quite satisfactory substitute.

Bolingbroke, Roger. An Oxford prelate who was also an astrologer and magician. In 1441 he was hanged for trying to murder Henry VI by demoniac means.

Bruce, Margaret. Miss Bruce sells ritual incenses and scents to practising magicians. She has also compiled a short book (*The Little Grimoire*) of folksy spells, charms and recipes. Her articles in the esoteric magazines have a refreshingly commonsensical approach to magic which, like the late Mr Crowley, she spells with a final 'k'.

Bulwer Lytton, E. G. E. L. (Lord Lytton), (1803–73). Author of works like *The Caxtons, The Last Days of Pompeii* and *Zanoni*, was a prolific writer of imaginative fantasies. Among these are *A Strange Story, The Coming Race* and *The Haunted and the Haunters*. He was a keen student of magic and was initiated, it is said, into its mysteries by Francis Barrett (q.v.). He was also a friend of Eliphas Lévi (q.v.), whom he entertained in London. With Lévi's assistance, Lytton is believed to have set up his own esoteric order which, according to the writer Montague Summers, still flourished in post-Second-World-War Cambridge.

Butler, W. E. A practising magician who is also the author of several books of which the first (*Magic: its Power, Ritual and Purpose* [Aquarian Press, London, 1961]) is by far the best. The others (*The Magician: his Training and Work*, 1963, *Apprenticed to Magic*, 1965, and *Magic and the Quaballah*, 1968, all Aquarian Press) are more wordy but less informative.

Cagliostro, Alessandro di, Count (1743–95). His real name was Guiseppe Balsamo but he changed it to Count Cagliostro during his early travels, which took him to Greece, Malta and Egypt. He also visited Rhodes, where he studied occultism under Althotas. On returning to Italy he married Lorenza Feliciani, and the happy couple promptly set out on a grand tour of Europe during which they amassed a considerable fortune through the sale of love philtres, rejuvenating potions and alchemical catalysts. But things did not always go well for the *soi-disant* count; he was incarcerated in the Bastille and later spent time in the Fleet Prison in London. His luck finally deserted him on a visit to Rome in 1789, when he was arrested and sentenced to death for being a heretic. The sentence was commuted to life imprisonment, and after enduring great hardship Cagliostro died in San Leo Prison in 1795.

Casanova, Giovanni Jacopo (1725–98). Casanova, son of an actor, was brought up in Venice where for a time he became a theatre violinist before setting out on his first round of travels. During these he became interested in the cognate sciences and was received into a Masonic Order in Lyons in 1750. Later he joined the Egyptian Order founded by Cagliostro. In 1755 he returned to Venice, where he was accused of practising sorcery and sentenced to five years' imprisonment. But Casanova had no intention of languishing in jail for that length of time. On October 31st, 1756, he achieved that spectacular escape which he was to describe in his famous *Histoire de ma Fuite* (1786). Once out of prison, he journeyed to Paris where he was entertained by all the best people. More travels followed, among them a trip to London. In spite of his reputation for magic, he received an honour from the Pope. After a period during which he was a spy for the Venetian authorities, he returned to Bohemia where he had a post as librarian and archivist. During his lifetime he composed verse and operatic libretti and even produced a translation of Homer's *Iliad*. More important were his *Mémoires* which provide us with a fascinating glimpse of the eighteenth-century *beau monde*.

Cellini, Benvenuto (1500–71). In his autobiography (*Vita scritta da lui medesimo*) the Florentine goldsmith and sculptor has given a valuable description of two necromantic conjurations he attended in Rome in 1534. The rites took place in the dead of night in, of all places, the ruin of the Coliseum. We quote an extract from his own description of the episode on pp. 199 ff. of this book.

Cobham, Eleanor. She was the wife of Humphrey, Duke of Gloucester, and this probably saved her life when in 1441 she was accused, together with Margery Jourdain, 'the witch of Eye', of practising necromancy and witchcraft. Her sentence was banishment to the Isle of Man, where she is said to have founded one of the covens that still meets there.

Crowley, Aleister (1875–1947). His real name was Edward Alexander Crowley, but he soon exchanged this for Aleister Crowley who, as the Master Therion, saw himself as 666, the Great Beast of Revelation or, more prosaically, 'The Wickedest Man Alive'. His magical pedigree was certainly a good one, for he claimed to be the re-incarnation of both Edward Kelley (q.v.) and Eliphas Lévi (q.v.). Originally associated with the Hermetic Order of the Golden Dawn (he was initiated on November 18th, 1898), Crowley, or Frater Perdurabo as he was called, decamped after an abortive attempt to gain control of the organization. Guided by astrology, the *I Ching* and, before he abandoned her, his wife's clairvoyance, he travelled to America, Mexico, Egypt and Hong Kong, practising magic as he went. In 1920 he established his famous Abbey of Thelema in Cefalu, Sicily, where, as in Rabelais' fictional abbey of the same name, the motto was 'Do as thou wilt.' Stories of drug-taking, sexual orgies and even child-sacrifice soon began to circulate, until in the end Mussolini ordered Crowley's expulsion from Italy. Back in England, Crowley's cultivated beastliness could scarcely compete with the increasing beastliness of Hitler, and the Master Therion was largely forgotten by the public when he died in 1947. Details of his life and magic may be found in *The Great Beast*, by John Symonds (Rider, London, 1951), *The Magic of Aleister Crowley*, by the same author (Muller, London, 1958), *Aleister Crowley*, by

Charles Cammell (University Books, New York, 1962) and *The Magical Dilemma of Victor Neuburg*, by Jean Overton Fuller (Allen, London, 1965).

The rituals Crowley describes in his writings are based mostly on those he learned while a member of the Order of the Golden Dawn, but he adapts these to suit his own personal philosophy. Not all the changes he made were happy ones and his work, while of immense value to the experienced occultist, cannot be recommended to beginners. Crowley's *Confessions* have recently been published (Jonathan Cape, London, 1969).

Dashwood, Sir Francis (1708–81). Founder of the notorious Hell Fire Club whose members, known as the Monks of Medmenham, met in the mid-eighteenth century. They were reputed to celebrate obscene parodies of the Mass, although it is more likely that all they went in for was a little communal debauchery. In a famous etching by Hogarth, Dashwood is depicted worshipping a tiny nude Venus.

Davies, Ann. This lady currently describes herself as 'Supreme Chief of Builders of Adytum', a cult based in Los Angeles and devoted to the 'Science of Ageless Wisdom'. Members are promised that their innate spiritual faculties will be developed through a study of the Tarot and kabbalah.

Dee, Dr John (1527–1608). A distinguished English mathematician and competent astronomer, Dr Dee taught at the universities of Louvain, Brussels and Paris before returning to England in 1551. There for the next thirty years he taught navigation to sea captains and indulged his lifelong enthusiasm for the occult sciences. It was these that eventually attracted the attention of the Court, and he was asked to decide the most astrologically propitious date for the coronation of Elizabeth I. Afterwards the queen used regularly to summon him to give her instruction in arcane matters.

Dee's practical experience of magic began when he met Edward Kelley, a younger man who possessed the mediumistic gifts which the Doctor, with all his learning, lacked. The new partnership turned out to be a great success with the two of them sharing everything, including their wives. In 1583 they set off together for Poland and Bohemia where they were entertained by kings and princes, all dabblers in occultism. It is sad to relate that despite his knowledge of magic and alchemy, Dr Dee died in poverty at Mortlake, while the unfortunate Kelley came to a mysterious and possibly violent end. Some of Dee's writings are now kept in the British Museum and the famous mirror, or *speculum*, in which Kelley had observed the spirits has also been preserved.

An account of Dee's magical work will be found in Charlotte Fell-Smith's biography, *John Dee* (London, 1909) and in Richard Deacon's more recent study, *John Dee, scientist, geographer, astrologer and secret agent to Elizabeth I* (London, Frederick Muller, 1968).

Encausse, Gérard (1865–1921). Best known as Papus, author of a standard textbook on the Tarot (*The Tarot of the Gipsies*), he was something of an occult 'all-rounder', famous for his talent as an alchemist, astrologer, healer and magician. His other books are now difficult to obtain; they include *The Knowledge of the Magi*, *The Kabbala* and a *Treatise on Practical Magic*. During the First World War Papus made several predictions about German strategy which are said to have been remarkably accurate. The members of his *Ordre des Inconnus Silencieux* are thought still to meet in Paris.

Faustus, Dr Johannes (?–1538). Immortalized in the etching by Rembrandt and plays of Marlowe and Goethe, the historical Dr Faustus was born in Würtemberg and earned a legendary reputation for his marvellous feats of magic. He was also the author of many books, although not all the *grimoires* later attributed to him are in fact his own work.

Fludd, Robert (1574–1637). A philosopher with a strong mystical bent, he became acquainted with the writings of Paracelsus (q.v.) on his travels in Europe. He himself was the author of two famous books, *The Mosaical Philosophy* and *Summum Bonum*, in which he presents his own version of the cosmogonic theories of the kabbalah. According to Fludd all creation proceeded from God, who is the sum total of everything, and all will eventually return to Him. The act of creation he saw as a separation of two principles, the active (light) and the passive (darkness), within the unity of God. Since then three 'worlds' have existed, the first being God or the divine archetype, the second the universe or macrocosm, and the third man or the microcosm. In addition to his interest in the kabbalah, Fludd was an ardent Rosicrucian. He is also claimed by the Freemasons as one of their own.

Modern occultists perform rituals dedicated to enlightenment on the anniversary of Fludd's death on September 8th. These involve meditating on the celebrated diagram of Man the Microcosm in his *Utriusque Cosmi-Historia*.

Forman, Dr. A highly respected occultist who lived in the seventeenth century. For a long time he was *persona grata* at the court of King James VI of Scotland.

Fortune, Dion (nom de plume *of Mrs V. M. Penry-Evans*, née *Firth*). Dion Fortune is the darling of contemporary occultists. She came to magic via the Hermetic Order of the Golden Dawn but later established her own Society of the Inner Light. For the rest of her life (she died in 1946) she wrote stories, essays and a treatise called *The Cosmic Doctrine* (Ernest Benn, London, new ed., 1970) which has often been compared with *The Secret Doctrine*, although the comparison is unfair to Mme Blavatsky.

Throughout Dion Fortune's work there is a curious contradiction between her many flights of fancy and the sober approach to magic she ceaselessly advocates. That this paradox was something inherent in Miss Fortune's own temperament is borne out by her tendency to condemn sexual emancipation while professing to be a disciple of Freud. Her book *An Esoteric View of Sex and Marriage* (Aquarian Press, London, new ed., 1964) is unintentionally hilarious.

Despite these faults, Miss Fortune's lucid prose is compulsory reading for all would-be magicians. Her books include *Applied Magic, The Esoteric Orders and their Work, Practical Occultism in Daily Life, Psychic Self-Defence* and *Sane Occultism*. All are published by the Aquarian Press in London.

The Society of the Inner Light still functions, although apart from conceding that its founder's books are in places rather dated, it has itself done little to modernize occultism.

Fox, Kate and Margaret. The sisters Fox were never magicians but are included here because they are generally regarded as the founders of modern spiritualism. Their story begins in Hydesville, a small town near Rochester, Pennsylvania, in 1848, where strange rapping sounds were heard one night coming from a room where the girls slept. When their frightened parents ventured into the room they found their daughters sitting up in bed conversing with the invisible agency responsible for the tapping. The adults, soon joined by curious neighbours, hastily devised a code by which the spirit could answer questions by giving an appropriate number of raps. In no time at all Kate and Margaret were demonstrating their mediumship to packed audiences in major American cities, being joined later by an older sister who, not to be outdone, had discovered that she too shared the family's psychic gifts. Other people copied them until the whole country was swept by a veritable fever of knockings, rappings and table-turnings. When this had reached its height the sisters astonished everyone by confessing that the manifestations were one big hoax. The raps, they explained, were produced by dislocating the toe and other small joints in their feet. But far from finishing the girls' career, this revelation gave it a boost. Crowds flocked more than ever to witness the dexterity with which the Misses Fox clicked their joints on command. Then one sister announced that her confession had been false and that the spirits did after all produce the raps. A confusing series of confessions, retractions and more confessions followed until it became impossible for anyone to tell where the truth lay. In the meantime rival mediums had begun to produce phenomena far more spectacular than anything managed by the toe-clicking Foxes. The three of them slipped unobtrusively off the spiritualist bandwagon which they above all others had helped to launch. They died, it is said, of drink.

The sisters are still remembered by spiritualists to the extent that most regard 1848 as the year when the modern movement began. But a discreet silence surrounds the young ladies and their noisy exploits. And who can blame the spiritualists? There are quite a few popes whom the Vatican would prefer to forget.

Gafferel, Jacques (1601–81). A practising French kabbalist of wide learning who had the post of librarian to Cardinal Richelieu.

Gardner, G. B. Before his death a few years ago, Gardner, who was already in his late seventies, became the self-appointed Pope of British witchcraft. His first book on the subject, *Modern Witchcraft* (Rider, London, 1954), is a vulgarization of Dr Margaret Murray's earlier findings, but his second, *Witchcraft Today* (Rider, London, 1957), is more interesting. On his retirement he became curator of his own museum of witchcraft at Castletown on the Isle of Man. This curious institution is now run by Gardner's heirs, who claim to have inherited also the high rank he had assumed for himself in the witch movement. Such a claim was more than some witches could stomach and so they promptly transferred their allegiance to a rival pontiff who lived in the north of England. As a result British witchcraft, like the fourteenth-century Church, is rent by schism.

Gaufridi, Louis. In his lifetime he was known as the Prince of Sorcerers, although no amount of sorcery could keep him from the gallows where he met his death in 1611.

Gessner. A German farmer who was convinced that treasure lay buried in his orchard. To discover its exact whereabouts he and two friends, called Heichler and Zenner, resolved to question the spirits. For this purpose they engaged the services of a young man, Weber, who was a student at the University of Jena. Weber possessed the magical instruments needed for the proposed evocation. The seance took place, without Heichler, in a small hut on Christmas Eve, 1715. When Heichler visited the hut some fifteen hours later, he found Gessner and Zenner both dead, the latter's body hideously mutilated, and Weber unconscious. That night three men were sent to guard the hut, but by the following morning one was dead and the other two gravely ill. There is a theory that the deaths were caused by the fumes from some charcoal burning inside the hut; but that in no way explains the mutilation of Zenner's body or the terrible story told by the surviving guards once they had regained their senses.

Grant, Kenneth. A disciple of the late Aleister Crowley and his successor as head of the *Ordo Templi Orentis*, a branch of a German order founded by Theodor Reuss. Its teachings are allegedly based on those of the Knights Templar. With John Symonds, Crowley's biographer and literary executor, Grant has recently edited *The Confessions of Aleister Crowley* (Jonathan Cape, London, 1969).

Guaita, Stanislas de. An active nineteenth-century occultist who tried to revive Rosicrucianism on the Continent. His philosophy was based on the acceptance of evil as the balancing force in life.

Guibourg, Etienne (1602–80). An elderly priest who between 1673 and 1679 conducted amatory masses for Mme de Montespan, whose nude body provided him with his altar. During this rite he would slit the throat of a small child and allow its blood to gush into a chalice resting on Mme de Montespan's stomach. Flour was added to the blood in order to make the wafer which, duly consecrated, was then dedicated to Astaroth and Asmodeus, twin powers of Darkness. Later the amatory Masses were succeeded by Masses intended to cause Louis XIV's death, which Mme de Montespan supplemented by trying to poison him. It was her attempts to administer these poisons that finally led to the investigation which brought the whole sordid business to light. It is not known how many children were immolated by Guibourg in his effort to serve the royal favourite, but he was executed for his pains.

Hermes Trismegistus. His name means Hermes Thrice Greatest, but his true identity is unknown. The neo-Platonists declared him to be the Egyptian god Ṭehuti (Thoth), but others have claimed that he was either Adam or Adam's grandson. His importance in magic is due to the so-called Emerald Tablet which succinctly sets out the 'as above, so below' principle on which most magical theory is based. He was also the fabled author of forty-two books about the life and philosophy of ancient Egypt.

'Honorius'. The accredited author of a famous *grimoire* called the *Constitution of Honorius* (1629), which has been attributed to Pope Honorius III (1216–27). Its rituals are a Christianized version of the sort of thing found elsewhere, notably in the *Key of Solomon*. Eliphas Lévi (q.v.), who claimed that the book's author was in fact the anti-pope Honorius II, argues that in it 'superstitious and sacriligious forms' are used to conceal its secrets from the un-initiated.

Iamblichus (250–325). This philosopher, founder of the Syrian school of neo-Platonism, is not highly thought of by historians of philosophy since he complicated Platonism by splitting up the assumed realities of the spiritual world and inserting intermediary categories between them. He was also the author of a theurgic treatise *On the Mysteries of the Egyptians, Chaldeans and Assyrians*, in which he aimed to reconcile Neo-Platonism with the beliefs of pagan religion. Like modern magicians, Iamblichus believed in the ritual conjuration of cosmic forces under the appearance of traditional god-forms.

'*Inquire Within*'. Anonymous author of two rather silly books, *Light-Bearers of Darkness* (1930) and *The Trail of the Serpent* (1936), which argue that behind occultism there lies a nefarious plot to assume control of society.

Kardec, Allan (Léon-Hyppolite-Denizart Rival) (1804–69). Kardec was the father of continental spiritualism. His *Spirits' Book* (Lake, Sao Paolo, new ed., n.d.), a series of questions and spirit answers, is described as the bible of modern spiritualism. Kardec's tomb at Père La Chaise cemetery in Paris remains a place of pilgrimage for the faithful.

Kelley, Edward (see Dee, Dr John).

King, George. Founder in 1956 of an occult group, whose aims were to disseminate the teachings of one Aetherius who lives on Venus and communicates through Mr King. As their effort towards world peace, members 'charge' mountains with a cosmic power channelled through certain space-intelligences who circle the earth in flying saucers.

Knight, Gareth. Author of *A Practical Guide to Occult Symbolism* (Helios Books, Toddington, 1964). This work contains Mr Knight's reflections on, among other things, the Tarot and the Tree of Life. He is also, with W. E. Butler (q.v.), responsible for a correspondence course on the kabbalah.

Koh Hung. A Chinese sage who lived in the fourth century and wrote a book on charms called the *Pao Poh-Tze*. His essays on alchemy still exist.

Kramer, Heinrich. His main claim to notoriety is that he was co-author with Jacob Sprenger of the *Malleus Maleficarum* or *Witches Hammer* (Hogarth Press, London, new ed., 1969). Published in the fifteenth century, this terrible book described ways of identifying and dealing with witches. The ecclesiastical authorities used it as their vade-mecum in the great witch-hunts that were to follow. A few years ago an English translation was produced by the Rev. Montague Summers.

La Voisin (d. 1681). An infamous sorceress whose real name was Catherine Monvoisin. She became the confidante of many ladies in the French Court to whom she sold love potions and other amorous charms. Her services extended also to the provision of Black Masses, for which she recruited the help of the renegade priest Etienne Guibourg (q.v.). Her most famous client was the Marquise de Montespan, mistress of Louis XIV, who sought Satanic help to retain the king's affection. The full extent of La Voisin's influence came to light after Louis ordered an investigation into her activities. So many important people were found to be involved in the scandal that things were hushed up, although La Voisin, being expendable, was put to death.

Leon, Moses de (d. 1335). A Jewish scholar who is thought to have brought the *Zohar*, a kabbalistic work, to Spain in the thirteenth century.

Lévi, Eliphas (*c.* 1810–75). Eliphas Lévi was the adopted Hebrew name of Alphonse-Louis Constant, later to become one of the important modern writers on magic. Originally destined for the Church, he was expelled from his seminary because of unorthodox views and a socialist conscience. After an unsuccessful marriage he turned his mind to occultism and became connected with a school of magic said to have been established in Cambridge by Francis Barrett (q.v.). His philosophy is contained in two books, *Le Dogme et rituel de la haute magie* (1854–6) and *Histoire de la Magie* (1860). Both have been translated into English and are still in print under the titles *Transcendental Magic* and *The History of Magic* (Rider, London, 1968 and 1969 respectively). Before completing his second book Lévi reverted to the Catholic faith, but though ceasing thereafter to regard magic as the one true science, he remained fascinated by it. The experienced student will find in Lévi's books much that is useful and interesting and much that is pretentious and nonsensical as well.

It was Eliphas Lévi who, though normally averse to necromancy, attempted in 1854 to communicate with the spirit of Apollonius of Tyana. Compared with the extravagances of Lévi's usual literary style the description of the evocation given in *Transcendental Magic* is remarkably straightforward.

Lewis, H. Spencer. The founder in 1915 and subsequently Imperator of the Ancient Mystical Order Rosae Crucis (A.M.O.R.C.), which has its headquarters in California and claims to be the sole guardian of Rosicrucian truths. For so many dollars down and the rest in instalments the organization offers nothing less than the complete mastery of life. This extraordinary service comes in the form of a correspondence course which can be supplemented – at extra cost – by the Imperator's own books on reincarnation, Atlantis and the meaning of the pyramids. The pyramids feature prominently in both the text and illustrations of the society's literature, the rest of which offers further courses to help disciples win high rank in the movement.

Other less prosperous Rosicrucian fraternities exist, but, rich or poor, none has been able to prove its direct descent from the original Christian Rosenkreuz.

Luly, Raymund (1235-1315). A Spanish alchemist and keen student of the kabbalah, which in his lifetime became popular among Jewish intellectuals living in Spain. He was apparently successful in obtaining alchemical gold, which is sometimes called *aurum raymundi* in memory of him.

Magus, Simon. The Samarian whose story is recounted in the New Testament (Acts viii). He was converted to Christianity on witnessing the superior skills of Philip as he went about healing the sick. To show his renunciation of magic Simon hurled his occult books into the sea, a foolhardy gesture he lived to regret, for his conversion did not last long. Non-biblical accounts of his subsequent career, for example those of Iranaeus and Hippolytus, tell how he launched a gnostic-type religion of his own. His end, however, was a sad one; convinced that anything Christ could do he could do better, Simon instructed his followers to bury him alive. When he failed to resurrect on the third day, he was dug up and found to be dead.

Master John. A shady character from the fourteenth century and an enthusiastic necromancer. He was accused of plotting to murder Edward II by magical means.

Maternus, Julius Firmicus. A Roman writer of the fourth century who studied magic at Alexandria. On his return to Rome he composed a lengthy defence of astrology and divination called the *Mathesis*.

Mathers, S. L. 'MacGregor'. S. L. Mathers (the MacGregor was a Scottish addition which both he and Aleister Crowley adopted in their Celtophile phase) first came into contact with what was to become the Hermetic Order of the Golden Dawn when a friend, Dr Woodward, showed him certain ritual texts he had come across in some old books. At Mathers's suggestion Woodward, himself the leader of the *Societas Rosicruciana in Anglia*, showed the texts to Rosicrucian colleagues in Nuremberg where they were recognized as genuine documents pertaining to a German branch of Rosicrucianism called the L... L... L... (Licht, Liebe und Leben). The Imperatrix of the German Order, one Anna Sprengel, authorized the Englishmen to set up a British Chapter to be known as the Golden Dawn. Its members included Annie Horniman, W. B. Yeats, Arthur Machin and A. E. Waite. The rituals set out in the ancient documents formed the basis of the ceremonial used by the Golden Dawn in their Isis-Urania Temple, but there is evidence that Mathers contributed much from his own head and his private researches in the British Museum – where, incidentally, he first encountered W. B. Yeats. Mathers married the sister of Henri Bergson, the French philosopher, and settled in Paris. His magical name was Deo Duce Comite Fero and his book, *The Kabbalah Unveiled* (Routledge, London, new ed., 1970), is still obtainable.

Merlin. The historical Merlin (Myrddin) was probably a bard who lived in the first half of the sixth century when, according to tradition, he attended the court of King Arthur. He is said to have been buried on Bardsey Island. The name was picked up by Geoffrey de Monmouth, whose fanciful *Vita Merlini* (*c.* 1145) was to provide the basis for subsequent legends about the great wizard of the Arthurian cycle. He has since become the patron of druidic magic (although it is unlikely that he ever met a Druid in the sixth century), and of many occultists of Celtic stock. An esoteric order known as the Lux Merlini was recently set up to establish contact with the Inner Planes tradition of which Merlin, rightly or wrongly, is believed to be the head. As Spenser has pointed out:

> For Merlin had in Magick more insight
> Than ever him before, or after living wight.

> (*The Faerie Queene*, Book III, Canto 3)

Molay, Jacques de (b. 1244). Founder and Grand Master of the Knights Templar, he was burned at the stake after King Philippe IV of France had ordered the arrest of all the Knights. Among other things they were accused of sodomy, trampling and spitting on the Cross, and worshipping a horned idol named Baphomet. The obscene kiss, or *osculum infame*, was another of their pastimes which shocked contemporary opinion. Eliphas Lévi claimed that the French Revolution represented the Templars' revenge for the persecution they had suffered in the thirteenth century. The Order is said to have been re-established in 1902 by a German, Theodor Reuss.

Mora, Pietro. A notorious magician who dwelt in Milan at the beginning of the seventeenth century. There he practised nigromancy, alchemy and, it was rumoured, the Satanic Mass. He was also accused of poisoning people and being responsible for spreading the plague. As our knowledge of these crimes stems entirely from a confession Mora made under torture, he may not have been so wicked after all. His book *Zekerboni* came into Casanova's possession and helped convict him of sorcery in 1755.

Murray, Jacqueline. Leader of an occult group, the Atlanteans, who as their name suggests derive their inspiration from the lost Continent of Plato's *Timaeus*. A former High Priest of Atlantis, Helio-Arcanophus, communicates with members through the mediumship of their leader. With the existence of Atlantis itself in doubt, that of its High Priest is yet more difficult for outsiders to accept.

Nectanebus. An Egyptian king who reigned in the fourth century B.C. and a magician of considerable prowess. He had a gift for prophecy which enabled him to see the outcome of battles, and on at least one occasion to escape disaster. Tradition maintains that he travelled to Greece, where he set himself up as a physician and occultist.

Neuburg, Victor (1883–1940). Neuburg, poet and critic, was also Frater Omnia Vincam in Crowley's magical Order, Argenteum Astrum. There he was subjected by his mentor to all sorts of indignities, although he probably accepted these as a necessary part of his magical training. In the East it is quite common for a *guru* to treat his *chela* or apprentice with studied cruelty, while nearer home the respected Gurdjieff was none too gentle with his pupils. In addition, Neuburg was Crowley's sexual partner in many magical operations.

Nostradamus (1503–66). Nostradamus, whose real name was Michel de Nostre-Dame, was a favourite of Catherine de Medici, physician-in-ordinary to Charles IX and a well-known figure at Court. His enduring celebrity is due to *Centuries* (Lyon, 1555), a book of prophetic poetry in which many world events are foretold. Unfortunately the ambiguous language in which the prognostications are couched makes it difficult to assess their accuracy. The book was put on the Index by the Church in 1781.

d'Olivet, Fabre (1768–1825). An occultist who wrote a famous work called *The Restitution of the Hebrew Tongue*, in which he sought to revive the religion of Pythagoras. His knowledge of that religion came by way of his wife who was clairvoyant. He was also the author of a *Catechism of Cabbalistic Principles*.

Papus (*see* Encausse, Gérard).

Paracelsus (*c.* 1490–1541). Born at Einsiedeln in the canton of Schwyz, his real name was Theophrastus Bombast von Hohenheim; he changed this to Aureolus Paracelsus partly in order to show his superiority to Celsus. After studying at Basel he became for a time the pupil of Tritheim (q.v.), who introduced him to occultism. Afterwards he lectured on medicine but was dismissed from his post on account of his controversial views. More travels followed, until he died at Salzburg where he had enjoyed the friendship and protection of the archbishop.

Paracelsus is often described as the father of modern medicine although his theories – like his esoteric speculation – owe a great deal to the misunderstandings and superstitions of his age. The mainstay of his occult system was the Hermetic view that human life is inseparable from that of the universe. From there Paracelsus went on to assert that the clay from which men are made, the *limus terrae*, was a compound of every chemical element in existence. Foremost among these chemicals were salt, sulphur and mercury which in healthy people were bound together by *Archaeus*, a subtle force situated in the stomach. Paracelsus sought to heal his ailing patients by immersing them in mineral baths so as to make up for any deficiency in their chemical composition and encourage the *Archaeus* to function properly. Of more interest to us nowadays are his views on the power of thought and the prevalence of the universal mind. He also has much of interest to say on the elemental kingdoms in his *De nymphis, sylphis, pygmeis, et salamandris*. His death is commemorated on September 24th, and healing operations which invoke his assistance are performed on that day.

Paris, Guillaume. A medieval magician who, like Pope Silvester II and the famous Robert of Lincoln (Robert Grossetête), manufactured talking statues.

Pasqually, Martines de (1715–79). A French occultist whose followers, the *Frères du Sieur de Pasqually*, still have a few Hermetic lodges in north-eastern France.

Postel, Guillaume de (1510–81). A noted astrologer and kabbalist who was often in trouble with the Inquisition. He claimed to have received hidden knowledge which he embodied in a book called *The Key to Things Kept Secret From the Foundation of the World*.

Prophetissa, Maria. Known also as Mary the Jewess, this lady was thought by her contemporaries to be none other than Miriam, the wily sister of Moses. She worked as an alchemist in Alexandria in the fourth century and designed a special furnace for spagyric experiments. The term 'bain-Marie' still used in chemistry and cooking owes its origin to her.

Pythagoras (569–470 B.C.). Occultists cannot truly claim the great philosopher-mathematician as one of their own. However, his theories on the transmigration of souls and the significance of numbers have earned for him their profound gratitude. How many of these theories are actually those of Pythagoras is uncertain, for according to Aristotle many disciples used falsely to claim that their own pet theories had been received from the lips of the Master. The Stoic philosopher Diogenes Laërtius associated the teachings of Pythagoras with those of druidism.

Rais, Gilles de (1401–40). After a distinguished military career, during which he accompanied Joan of Arc to Orleans, he began to squander his vast fortune until at last he had to resort to magic in an effort to replenish the empty coffers. His first experiments were unsuccessful, but things began to look brighter when a Florentine priest called Prelati offered him his services. Unfortunately, Prelati's familiar, Barron by name, had a liking for small children, 140 of whom were sacrificed in his honour. Gilles's confession, though made under torture, makes gruesome reading. He was hanged, repentant, on October 26th, 1440.

Rasputin, Gregor Efimovitch (1871–1916). Many stories surround the Russian monk, including, inevitably perhaps, one that makes him out to be a practising magician. During his lifetime he exercised tremendous power over those who came in contact with him, but this was probably due to the force of his personality rather than magic. Rasputin believed that within him there burned a divine spark enabling him to offer salvation to those who sought it. Salvation, however, demanded repentance, and repentance presupposed sin. Thus Rasputin is said to have encouraged his followers to sin heartily so as to have something worth repenting later.

The circumstances of his death after a supper party at Prince Youssupoff's palace are well known.

Regardie, Dr Israel. Since 1920 Dr Regardie has done much to remove the excessive secrecy surrounding modern occultism. His account of the Golden Dawn rituals, once a collectors' piece, is now generally available (*The Golden Dawn, an encyclopaedia of practical occultism* [Llewellyn Press, St Paul, Minnesota, 1970]) as are his other books. These include, from the same publishers, *The Philosophers' Stone*, *The Middle Pillar* and *The Eye in the Triangle*, this last being a study of Aleister Crowley. All appeared in new editions in 1970.

Reuss, Theodor. In 1902 Reuss set up a German Order (*Ordo Templi Orientis*) which still exists and claims to continue the teachings of the Knights Templar. Aleister Crowley was initiated by Reuss and allowed to establish an English branch of the Order known as the *Mysteria Mystica Maxima*. The M.M.M. was later assimilated into Crowley's own Argenteum Astrum.

Ripley, George. A fifteenth-century occultist who claimed to have discovered the Philosophers' Stone. He also experimented with an *aurum potabile* which he had distilled and which he hoped might provide him with the elixir of life. He died of old age.

Rosenkreuz, Christian (1378–?1484). Rosenkreuz and Rosicrucianism are first mentioned in a book called *Fama Fraternitas* which turned up between 1610 and 1615. It tells how Rosenkreuz journeyed to Damascus, Arabia and Egypt, where he acquired great wisdom. On his return to Germany he chose eight friends to whom he imparted the secrets he had learned. Each then departed to a different country in search of recruits. For the next 120 years the fraternity remained secret, until one day a member came across the vault in which lay the perfectly preserved body of its founder and some valuable documents. Once these papers had been distributed among the brothers the tomb was resealed and its whereabouts is now unknown.

Some commentators contend that Rosenkreuz is a mythical character whose 'life' is an allegorical history of the Rosicrucian movement. In modern times there are some fifty Rosicrucian groups in existence, not to mention the Rose–Croix Order in Freemasonry. The largest existing fraternities are based in America where H. Spencer Lewis (q.v.) founded the Ancient Mystical Order Rosae Crucis while his rival R. Swinburn Clymer created the *Fraternitas Rosae Crucis*. Both claimed to have inherited the ancient wisdom of their Rosicrucian predecessors, Lewis going as far as claiming that his group is directly descended from a secret brotherhood that has numbered Solomon, Plato, Jesus and Benjamin Franklin among its members.

Saint-Germain, Comte de (c. 1710–?80). Said to have been of Portuguese-Jewish origin, the mysterious Count appeared at the French Court in 1748 where he astonished everyone with his vast knowledge and fluency in every major European language. The thing which really intrigued his contemporaries was his claim to be over two thousand years old. The story he gave was that having discovered an alchemical elixir which halted senescence, he had succeeded in staying a perennial thirty-year-old. The tale was widely believed and its teller credited with the most wondrous magical secrets. He was the author of a manual *La Très Sainte Trinosophie*, and Cagliostro tells us that Saint-Germain was the founder of Freemasonry in France.

In 1760 he journeyed to England and stayed there for two years before going off to Russia where he captivated the Empress Catherine. More travels followed before he eventually settled in Schleswig-Holstein. There he taught magic to Landgrave Charles of Hesse-Cassel until his death in 1780. There are reports, however, that he was seen in Paris in 1789 and then elsewhere in Europe. He is even believed to have turned up, as spry and erudite as ever, at a diplomatic reception on the eve of the last war.

These and similar stories have made Saint-Germain something of a hero among occultists. According to the Theosophical Society, he is to be counted amongst the Masters, but before accepting this claim the reader should examine the chapter devoted to him in Professor E. M. Butler's *Myth of the Magus* (Macmillan, London, 1948).

Sanders, Alec. A male witch, rather given recently to boasting in the press of his familiarity with demons and devils. As will be gathered, he and his coven are not averse to publicity. They are even happy to perform their rituals on the stages of suburban cinemas.

Schröpfer, Johann Georg (1730–74). A teacher and practitioner of the magical art, he was known as the 'Illuminatus of Leipzig'. On one occasion he conducted a seance for Prince Charles of Saxony. It is recounted that he once dispatched a fiend to torment one of his adversaries. However, the demon found its intended victim dead on arrival, and furious at being thwarted returned to plague Schröpfer. In desperation the magician shot himself one morning in a wood on the outskirts of Leipzig.

Scot, Michael (*c.* 1175–1232). After studying at Oxford and Paris, Scot became one of the many scholars at the Court of Frederick II. There he produced several books dealing with the occult sciences (*Super actorem spherae, De Sole et Luna, De chiromantia*). These became exceedingly popular in the fifteenth and sixteenth centuries when new editions regularly appeared.

Many legends grew up around Scot, the most famous being one that tells how he met his death. According to this, Scot had once predicted that he would be killed by a stone weighing not more than two ounces. In order to protect himself, therefore, he always went about with a helmet on his head. But Fate was not to be cheated. One morning in church, just as the unsuspecting Scot raised his helmet at the elevation of the host, down fell the fatal stone.

Sir Walter Scott has more to say about him in a note to his *Lay of the Last Minstrel*, where the opening of the magician's tomb is described. Michael Scot is also mentioned by Boccaccio and figures in Dante's *Inferno* (Canto xx, 115–17).

Scot, Reginald. He was the author of a book called *Discouerie of Witchcraft* (1584) which he intended to be an exposure of ceremonial magic and the 'cozenors' who practised it. In it he gives a description of many ritual processes, most of them derived from the *Pseudomonarchia daemonum* of Wierus (q.v.). However, his contemporaries, far from being put off by what they read, were fascinated. The book was frequently reprinted and emerged in 1665 with copious additions by an anonymous author who, unlike Scot, took his magic seriously. The most substantial additions are to the section called 'A Discouerie of Devils and Spirits'.

Sibly, Ebenezer (b. 1757). Known as the Prophet Sibly, he was a physician who in 1790 published his *New and Complete Illustration of the Occult Sciences*. He held that all in nature had a prophetic meaning, and sought in his lifetime to make that meaning known to his contemporaries.

Solomon. With the passing of time, Solomon's wisdom was extended to occult law, so that by the first century A.D. the historian Josephus could report that the biblical king had power over all the spirits of the infernal world. Soon afterwards his name began to recur in the folklore not only of Europe but also of India, Ethiopia and China. By the Middle Ages he had become a universal figure, a Lord of the Occult, who was expert at magic, alchemy, astrology and much else besides. Many magical textbooks were ascribed to him, the most famous being the *Testament of Solomon* which recounts the king's magical exploits in autobiographical form, the *Lemegeton* or *Lesser Key of Solomon* which contains a catalogue of the demoniac powers, and most notable, the *Clavicle* or *Key of Solomon* which remained for centuries the happy hunting-ground of magicians and scholars.

Solomon is revered also by the Freemasons. A legend surrounding his construction of the Temple lies at the heart of their *corpus symbolicum*.

Spearman-Cook, Gladys. This lady presides over an organization known as the School of Universal Philosophy and Healing. Students of the School, which is situated in the Holland Park area of London, receive their instruction from an enlightened Venusian whose mouthpiece is none other than Mrs Spearman-Cook herself. Recently the Venusian has entered the political arena on the side of the Labour Party. Apart from his opinions on the Socialist Theocracy, the same Venusian has to his credit some bizarre views on flying saucers, nutrition and sex.

Steiner, Rudolf (1861–1925). It was while at Berlin in the 1890s that Steiner began to develop his theories about a state of perception totally independent of the senses. This spiritual perception was a product of the higher self and enabled man to become aware of an otherwise imperceptible spiritual world. This world is probably identical to the astral world of esoteric tradition. In 1902 Steiner became associated with the Theosophical Society but ten years later founded his own Anthroposophical Society, whose headquarters were the Goetheanum at Dorlach in Switzerland. The original Goetheanum was burned down in 1922 but a new edifice soon took its place. There Steiner died in 1925. A philosopher, scientist and artist of considerable merit, he is remembered also for his practical contribution to education, agriculture and the cure of mental illness.

Tritheim, Johann (1462–1516). Abbot of Spanheim and friend of Agrippa (q.v.), he was profoundly interested in alchemy and hermetic science. His book *Liber octo quaestionum* contains a classification of demons which is still accepted by some magical lodges. Tradition has it that Tritheim once exorcized Mary of Burgundy, wife of the Emperor Maximilian.

Waite, A. E. In the 1890s, when its members were quarrelling among themselves, Arthur Edward Waite took over the stewardship of the London branch of the Hermetic Order of the Golden Dawn. At once he set about Christianizing its rituals to the dismay of his more pagan brethren, who resigned by the score. A formidable scholar, Waite was responsible for, among other things, translating Eliphas Lévi's books into English. Waite's autobiography, *Shadows of Life and Thought*, has two chapters on the history and organization of the Golden Dawn.

Wierus, Johannes (1516–88). A pupil of Agrippa (q.v.) and author of a manual *De praestigiis daemonum et incantationibus et veneficiis*, which gives advice on demoniac conjuration, sorcery and the concoction of magic potions. His book *Pseudomonarchia daemonum* contains a list of nearly seventy demons together with details of their offices and activities.

Yeats, W. B. (1865–1939). The Irish poet and mystic established a small esoteric group of his own in Dublin called the Hermetic Students. On coming to London he was initiated by S. L. Mathers into the Hermetic Order of the Golden Dawn. There Yeats, as Frater Daemon est Deus Inversus, quickly rose to high rank, eventually obtaining control of the London branch after Mathers had decamped to France. Yeats saw his position threatened by Aleister Crowley (q.v.), who had managed to win over Mathers during a visit to Paris. After lengthy and undignified squabbling, Yeats resigned from the Golden Dawn and, like Dr Dee before him, burnt his magical books. A general account of all this activity can be found in Yeats's autobiography *The Trembling of the Veil* (Macmillan, London, 1926). He was also the author of *Studies in Mysticism and Certain Aspects of the Secret Tradition* (Hodder, London, 1906) and *The Real History of the Rosicrucians* (Kegan Paul, London, 1909).

Ziito. A fourteenth-century magician at the Court of King Wenceslas IV of Bohemia, his feats are recounted by the historian Dubravius.

NOTES

CHAPTER 1. MAGIC AND NATURAL LAW

1. Cf. Virgil, *Georgics* iv, 219–21: *His quidam signis atque haec exempla secuti esse apibus partem divinae mentis et haustus aetherios dixere; deum namque ire per omnis terrasque tractusque maris caelumque profundum.*

2. On these points, see H. H. Price, 'Parapsychology and Human Nature', *Journal of Parapsychology*, vol. XXIII (1959), pp. 180–95; 'Survival and the Idea of another world', *Proceedings*, Society for Psychical Research (1953), pp. 3–25.

3. For Sir Alister Hardy's thoughts on telepathy and its significance, see his book *The Divine Flame* (Collins, London, 1966), pp. 176–97.

4. See, for example, *Philosophy*, vol. XXIV (1949), pp. 291–308.

5. Cf. the first verse of the *Dhammapada*: 'All that we are is the result of what we have thought; it is founded on our thoughts, it is made up of our thoughts.'

CHAPTER 2. THE MAGICAL UNIVERSE

1. See Ezek. i 26 and Dan. vii 13.

2. Those who read German will find the *Sefer-hab-Bahir*, together with other kabbalistic literature, in G. Scholem's *Quellen und Forschungen zur Gesch. d. Jud. Mystik* (Leipzig, 1923).

3. Eliphas Lévi, *Transcendental Magic*, tr. Waite (Rider, London, new ed., 1968, p. 19).

4. *Raymond or Life After Death* (Methuen, London, 1916). This book caused a sensation when it appeared, marking as it did the conversion of a world-famous scientist to spiritualism.

5. E. Lévi, new ed., op. cit., pp. 122 ff.

CHAPTER 3. THE WORLD AND THE MAGICIAN

1. See Lucretius, *De rerum natura* ii. 216–93.

CHAPTER 5. THE MEANING OF RITUAL

1. See Aristotle, *Metaphysics* i, chs. 5 and 8.

2. Dr Mervyn Stockwood, Bishop of Southwark, *The Times*, May 2nd, 1969. His article is mild stuff compared with the ravings of the late Rev. Montague Summers, a Roman Catholic priest, who is the nearest thing to a 20th-century Witchfinder General. For him, the slap and tickle of a witches' sabbat was the most heinous crime in Christendom. See his *Witchcraft and Black Magic* (Rider, London, 1945), and the same author's *History of Witchcraft and Demonology* (Routledge, London, 1956).

3. To meet this interest, Reich's treatise *The Function of the Orgasm* was published in paperback in London by Panther Books (1968; new ed., 1970). See also Charles Rycroft's recent study, *Reich* (Fontana, London, 1971).

4. Details of the ritual may be found in H. T. F. Rhodes's book *The Satanic Mass* (Pedigree Books, London, 1960).

5. Margaret Murray, *The Witch Cult in Western Europe* (Clarendon Press, Oxford, 1921); *The God of the Witches* (Sampson Low, London, 1931; Faber and Faber, London, 1952).

6. E.g. G. B. Gardner, *Modern Witchcraft* (Rider, London, 1954).

7. K. Preisendari, *Papyri Graecae Magicae* (Leipzig, 1928–31), vol. I, p. 91. My translation.

CHAPTER 6. THE PREPARATION

1. For details of research in this field see Ingrid Lind, *Astrology and Commonsense* (Hodder, London, 1962), pp. 17 ff.; and Michel Gauquelin, *Astrology and Science* (Peter Davies, London, 1969).

2. Michel Gauquelin, op. cit., pp. 211 ff.

3. Details of the movements of planets through the zodiac may be obtained quite easily from almanacks, ephemerides, astrological magazines and the astronomical data given in some newspapers.

4. Herbert Trench, 'She Comes Not When Noon is on the Roses'.

CHAPTER 7. THE MASTER RITUALS

1. Cf. Ps. xci 10, 11.

2. See, for example, J. Vandier, *La Religion égyptienne* (Paris, 1944).

CHAPTER 8. ASTRAL PROJECTION

1. Among the best are those of R. Crookall, *Out-of-the-Body Experiences* (University Books, New York, 1970), *The Techniques of Astral Projection* and *More Astral Projections* (both Aquarian Press, London, 1964). Also of immense value are Sylvan Muldoon, *The Case for Astral Projection*, and Muldoon and Carrington, *The Phenomena of Astral Projection* and *The Projection of the Astral Body*. The last two books are

published (new editions 1969) in London by Rider and are highly esteemed in occult circles.

2. See Eccles. xii 6.

3. Cf. Jer. i 6: 'Then said I, Ah, Lord God, behold I cannot speak: for I am a child.'

CHAPTER 10. THE ART OF PROPHECY

1. Details of experimental work in this field will be found in D. J. West, *Psychica Research Today* (Duckworth, London, 1954; Penguin Books, Harmondsworth, 1962). See also *New Scientist*, October 18th, 1969.

2. See S. G. Soal, 'A Report on Some Communications Received through Mrs Blanche Cooper', *Proceedings*, Society for Psychical Research, vol. XXXV (1926), pp. 471–594. The case is mentioned by most writers on psychic research, among them West (op. cit.).

3. J. B. Priestley, *Man and Time* (Aldus, London, 1964).

4. J. W. Dunne, *An Experiment with Time* (Faber, London, 1929).

5. This took place in January 1914 and an account of it is given in Jean Overton Fuller's book *The Magical Dilemma of Victor Neuburg* (Allen, London, 1965), pp. 203–16.

CHAPTER 11. A WORD ABOUT DEMONS

1. For example, see R. H. Robbins, *The Encyclopaedia of Witchcraft and Demonology* (Spring Books, London, 1959). The most comprehensive catalogue of angels, good and bad, has been compiled by Gustav Davidson in his *Dictionary of Angels* (The Free Press, London, 1967).

2. Benvenuto Cellini, *Vita scritta da lui medesimo* (1558–66).

CHAPTER 12. THREE MAGICAL INTENTIONS

1. See E. M. Butler, *The Myth of the Magus* (Macmillan, London, 1948), pp. 185–214. Saint-Germain was the inspiration of Bulwer-Lytton's novel *Zanoni*, and is also a 'Master' of the Theosophical Society.

2. See, for example, *Eclogue* VIII. Virgil's work was used for random divinatory experiments (*Sortes Virgilianae*) throughout the Middle Ages.

3. *Early English Prose Romances*, ed. Thoms (London, 1858), II, p. 58. The story is retold by Professor E. M. Butler, op. cit. More recent than Virgil's alleged rejuvenation by these means is that of Cardinal de Cusa who, in the 15th century, is said to have forced his astral self upon the infant Copernicus. The story is recounted by Mme Blavatsky in her *Secret Doctrine* (Theosophical Publishing House, Adyar, new ed., 1962), p. 355.

4. Eliphas Lévi, *History of Magic* (Rider, London, new ed., 1969), pp. 303 ff.

CHAPTER 13. DEATH AND THE MEANING OF LIFE

1. See particularly Karlis Osis, *Deathbed Observations* (Parapsychology Foundation, New York, 1961).

2. Lepsius, *Das Todtenbuch der Aegypten nach dem hieroglyphischen Papyrus in Turin*, cap. LXXXIX, p. 6.

3. Ibid., p. 5.

CHAPTER 14. THE WAY OF HIGH MAGIC

1. Cf. M. Barbanell, *Modern Spiritualism* (Herbert Jenkins, London, 1959), p. 52: 'The knowledge [he] has gained is astonishing. Men would give kingdoms to have it.' (A spirit guide is speaking.) See also P. Andreas and G. Adams., *Between Heaven and Earth* (Harrap, London, 1967), pp. 41–65.

2. For a detailed report on this see *Nature* (August 1961).

3. J. V. Luce, *The End of Atlantis* (Thames and Hudson, London, 1969), and A. G. Galanopoulos and E. Bacon, *Atlantis: The Truth Behind The Legend* (Nelson, London, 1969). The latter book contains a light-hearted examination of some of the more extravagant theories of Atlantis.

First-hand evidence of such theories will be found in Volumes 3 and 4 of Mme Blavatsky's *Secret Doctrine* and in Ignatius Donnelly's classic, *Atlantis and the Antediluvian World* (1882) which has recently (1970) been reissued by Sidgwick and Jackson, London.

4. Dion Fortune, *Applied Magic* (Aquarian Press, London, 1962), pp. 85–6.

5. Num. ix 15–23.

DUTTON PAPERBACKS OF RELATED INTEREST